THE GOOD WOMEN
OF CHINA

Xinran was born in Beijing in 1958. In 1997 she moved
to London. This is her first book.

Xinran

THE GOOD WOMEN
OF CHINA

Hidden Voices

TRANSLATED BY
Esther Tyldesley

VINTAGE

Published by Vintage 2003

2 4 6 8 10 9 7 5 3 1

First published in Great Britain in 2002 by
Chatto & Windus

Vintage
Random House, 20 Vauxhall Bridge Road,
London SW1V 2SA

Random House Australia (Pty) Limited
20 Alfred Street, Milsons Point, Sydney
New South Wales 2061, Australia

Random House New Zealand Limited
18 Poland Road, Glenfield,
Auckland 10, New Zealand

Random House (Pty) Limited
Endulini, 5A Jubilee Road, Parktown 2193,
South Africa

The Random House Group Limited Reg. No. 954009
www.randomhouse.co.uk

A CIP catalogue record for this book
is available from the British Library

ISBN 0 09 945206 5

Papers used by Random House are natural, recyclable products made from wood grown in sustainable forests. The manufacturing processes conform to the environmental regulations of the country of origin

Printed and bound in Great Britain by
Bookmarque Ltd, Croydon, Surrey

For every Chinese woman

and for my son PanPan

Author's Note

The stories told here are true, but names have been changed in order to protect the people concerned.

In Chinese, 'Xiao' in front of a surname means 'young'. When it precedes a first name, it creates a diminutive and indicates that the speaker is close to the person being addressed.

Contents

Prologue

At nine o'clock on 3 November 1999, I was on my way home from teaching an evening class at London University's School of Oriental and African Studies. As I walked out of Stamford Brook tube station into the dark autumnal night, I heard a rushing sound behind me. I had no time to react before someone hit me hard on the head and pushed me to the ground. Instinctively, I tightened my grip on my handbag, which contained the only copy of a manuscript I had just finished writing. But my assailant wasn't deterred.

'Give me your bag,' he shouted again and again.

I struggled with a strength I had not known I possessed. In the darkness, I could not see a face. I was aware only that I was fighting a pair of strong yet invisible hands. I tried to protect myself and, at the same time, kick with my feet at where I thought his groin might be. He kicked back and I felt sharp bursts of pain in my back and legs, and the salty taste of blood in my mouth.

Passers-by started running towards us, shouting. Soon the man was surrounded by an angry crowd. When I staggered to my feet, I saw that he was over six feet tall.

Later, the police asked me why I had risked my life fighting for a bag.

Trembling and in pain, I explained, 'It had my book in it.'

'A book?' a policeman exclaimed. 'Is a book more important than your life?'

Of course, life is more important than a book. But in so many ways my book was my life. It was my testimony to the lives of

Chinese women, the result of many years' work as a journalist. I knew I had been foolish: if I had lost the manuscript, I could have tried to recreate it. However, I wasn't sure that I could put myself through the extremes of feeling provoked by writing the book again. Reliving the stories of the women I had met had been painful, and it had been harder still to order my memories and find language adequate to express them. In fighting for that bag, I was defending my feelings, and the feelings of Chinese women. The book was the result of so many things which, once lost, could never be found again. When you walk into your memories, you are opening a door to the past; the road within has many branches, and the route is different every time.

1

My Journey Towards the Stories of Chinese Women

Early one spring morning in 1989, I rode my Flying Pigeon bicycle through the streets of Nanjing dreaming about my son PanPan. The green shoots on the trees, the clouds of frosty breath enveloping the other cyclists, the women's silk scarves billowing in the spring wind, everything merged with thoughts of my son. I was bringing him up on my own, without the help of a man, and it was not easy caring for him as a working mother. Whatever journey I went on, though, long or short, even the quick ride to work, he accompanied me in spirit and gave me courage.

'Hey, big-shot presenter, watch where you're going,' shouted a colleague as I wobbled into the compound of the radio and TV station where I worked.

Two armed policemen stood at the gates. I showed them my pass. Once inside, I would have to face further armed guards at the entrances to the offices and the studios. Security at the broadcasting station was extremely tight and workers were wary of the guards. A story circulated of a new soldier who fell asleep on night duty and was so keyed up that he killed the comrade who woke him.

My office was on the sixteenth floor of the forbidding, twenty-one-storey modern building. I preferred to climb the stairs rather than risk the unreliable lift, which broke down frequently. When I arrived at my desk, I realised I had left my bicycle key in the lock. Taking pity on me, a colleague offered to go and telephone down to the gatekeeper. This was not so easy since no junior employee at that time had a telephone and my colleague would have to go to the section head's office to make the call. In the end, someone brought me up my key with my mail. Amidst the large pile of letters, one immediately caught my attention: the envelope had been made from the cover of a book and there was a chicken feather glued to it. According to Chinese tradition, a chicken feather is an urgent distress signal.

The letter was from a young boy, and had been sent from a village about 150 miles from Nanjing.

> Most respected Xinran,
>
> I listen to every one of your programmes. In fact, everyone in our village likes listening to them. But I am not writing to tell you how good your programme is; I am writing to tell you a secret.
>
> It's not really a secret, because everyone in the village knows. There is an old, crippled man of sixty here who recently bought a young wife. The girl looks very young – I think she must have been kidnapped. This happens a lot around here, but many of the girls escape later. The old man is afraid his wife will run off, so he has tied a thick iron chain around her. Her waist has been rubbed raw by the heavy chain – the blood has seeped through her clothes. I think it will kill her. Please save her.
>
> Whatever you do, don't mention this on the radio. If the villagers find out, they'll drive my family away.
>
> May your programme get better and better.
>
> Your loyal listener,
> Zhang Xiaoshuan

This was the most distressing letter I had received since I had started presenting my evening radio programme, *Words on the Night Breeze*, four months earlier. During the programme I discussed various aspects of daily life and used my own experiences to win the listeners' trust and suggest ways of approaching life's difficulties. 'My name is Xinran,' I had said at the beginning of the first broadcast. ' "Xinran" means "with pleasure". "*Xin xin ran zhang kai le yan*," wrote Zhu Ziqing in a poem about spring: "With pleasure, Nature opened its eyes to new things."' The programme was a 'new thing' for everyone, myself included. I had only just become a presenter and I was trying to do something that hadn't been done on the radio before.

Since 1949, the media had been the mouthpiece of the Party. State radio, state newspapers and, later, state television provided the only information Chinese people had access to, and they spoke with one identical voice. Communication with anyone abroad seemed as remote as a fairy tale. When Deng Xiaoping started the slow process of 'opening up' China in 1983, it was possible for journalists, if they were courageous, to try and make subtle changes to how they presented the news. It was also possible, although perhaps even more dangerous, to discuss personal issues in the media. In *Words on the Night Breeze* I was trying to open a little window, a tiny hole, so that people could allow their spirits to cry out and breathe after the gunpowder-laden atmosphere of the previous forty years. The Chinese author and philosopher Lu Xun once said, 'The first person who tasted a crab must also have tried a spider, but realised that it was not good to eat.' As I awaited the reaction of my listeners to the programme, I wondered whether they would think it was a crab or a spider. The number of enthusiastic letters that piled up on my desk convinced me that it was the former.

The letter I received from the young boy Zhang Xiaoshuan was the first that had appealed for my practical help and it threw me into confusion. I reported it to my section head and asked what I should do. He suggested indifferently that I contact the local Public Security Bureau. I put a call through and poured out Zhang Xiaoshuan's story.

The police officer on the other end of the line told me to calm down. 'This sort of thing happens a lot. If everyone reacted like you, we'd be worked to death. Anyway, it's a hopeless case. We have piles of reports here, and our human and financial resources are limited. I would be very wary of getting mixed up in it if I were you. Villagers like that aren't afraid of anyone or anything; even if we turned up there, they'd torch our cars and beat up our officers. They will go to incredible lengths to make sure that their family lines are perpetuated so as not to sin against their ancestors by failing to produce an heir.'

'So,' I said, 'Are you telling me you are not going to take responsibility for this girl?'

'I didn't say I wouldn't, but . . .'

'But what?'

'But there's no need to hurry, we can take it step by step.'

'You can't leave someone to die step by step!'

The policeman chuckled. 'No wonder they say that policemen fight fire and journalists start fire. What was your name again?'

'Xin . . . ran,' I said through gritted teeth.

'Yes, yes, Xinran, good name. All right, Xinran, come over. I'll help you.' He sounded as if he was doing me a favour rather than performing his duty.

I went straight to his office. He was a typical Chinese police officer: robust and alert, with a shifty expression.

'In the countryside,' he said, 'the heavens are high and the emperor is far away.' In his opinion the law had no power there. The peasants feared only the local authorities who controlled their supplies of pesticide, fertiliser, seeds and farming tools.

The policeman was right. In the end, it was the head of the village agricultural supplies depot who managed to save the girl. He threatened to cut off the villagers' supply of fertiliser if they did not release her. Three policemen took me to the village in a police car. When we arrived, the village head had to clear the way for us through the villagers, who were shaking their fists and cursing us. The girl was only twelve years old. We took her away from the old man, who wept and swore bitterly. I dared not ask after the schoolboy who had written to me. I wanted to thank him, but the police officer told me that if the villagers found out what he had done, they might murder him and his family.

Witnessing the power of the peasants first-hand, I began to understand how Mao had defeated Chiang Kai-shek and his British and American weapons with their help.

The girl was sent back to her family in Xining – a twenty-two-hour train journey from Nanjing – accompanied by a police officer and someone from the radio station. It turned out that her parents had run up a debt of nearly 10,000 yuan searching for her.

I received no praise for the rescue of this girl, only criticism for

4

'moving the troops about and stirring up the people' and wasting the radio station's time and money. I was shaken by these complaints. A young girl had been in danger and yet going to her rescue was seen as 'exhausting the people and draining the treasury'. Just what was a woman's life worth in China?

This question began to haunt me. Most of the people who wrote to me at the radio station were women. Their letters were often anonymous, or written under an assumed name. Much of what they said came as a profound shock to me. I had believed that I understood Chinese women. Reading their letters, I realised how wrong my assumption had been. My fellow women were living lives and struggling with problems I had not dreamed of.

Many of the questions they asked me related to their sexuality. One woman wanted to know why her heart beat faster when she accidentally bumped into a man on the bus. Another asked why she broke out into a sweat when a man touched her hand. For so long, all discussion of sexual matters had been forbidden and any physical contact between a man and woman who were not married had led to public condemnation – being 'struggled against' – or even imprisonment. Even between a husband and wife 'pillow talk' could be taken as evidence of delinquent behaviour, and, in family quarrels, people would often threaten to denounce their partners to the police for having indulged in it. As a result, two generations of Chinese had grown up with their natural instincts in confusion. I myself was once so ignorant that, even at the age of twenty-two, I refused to hold hands with a male teacher at a bonfire party for fear of getting pregnant. My understanding of conception was gleaned from a line in a book: 'They held hands under the light of the moon . . . In spring they had a bouncing baby son.' I found myself wanting to know much more about the intimate lives of Chinese women and decided to start researching their different cultural backgrounds.

Old Chen was the first person I told about my project. He had been a journalist for a very long time and was highly respected. It was said that even Nanjing's mayor came to him for advice. I often consulted him about my work, out of deference to his seniority, but also to draw on his considerable experience. This time, however, his reaction surprised me. He shook his head, which was so bald you couldn't tell where his scalp ended and his face began, and said, 'Naive!'

I was taken aback. Chinese people consider baldness a sign of wisdom. Was I wrong? Why was it so naive to want to understand Chinese women?

I told a friend who worked at the university about Old Chen's warning.

'Xinran,' he said, 'have you ever been inside a sponge cake factory?'

'No,' I replied, confused.

'Well, I have. So I never eat sponge cake.' He suggested that I try visiting a bakery to see what he meant.

I am impatient by nature, so at five o'clock the next morning I made my way to a bakery that was small but had a good reputation. I hadn't announced my visit, but I didn't expect to encounter any difficulty. Journalists in China are called 'kings without crowns'. They have the right of free entry to almost any organisation in the country.

The manager at the bakery did not know why I had come but he was impressed by my devotion to my job: he said that he had never seen a journalist up so early to gather material. It was not yet fully light; under the dim light of the factory lamps, seven or eight female workers were breaking eggs into a large vat. They were yawning and clearing their throats with a dreadful hawking noise. The intermittent sound of spitting made me feel uneasy. One woman had egg yolk all over her face, most probably from wiping her nose rather than some obscure beauty treatment. I watched two male workers add flavouring and colour to a thin flour paste that had been prepared the day before. The mixture had the eggs added to it and was then poured into tins on a conveyor belt. When the tins emerged from the oven, a dozen or so female workers packed the cakes into boxes. They had crumbs at the corners of their mouths.

As I left the factory, I remembered something a fellow journalist had once told me: the dirtiest things in the world are not toilets or sewers, but food factories and restaurant kitchens. I resolved never to eat sponge cake again, but could not work out how what I had seen related to the question of understanding women.

I rang my friend, who seemed disappointed with my lack of perception.

'You have seen what those beautiful, soft cakes went through to become what they are. If you had only looked at them in the shop, you would never have known. However, although you might succeed in describing how badly managed the factory is and how it contravenes health regulations, do you think it will stop people wanting to eat sponge cake? It's the same with Chinese women. Even if you manage to get access to their homes and their memories, will you be able to judge or change the laws by which they live their lives? Besides, how many women will actually be willing to give up their self-respect and talk to you? I'm afraid I think that your colleague is indeed wise.'

2

The Girl Who Kept a Fly as a Pet

Old Chen and my friend at the university were certainly right about one thing. It would be very difficult to find women who would be prepared to speak freely to me. For Chinese women, the naked body is an object of shame, not beauty. They keep it covered. To ask women to let me interview them would be like asking them to take off their clothes. I realised that I would have to try more subtle ways to find out about their lives.

The letters I received from my listeners, full of longing and hope, were my point of departure. I asked my director whether I could add a special women's mailbox feature to the end of my programme, in which I would discuss and perhaps read out some of the letters I received. He was not opposed to the idea: he too wanted to understand what Chinese women were thinking so that he could address his tense relationship with his wife. However, he could not authorise the feature himself; I would have to send an application to the central office. I was only too familiar with this procedure: the ranks of officials in our station were merely glorified errand boys, with no executive power. The upper echelons had the last word.

Six weeks later, my application form was sent back, festooned with four red seals of official approval. The time of my proposed feature had been cut down to ten minutes. Even so, I felt like manna had fallen from heaven.

The impact of my ten-minute women's mailbox slot went far beyond my expectations: the number of listeners' letters increased to a point where I was receiving over a hundred a day. Six university students had to help me with my post. The subject matter of the letters was becoming more varied too. The stories the listeners told me had taken place all over the country, at many different times during the past seventy or so years, and came from women of very different social, cultural and professional backgrounds. They revealed worlds that had been hidden from view to the majority of the population, including myself. I was deeply moved by the letters. Many of them included personal touches such as pressed flowers, leaves or bark, and hand-crocheted mementos.

One afternoon, I returned to my office to find a parcel and a short note from the gatekeeper on my desk. Apparently, a woman of about forty had delivered the parcel and asked the gatekeeper to pass it on to me; she had not left a name or address. Several colleagues advised me to hand the parcel to the security department for inspection before opening it, but I resisted. I felt that fate could not be second-guessed, and a strong impulse urged me to open the parcel at once. Inside was an old shoebox, with a pretty drawing of a human-looking fly on the lid. The colours had almost completely faded. A sentence had been written next to the fly's mouth: 'Without spring, flowers cannot bloom; without the owner, this cannot be opened.' A small lock had been cleverly fitted to the lid.

I hesitated: ought I to open it? Then I spotted a tiny note which had clearly been pasted on recently: 'Xinran, please open this.'

The box was filled with yellowing, faded pieces of paper. Covered in writing, the pieces of paper were not uniform in size, shape or colour: they were mostly scrap paper of the kind used for hospital records. It looked like a diary. There was also a thick recorded-delivery letter. It was addressed to Yan Yulong at Production Team X, Shandong Province, and was from someone called Hongxue, who gave as her address a hospital in Henan Province. The letter was postmarked 24 August 1975. It was also open, and written at the top of it were the words, 'Xinran, I respectfully ask you to read every word. A faithful listener.'

Since I did not have time to look at the scraps of paper before I went on air, I decided to read the letter first:

Dear Yulong,

Are you all right? I am sorry not to have written sooner, there is no real reason for it, it's just that I have too much to say, and I don't know where to start. Please forgive me.

It is already too late to beg you to forgive my terrible, irrevocable mistake, but I still want to say to you, Dear Yulong, I am sorry!

You asked me two questions in your letter: 'Why are you unwilling to see your father?' and 'What made you think of drawing a fly, and why did you make it so beautiful?'

Dear Yulong, both of these questions are very, very painful for me but I will try to answer them.

What girl does not love her father? A father is a big tree sheltering the family, the beams that support a house, the guardian of his wife and children. But I don't love my father – I hate him.

On New Year's Day of the year I turned eleven, I got out of bed early in the morning to find myself bleeding inexplicably. I was so frightened that I burst into tears. My mother, who came when she heard me, said, 'Hongxue, you've grown up.' No one – not even Mama – had told me about women's matters before. At school nobody had dared ask such outrageous questions. That day, Mama gave me some basic advice about how to cope with the bleeding, but did not explain anything else. I was excited: I had become a woman! I ran about in the courtyard, jumping and dancing, for three hours. I even forgot about lunch.

One day in February, it was snowing heavily and Mama was out visiting a neighbour. My father was back home from the military base, on one of his rare visits. He said to me, 'Your mother says you've grown up. Come, take off your clothes for Papa to see if it is true.'

I didn't know what he wanted to see, and it was so cold – I didn't want to get undressed.

'Quick! Papa will help you!' he said, deftly removing my clothes. He was totally unlike his usual slow-moving self. He rubbed my whole body with his hands, asking me all the time: 'Are those little nipples swollen? Is it here that the blood comes from? Do those lips want to kiss Papa? Does it feel nice when Papa rubs you like this?'

I felt mortified. Ever since I could remember, I had never been naked in front of anyone except in the segregated public baths. My father noticed me shivering. He told me not to be afraid, and warned me not to tell Mama. 'Your mother has never liked you,' he said. 'If she finds out I love you this much she will want even less to do with you.'

This was my first 'woman's experience'. Afterwards, I felt very sick.

From then on, as long as my mother was not in the room, even if she was just cooking in the kitchen or in the toilet, my father would corner me behind the door and rub me all over. I became more and more afraid of this 'love'.

Later, my father was moved to a different military base. My mother could not join him because of her job. She said she had exhausted herself bringing up my brother and me, she wanted my father to fulfil his responsibilities for a while. And so it was that we went to live with my father.

I had fallen into the wolf's lair.

Every midday, from the day my mother left, my father climbed into my bed while I was resting. We each had a room in a collective dormitory and he used the excuse that my little brother did not like taking a midday nap to lock him out.

For the first few days, he only rubbed my body with his hands. Later, he started to force his tongue into my mouth. Then he began shoving at me with the hard thing on his lower body. He would creep into my bed, not caring if it was day or night. He used his hands to spread me open and mess about with me. He even put his fingers inside me.

By then, he had stopped pretending it was 'father's love'. He threatened me, saying that if I told anyone I would have to endure a public criticism and be paraded through the streets with straw on my head, because I was already what they called a 'broken shoe'.

My rapidly maturing body made him more excited by the day, but I grew increasingly terrified. I fitted a lock to the bedroom door, but he did not care if he woke all the neighbours by knocking until I opened it. Sometimes he deceived the other people in the dormitory into helping him force open my door, or told them that he had to climb through the window to collect something because I was sleeping so soundly. Sometimes it was my brother who helped him without realising what he was doing. So, regardless of whether I had locked the door or not, he would enter my bedroom in full view of everyone.

When I heard the knocking, I was often paralysed with fear, and just curled up in my quilt shivering. The neighbours would say to me, 'You were sleeping like the dead, so your father had to climb in to collect his things, poor man!'

I did not dare sleep in my room, I did not dare to be alone in it at all. Father realised I was finding more and more excuses to go out, so he made a rule that I had to be back home in time for lunch every day. But I often collapsed before I had even finished eating: he had put sleeping pills in my food. There was no way I could protect myself.

I thought of killing myself many times, but could not find it in my heart to abandon my little brother, who had no one to turn to. I grew thinner and thinner, and then fell seriously ill.

The first time I was admitted to the military hospital, the duty nurse told the consultant, Dr Zhong, that my sleep was very disturbed. I would shake with fright at the slightest noise. Dr Zhong, who did not know the facts, said it was because of my high fever.

However, even when I was dangerously ill, my father would come to the hospital and take advantage of me when I was on a drip and could not move. Once when I saw him walking into my room, I started screaming uncontrollably, but my father just told the duty nurse who came running that I had a fierce temper. That first time, I only spent two weeks in hospital. When I came home, I found a bruise on my brother's head, and bloodstains on his little coat. He said that while I had been in hospital, Papa had been in a foul temper and had beaten him on the slightest pretext. That day my sick beast of a father pressed my body – still desperately frail and weak – to him madly and whispered that he had missed me to death!

I could not stop crying. Was this my father? Had he had children just to satisfy his animal lusts? What had he given life to me for?

My experience in hospital had shown me a way to go on living. As far as I was concerned, injections, pills and blood tests were all preferable to living with my father. And so I started to hurt myself, again and again. In the winter, I would soak myself in cold water, then stand outside in the ice and snow; in autumn I would eat food that had gone off; once, in despair, I stuck my arm out to catch a falling piece of iron so that it would cut off my left hand at the wrist. (If not for a piece of soft wood underneath, I would certainly have lost my hand.) That time I won myself a whole sixty nights of safety. Between the self-injury and the drugs, I grew painfully thin.

More than two years later, my mother got a job transfer and came to live with us. Her arrival did not affect my father's obscene desire for me. He said that my mother's body was old and withered, and that I was his concubine. My mother did not seem to know about the situation until one day last February, when my father was beating me because I had not bought him something he wanted, I shouted at him for the first time in my life, caught between sorrow and fury: 'What are you? You beat anyone as you please, you mess about with anyone as you wish!'

My mother, who was watching from the sidelines, asked me what I meant. As soon as I opened my mouth, my father said, glaring at me fiercely, 'Don't talk nonsense!'

I had taken all I could, so I told my mother the truth. I could see that she was terribly upset. But just a few hours later, my 'reasonable' mother said to me, 'For the security of the whole family, you must put up with it. Otherwise, what will we all do?'

My hopes were completely crushed. My own mother was persuading me to put up with abuse from my father, her husband – where was the justice in that?

That night my temperature reached 40°. Once again I was taken to hospital, where I have stayed until now. This time I didn't have to do anything to provoke my illness. I just collapsed, because my heart had collapsed. I have no intention of going back to that so-called home now.

Dear Yulong, this is why I don't want to see my father. What sort of father is he? I am keeping quiet for the sake of my little brother and my mother (even though she doesn't love me); without me they are still a family like before.

Why did I draw a fly, and why did I make it look so beautiful?

Because I long for a real mother and father: a real family where I can be a child, and cry in my parents' arms; where I can sleep safely in my bed at home; where loving hands will stroke my head to comfort me after a bad dream. From my earliest childhood, I have never felt this love. I hoped and yearned for it, but I have never had it, and I will never have it now, for we only have one mother and father.

A dear little fly once showed me the touch of loving hands.

Dear Yulong, I don't know what I am going to do after this. Perhaps I will come to look for you, and help you in some way. I can do many things, and I am not afraid of hardship, as long as I can sleep in peace. Do you mind if I come? Please write and let me know.

I would really like to know how you are. Are you still practising your Russian? Do you have any medicine? Winter is coming again, you must take good care of yourself.

I hope you will give me a chance to make it up to you and do something for you. I have no family, but I hope I can be a younger sister to you.

Wishing you happiness and good health!

I miss you.

Hongxue, 23 August 1975

I was deeply shaken by this letter, and found it difficult to maintain my composure during that evening's broadcast. Later, many listeners wrote in to ask if I had been ill.

After my programme had finished, I called a friend to ask if they would go to my house to check that my son and his nanny were all right. Then I sat in the empty office and put the scraps of paper in order. So it was that I read Hongxue's diary.

27 February – Heavy snow

How happy I am today! My wish has come true again: I'm back in hospital. This time it wasn't too hard, but I'm suffering so much already!

I don't want to think any more. 'Who am I? What am I?' These questions are useless, like everything about me: my brains, my youth, my quick wit and nimble fingers. Now I just want to have a good, long sleep.

I hope the doctors and nurses will be a bit lax, and not check the wards too diligently on their rounds this evening.

The hospital room is so warm, and comfortable to write in.

2 March – Sunny

The snow has melted very quickly. Yesterday morning it was still pure white; today when I ran outside, the little snow left had turned a dirty yellow, stained like the fingers of my fellow patient Old Mother Wang, who smokes like a chimney.

I love it when it snows heavily. Everywhere is white and clean; the wind traces patterns in the surface of the snow, hopping birds leave delicate prints, and people too, unwittingly leave beautiful tracks. Yesterday I sneaked outside several times. Dr Liu and the head nurse scolded me: 'You must be crazy, running outside with a high temperature! Are you trying to kill yourself?' I don't mind what they say to me. Their tongues may be sharp, but I know they are soft underneath.

It's a pity I don't have a camera. It would be nice to take a picture of the landscape blanketed in snow.

17 April – Sunshine (wind later?)

There is a patient here called Yulong: her chronic rheumatism brings her to hospital several times a year. Nurse Gao is always tutting sympathetically, wondering how such a pretty, clever girl could have got such a troublesome illness.

Yulong treats me as a dear younger sister. When she is here, she keeps me company in the courtyard whenever I can leave my room (patients aren't allowed to visit other wards. They are afraid we'll infect each other or affect the treatment). We play volleyball, badminton or chess, and chat. She won't let me get lonely. When she has something nice to eat or to play with, she shares it with me.

Another reason I like Yulong is that she's very pretty. A long time ago I heard somebody say that friends start looking alike after some time. If I could have half Yulong's beauty, that would be good enough. It's not just me who likes Yulong, everyone else does too. If she needs something done, everyone is willing to give her a hand. She also gets special favours that other people don't. For example, her sheets are changed twice a week rather than once, she is allowed to have visitors in her room, and she never has to wait for a nurse's attention. The male nurses always find a reason to hang about her room. I'm sure Yulong gets better food too.

I really envy her – as Old Mother Wang says, her face is her fortune. Old Mother Wang doesn't like Yulong, though. She says she's like the fox fairy in the legends, who lures men to their deaths.

. . .

I got up secretly to write, but Dr Yu found me on her night rounds. She asked if I was hungry, and invited me to have a late-night snack. She said that a full stomach would help me sleep.

In the duty room, Nurse Gao lit the stove and started to prepare noodles with crispy fried green onions. Suddenly there was a power cut. The only light came from the stove. Dr Yu hurriedly went to check on the patients with a torch. Nurse Gao carried on cooking. She seemed to be used to doing things in the dark, and very soon the scent of fried onions filled the air. Kind Nurse Gao knew I loved crispy onions, so she picked out two spoonfuls of them specially for me. Soon the power came back on and Dr Yu returned and the three of us settled down to eat. While I was enjoying my second spoonful, I told Dr Yu how Nurse Gao had spoiled me by picking out the onions specially.

Suddenly, Dr Yu pushed away my spoon and asked urgently, 'Have you swallowed any?'

I nodded, puzzled: 'This is my second spoonful.'

Nurse Gao was also bemused. 'What's wrong? Why are you frightening us?'

Dr Yu pointed anxiously at the crispy onions scattered on the floor. Among the green onions were countless dead flies, burned to a crisp. The flies had been drawn out of hiding by the heat and light of the stove. Weakened by the winter, they dropped into the pot. In the darkness, nobody had noticed.

Dr Yu and Nurse Gao quickly found some medicine. They had two pills each and I had four, washed down with glucose solution. The noodles, which had smelled so wonderful, were tipped into the toilet. They tried to reassure me that I would not get sick.

My head is full of those flies I swallowed. Did I break their bones and crush their bodies with my teeth? Or did I swallow them whole?

Goodness! But I've written a funny little story!

21 April – Light rain

I have decided to keep a baby fly as a pet.

Last Sunday I did not have any drip treatment, so I slept well until I was woken by a soft, shivery feeling on my skin. Only half awake, I felt too lazy to move, and lay there wondering where the feeling came from. Whatever caused it was still there, moving busily up and down my leg, but it didn't disturb or scare me at all. I felt as if a pair of tiny hands was gently stroking me. I was very grateful to that pair of little hands, and wanted to know whose they were. I opened my eyes and looked:

It was a fly! How horrible! Flies are covered with sewage and germs!

But I never knew that the feet of a fly could feel so soft and gentle, even if they are dirty.

For several days, I waited for those 'little hands', but they did not come again.

While I was being X-rayed after a barium meal this morning, I suddenly thought of the time I visited the specimen room in the hospital, and of the little animals the doctors raised for medical experiments. I could raise a clean fly! Yes, I would find a baby fly and keep it in my mosquito net.

25 April – Overcast

It is very hard to find a baby fly. The world is full of big flies, buzzing all over the place, landing on the filthiest, smelliest things, but I don't dare touch them. I really want to ask Dr Zhong for advice; he is a biology expert, and would definitely know where to find a baby fly. But if I ask him, he'll think I'm mad.

8 May – Sunny

I'm so tired, so very tired.

Two days ago, I finally caught a baby fly. It is very little. It was struggling in a spider's web on a small apple tree in the thicket behind the canteen. I covered the fly and web with a gauze bag made out of a face mask, and took it back to my room. As I was passing the treatment room, Nurse Zhang asked me what I'd caught. I blurted out the first thing that came into my head, that it was a butterfly, then hurried back to my room and dived into my mosquito net. As soon as I was inside, I slowly opened the gauze bag. To my surprise, the gauze fibres had unstuck the spider's web, and the baby fly could move freely. I thought it must be very tired and hungry after having been stuck for goodness knows how long, so I ran to the duty room, stole a little bit of gauze, and poured some glucose solution on to it. Then I ran to the kitchen and picked a piece of meat from the pot of leftovers. When I got back to my mosquito net, the baby fly seemed not to have moved. Its tiny wings were waving feebly; it looked hungry and tired. I put the meat down on the sugared gauze, and gently pulled it close to the baby fly. Just then I heard the sound of the medicine trolley. It was time for the afternoon treatment. I had to find something to cover the fly with, I couldn't let it be discovered. I like collecting little containers, so it was very easy for me to find a box with a transparent plastic lid in which to put the fly and its gauze 'nest'. I had just finished doing this when Nurse Zhang pushed the trolley in.

Nurse Zhang said, 'What about your butterfly then? Let's see if it's pretty or not.'

'I . . . I thought it wasn't very pretty after all, so I let it go,' I lied, stammering.

'Never mind, next time I'll catch you a beautiful one,' he consoled me.

I thanked him, but wished he would hurry up and leave. I was worried about my baby fly.

It's much harder to keep a baby fly than a kitten. Everybody likes kittens, so if you have a kitten, many people will help you. But nobody likes flies. I'm worried that someone might kill it, or that it will escape. I haven't dared venture outside for exercise for the last few days because I'm afraid the baby fly will have an accident. I can't sleep easily at night either because I'm worried the doctors and nurses will chase the fly away. I listen for their footsteps, and thrust my arm out of the mosquito net before they come in, so that they can take my pulse and temperature without lifting the net. It's been like this every day, for several days. I am really so very tired.

This is much better than sleeping at home, though. Besides, my baby fly really looks much better now. It's growing very slowly, it hardly seems to be getting any bigger. But that's fine, I don't like those big, green-headed flies at all. The baby fly is always landing on me: I love the gentle, sometimes ticklish feeling on my skin. I like it too when it plays on my cheeks, but I don't let it kiss me.

11 May – Sunny

I haven't had to have any drips for the last few days. Dr Zhong says they'll keep me in for a few more days of observation, and a new treatment. I don't care what they do, so long as I can stay here and not go home.

My baby fly is wonderful.

I've made a house for it, where it can be safe, and move around too: it's a gauze cover, the sort the canteen uses to cover the food. The head cook gave it to me because I said that I had to have drips every day and couldn't have meals at the regular times and wanted something to stop flies and bugs crawling all over my food. The head cook is a good person. He agreed at once, and even sewed on a little gauze bag especially for me to keep clean bowls and utensils in. And so the little fly has its own special house, but the most important thing is that he is very safe there. Nobody would suspect that there was a fly inside an anti-fly cover. Also, I don't have to run to the canteen to get food for it: it can enjoy my rice and vegetables with me.

I can sleep in peace again.

It's beautifully sunny today. I put the fly in its house at the foot of my bed, and borrowed Old Mother Wang's magnifying glass to watch it eating sugar.

The fly looks like a little old man under the microscope – it's hairy all over! I was so startled, I had to put down the magnifying glass in a hurry. I don't want to see it looking so ugly. Seen with the naked eye it's ever so cute: its body is tiny, you can't say for sure whether it's grey, brown or black (maybe it's patterned); its wings glitter in the sun like two little diamonds; its legs are so slender they make me think of a dancer's legs; its eyes are like small glass balls. I have never managed to find its pupils; it never seems to look at anything.

My baby fly looks really funny on the sugared gauze: its front feet busy all the time, moving back and forth, rubbing together, like people do when they wash their hands.

9 June – Cloudy, clear later

I've been feeling very faint for the last couple of days, but when it's time for the daily examination, I don't have a high temperature, and my blood pressure isn't particularly low either. Today, I could hardly see the shuttlecock when I was playing badminton with Yulong; once, I almost collapsed trying to return her serve. My vision is blurred, everything seems to have a flickering shadow. Luckily, Dr Zhong was on duty today. When I spoke to him about the situation, he said that I would have to go back to the main hospital for another blood test.

Okay, I won't write anything more. I am seeing double.

I can't see my baby fly properly either, he's too small. Today, there seem to be two of him.

Nurse Zhang says he's going to give me something nice today, but I'm about to go to sleep now and he still hasn't come. He must have been teasing. I won't write any more today, I'm too sleepy. Good night, dear diary.

11 June – ?

I have only just stopped crying. Nobody knew why I was crying, the doctors, nurses and other patients all thought I was scared of dying. As a matter of fact, I'm not scared of dying. Old Mother Wang says, 'Life and death are separated by a thread.' I think that must be right. Death must be like sleep; I like being asleep and away from this world. Besides, if I died, I wouldn't have to worry about being sent home. I'm only seventeen, but I think this is a good age to die. I will be a young girl for ever, and never turn into an old woman like Old Mother Wang, with a face scored with lines.

I was crying because my baby fly is dead.

The evening of the day before yesterday, I had only written a few lines of my diary when I felt so dizzy I could not carry on. I got up to go to the toilet, then, just as I was about to get back into bed, I saw a pair of demonic eyes staring at me from the headboard of my bed. I was so frightened, I screamed and fainted.

Dr Liu said I was delirious for half a day, shouting all the time about flies, demons and eyes. Old Mother Wang told all our fellow patients I was possessed, but the head nurse told her not to talk nonsense.

Dr Zhong knew the reason for my collapse, and gave Nurse Zhang a terrible telling-off because of it. Nurse Zhang had spent several hours catching a big, patterned butterfly as a present for me. He had pinned the live butterfly to my bedhead, hoping to give me a nice surprise, never dreaming that I would be scared out of my wits by it.

While I was delirious, I couldn't look after my baby fly. In that time, somebody had put things on to my bedside table that had squashed my baby fly flat in its gauze bag. I had great difficulty finding it, but by that time, its tiny body was already dried out.

Poor little fly, it died before it had even grown up.

I put the baby fly gently into a matchbox I had been saving for a long time. I pulled out a bit of white cotton wadding from my quilt, and padded the matchbox with it. I wanted the baby fly to sleep a little more comfortably.

Tomorrow, I will bury the baby fly in the little wood on the hill behind the hospital. Not many people go there, it's very peaceful.

12 June – Overcast, cloudy later

This morning the skies were dark and gloomy. It was dull grey in the wards too: everything around me reflected my feelings. I was constantly on the verge of tears, thinking about the little fly, who would never play with me again.

Dr Zhong says my white blood-cell count is too low, and that is why I feel faint. From today, I must have three bottles of a new medicine on a drip; each 500ml bottle takes about two hours, three bottles will take nearly six hours. It will be so hard to lie here alone, counting every drop of medicine. I will miss my baby fly.

At noon, the sun came out hesitantly, but it kept ducking behind the clouds. I don't know if it was mischievously playing hide-and-seek, or if it was too ill or too lazy to shine down on us. Perhaps its heart was aching for the baby fly too, and it was crying in secret?

I didn't finish the drips until after supper, but I did not have much appetite. I wanted to bury my baby fly while it was still light.

I wrapped the matchbox up in my favourite handkerchief,

and, taking the long way round to avoid the duty room, slipped out of the hospital to the little wood on the hill. I chose a spot next to a rock that could be seen from below the hill, and planned to bury the fly there. I wanted to use the rock as a gravestone, that way I could easily see it from the back door of the hospital. The ground was very hard – digging with my hands didn't work. I tried using a twig but it was very difficult, so I decided to look for a thicker branch instead. I rested the matchbox on the rock, and climbed further up the hill to look for one.

Suddenly, I heard someone breathing hard and a strange moaning cry. Soon after, I saw a woman and a man rolling around on a grassy patch in the wood. I couldn't see very clearly, but they seemed to be wrestling. The breathing sounded like the last struggle of a dying person.

I started shivering with fright. I didn't know what to do: I'd seen scenes like this in films, but never in real life. I knew I was very weak, and didn't have the strength to help the woman, let alone hold back the man. I thought I had better fetch help. I hurriedly grabbed my matchbox – I could not leave my baby fly there alone – and ran back to the hospital.

The first person I saw when I had reached the bottom of the hill was the head nurse, who had been looking for me by the door of the hospital. I was so tired, and was panting so hard that I couldn't speak, but I pointed urgently at the hill. Dr Zhong, who had just finished his shift and was leaving the hospital, came out and asked what had happened.

I didn't know what to say to make them understand. 'I think someone's going to die!'

Dr Zhong ran off up the hill and the head nurse gave me some oxygen. I was so exhausted that I fell asleep while I was inhaling it.

When I woke up, I went to the duty room. I wanted to know if the woman in the wood had been saved, and how she was.

Strangely, Nurse Gao, who was on duty, did not tell me anything. She just patted me on the head and said, 'Oh, you . . . !'

'What about me?' I felt very put out. I still don't know what happened.

13 June – Sunny

I have found a safe place for the baby fly: one of the nurses gave me a box of liqueur chocolates this afternoon. I love liqueur chocolates: I like piercing two holes in them with a needle, and then sucking out the liqueur (you can't suck it out if there's only one hole). Today, as I was doing this, I suddenly had a novel idea. I could put the baby fly in a hollow liqueur chocolate, which I could keep in the fridge in the duty office (the head nurse said I can store food there). And so I laid the baby fly in a liqueur chocolate, which he would certainly have enjoyed eating. This way, I can visit him often too.

I'm ingenious, aren't I? I am! At least, I think so.

23 June – Hot and windy

Yulong will be discharged tomorrow – I don't want her to go. Leaving the hospital is good for her, of course.

What shall I give Yulong as a leaving present?

24 June – Hot and humid

Yulong has left – I couldn't see her off because I was on a drip. Just before she left she got permission to come to my room to say goodbye. She gently stroked my hand, which was covered with needle punctures, and spoke to me affectionately. She advised me not to wash my hands in cold water, but to soak them in hot water instead, so the blood vessels would heal more quickly.

She also gave me a pair of gloves she had knitted specially for me. She had originally planned to give me them later, when winter began. She took a good look round my room, piled high with medical equipment, and praised me for keeping it so clean and tidy.

I asked if she knew what had happened to the woman on the hill. She didn't know what I was talking about so I told her about what I had seen. She went very quiet and her eyes filled with tears.

I gave Yulong a picture I had drawn of a beautiful baby fly, which I had framed with old rubber, bits of cellophane and cardboard. Yulong said she had never seen a fly drawn so beautifully, she also praised the originality of my frame.

I sent her on her way with good wishes, but secretly hoped she would come back to the hospital soon to keep me company.

16 July – Rain

I would never, ever have imagined that I could have been responsible for ruining Yulong's life.

Today I received a letter from Yulong in her village:

Dear Hongxue,

Are you well? Are you still having drips? Your family is unable to look after you, so you must learn how to take care of yourself. Luckily, the doctors and nurses at the hospital all love you, and so do the other patients. We all hope you can soon return to where you should be, among your family and friends.

I have been expelled from the military academy and sent back to my village under escort: all the villagers say I have shattered their hopes.

I have never told you that I am an orphan. My parents died one after the other – one of illness and the other probably from starvation – not long after I was born. The villagers took pity on me, and brought me up in turns. I lived on food from a hundred households, and grew up wearing clothes from a hundred families. The village was extremely poor. The villagers made their own children go without in order to send me to school: I was the first girl from my village ever to do so. Four years ago, the military academy came to the region to recruit students from among the peasants and workers. Our Party branch secretary travelled with me through the night to the prefecture army camp to beg the army leaders to accept me. He said it was the dearest wish of all in our village. The leaders told my story to their comrades, and I was eventually given special permission to participate in the practical training, and later to join the military academy.

I studied Russian and Military Communications at the academy, where almost all my classmates came from the countryside. Because the main admission requirement was the right political background, there were enormous differences in our levels of education. I was the best student in the class because I had attended one year of senior middle school. On top of that, I seemed to have a gift for languages, for my Russian marks were always very good. The instructors in the department all said I had the makings of a diplomat, and that it would be no problem for me to be an interpreter at the very least. I worked very hard, and never stopped studying on account of the rheumatism that I had had since I was a child. I wanted to repay the kindness of the villagers who had raised me.

Hongxue, a year ago, I was no longer able to avoid the reality that I had grown up, and I was painfully aware of being a mature woman. You don't understand this yet, but you will in a few years.

Little sister, I was the woman you wanted to 'save' on the hill behind the hospital.

I wasn't being hurt, I was with my boyfriend . . .

Dr Zhong and the others sent us to the Department of Military Discipline. My boyfriend was locked up and interrogated, and I was sent back to the hospital under house arrest because I needed medical treatment. That night, my boyfriend, who had a very strong sense of honour, killed himself. The next day, officials from the Department of Military Discipline, the Public Security Bureau – and other departments too, perhaps – arrived at the hospital to investigate. They said I had supplied my boyfriend with the 'means to commit the crime of making himself dead to the Party and the people for ever' (they said that suicide is a crime). I refused to say I had been raped and swore undying love to my boyfriend instead.

The price I am paying for my love is to be back in this poor village as a peasant. The villagers shun me now – I don't know if there is a place for me here.

My boyfriend was a good man, I loved him very much.

I am not writing you this letter because I blame you in the slightest. I know you are still young, you were trying to save someone out of the goodness of your heart. Promise me not to be unhappy because of this. Otherwise, the price I am paying will be even higher.

Finally, little sister, are you prepared to answer these questions:

Why are you unwilling to see your father?

What made you think of drawing a fly, and why did you make it so beautiful?

I hope you will be happy and well soon.

I miss you.

Yulong

By candlelight, evening, 30 June 1975.

Now I know why many people have been ignoring me recently. They all know about Yulong's tragic end, and that I am the culprit, the criminal who has brought her such unhappiness.

Yulong, I have done something unforgivable to you.

Who can forgive me?

30 July – Oppressive heat before a storm

I have hardly been outside for days. I don't want to see anybody. Every word of Yulong's letter has been carved into my brain. Her questions will not go away:

Why are you unwilling to see your father?

What made you think of drawing a fly, and why did you make it so beautiful?

To answer Yulong, I will have to remember, and return to hell. But Yulong has been banished to hell because of me. So I must make the journey. I cannot refuse her.

The baby fly is still sleeping in the heart of the liqueur

chocolate; nothing more can trouble it now.

When I was looking at it today, I was filled with envy.

8 August – Hot

For the last half month it has been constantly hot and humid. I don't know what is brewing up in the heavens to bring people down here out in sweat like this.

I need courage, courage to remember. I need strength, and I need willpower.

Wading through my memories, the pain clings like mud; the hate, which had faded in this white world of illness, suddenly rushes back.

I want to write back to Yulong, but don't know where to begin. I don't know how to answer her questions clearly. I only know that it will be a very long letter.

For the last three days, I haven't dared to look in on the baby fly. It talks to me in my dreams . . . oh, it's too hot!

18 August – Cool

The heavens have given vent to their feelings at last. The autumn skies are high and the air is clean and fresh. Everyone seems to have heaved a sigh of relief, and expelled the gloom of so many days. The patients, who were sweltering in the hospital, afraid of the heat, now find reasons to go out.

I don't want to go anywhere. I have to write to Yulong. This morning, though, I took the baby fly out for a half-hour stroll in a matchbox. But I was afraid that the chocolate would melt and hurt the baby fly, so I put it back in the fridge as soon as possible.

Yesterday, Dr Zhong gave me a warning when he did the rounds. He said that even though the results of my blood test had shown that I had no serious blood disease, my blood was abnormal because of repeated high fevers and the side effects of the medicine. If I didn't rest properly, I would be very likely to get septicaemia. Nurse Gao frightened me by saying that people die of septicaemia. She also pointed out that after ten hours on a drip I shouldn't sit at the desk writing, without rest or exercise. Nurse Zhang thought I was writing another essay for the People's Liberation Army or Youth of China magazines and asked me eagerly what I was writing about. I have managed to get several of my essays published and Nurse Zhang must be my most enthusiastic reader.

24 August – Sunny

Today I sent a letter to Yulong by recorded delivery. The letter was very thick, so it took all the money I had received for one of my essays to pay for the postage.

I used to dream that my pain could be cleared away somehow, but can I clear away my life? Can I clear away my past and my future?

I often examine my face closely in the mirror. It seems smooth with youth, but I know it is scarred with experience: heedless of vanity, two frown-lines often appear, signs of the terror I feel by day and night. My eyes have none of the lustre or beauty of a young girl's, in their depths is a struggling heart. My bruised lips have had all hope of feeling ground from them; my ears, weak from constant vigilance, are unable even to support a pair of glasses; my hair is lifeless with worry, when it should shine with health.

Is this the face of a seventeen-year-old girl?

Just what are women, exactly? Should men be classed in the same species as women? Why are they so different?

Books and films may say it is better to be a woman, but I cannot believe it. I have never felt it to be true, and I never will.

. . .

Why is this big fly that came buzzing in here this afternoon always landing on the picture I've just finished? Can it be that it knows the baby fly in the picture? I shoo it away but it is fearless. Instead, I'm afraid – what if it is the baby fly's mother?

This is serious. I must . . .

25 August – Sunny

Yesterday I hadn't finished when it was time for lights out.

That big fly is still in my room today. It is very clever. Every time anybody comes in, it goes into hiding, I don't know where. As soon as the coast is clear, it either lands on my picture or buzzes all around me. I don't know what it's doing. I have a feeling that it doesn't want to leave me.

In the afternoon Dr Zhong said that if my condition stabilises, the treatment will be proved effective, and I will be discharged to build up my strength at home on a course of medication. The head nurse said that they will be very short of beds from the autumn on, so the people with lingering illnesses will all have to leave the hospital.

Go home? That would be dreadful!

I've got to think of a way to stay on.

26 August – Overcast

I hardly slept all night. I thought of many ways out, but they all seem impossible. What can I do?

It's probably quickest to infect myself with a disease, but access to the contagious-disease wards is restricted.

Today my head was so full of how to stay on that I missed a step at the canteen. One foot stepped into mid-air and I fell down. I got a big purple bruise on my thigh and a gash on my arm. When the shift changed, Dr Yu told the nurse to dab some more ointment on my arm. She said I had a weak constitution and could easily get septicaemia, and urged the nurse to watch out for flies when she changed my bandage, saying that flies were great carriers of disease.

At night the duty nurse said there were flies in my room and he wanted to spray it.

I didn't want the big fly to be killed, so I told him I was allergic to fly spray. He said he'd swat the flies for me tomorrow instead. I don't know where the big fly is hiding. I plan to leave the window open while I'm sleeping so it can escape. I don't know if that will save it.

27 August – Drizzling

I couldn't save the big fly. At 6.40 a.m. Dr Yu came to check the room and swatted it on my picture. Saying that I wanted to keep the picture, I stopped Dr Yu from getting rid of the big fly, and put it in the fridge with the baby fly. I don't know why, but I've always felt they had a special relationship.

I think the wound on my arm is slightly infected. It's come up in a big red lump, and I'm finding it very uncomfortable to write. But I told the trainee nurse who changed the bandage that it was all right and there was no need to apply fresh ointment. To my surprise, she believed me! The long-sleeved hospital pyjama top covers my arm completely.

I hope this will work.

'Flies are great carriers of disease.' Dr Yu's words have given me an idea, which I've decided to try out. I don't care about the consequences, even death is better than going home.

I'm going to squash the big fly into the cut on my arm.

30 August – Sunny

Success! My temperature has been going up and up for the last two days. I feel very ill, but happy. Dr Zhong is very surprised at my turn for the worse; he is going to do another full blood test on me.

I haven't visited my dear little fly for the last few days. I feel like I've got cramp all over my body.

Baby fly, I'm sorry.

7 September

Yesterday evening I was taken to the main hospital here.

I'm very tired and sleepy. I miss my baby fly, I really do.

And I don't know if Yulong has replied to my letter . . .

*

I finished reading this diary as the sun cast its first rays in the east, and the noise of people arriving for work began to filter through from neighbouring offices. Hongxue had died of septicaemia. A death certificate was included in the box of papers, dated 11 September 1975.

Where was Yulong? Did she know about Hongxue's death? Who was the woman in her forties who had left the box for me? Were the essays that Hongxue had published as beautifully written as the papers in the box? When he learned of his daughter's suicide, did Hongxue's father feel remorse? Did Hongxue's mother, who had treated her daughter as an object of sacrifice, ever discover anything of a maternal nature?

I did not know the answers to these questions. I did not know how many sexually-abused girls were weeping amongst the thousands of dreaming souls in the city that morning.

3

The University Student

Hongxue haunted me. She seemed to gaze at me with helpless and expectant eyes, as if begging me to do something. An incident that took place a few days later deepened my resolve to find a way to make my radio programme more helpful to women.

At about ten o'clock that morning, I had just cycled up to the radio station when a colleague leaving after the early shift barred my way. She told me that an old couple had arrived at the station, ranting about having a score to settle with me.

'What for?' I asked, astonished.

'I don't know. They seem to be saying that you're a murderer.'

'A murderer? What do they mean?'

'I don't know, but I think you'd better keep out of their way. When some of these listeners get going, there's no reasoning with them.' She yawned. 'Sorry, can't fight it. I've got to go home and sleep. It's torture having to come in at four thirty for the early news. Bye.'

I waved goodbye distractedly.

I was anxious to find out what was happening, but had to wait for the External Affairs Office to deal with the matter.

At nine o'clock that evening, the office finally passed on a letter that the old couple had given them. The colleague who delivered it said it was the suicide note of the couple's only child, a nineteen-year-old girl. Afraid that I would be too disturbed to go on air after reading it, I put the letter in my jacket pocket.

It was after half past one in the morning by the time I left the studio. It was only when I had fallen into bed at home that I dared open the letter. It was stained with tears.

Dear Xinran,

Why didn't you reply to my letter? Didn't you realise that I had to decide between life and death?

I love him, but I have never done anything bad. He has never touched my body, but a neighbour saw him kiss me on the forehead, and told everyone I was a bad woman. My mother and father are so ashamed.

I love my parents very much. Ever since I was small, I have hoped that they would be proud of me, happy that they had a clever, beautiful daughter rather than feeling inferior to others because they did not have a son.

Now I have made them lose hope and lose face. But I don't understand what I have done wrong. Surely love is not immoral or an offence against public decency?

I wrote to you to ask what to do. I thought you would help me explain things to my parents. But even you turn away.

Nobody cares. There is no reason to go on living.

Farewell, Xinran. I love you and hate you.

A loyal listener in life,

Xiao Yu

Three weeks later, Xiao Yu's first letter begging for help finally arrived. I felt crushed by the weight of this tragedy. I hated to think of the number of young Chinese girls who might have paid for their youthful curiosity with their lives. How could love be equated with immorality and offending public decency?

I wanted to put this question to my listeners and asked my director if I could take calls on the subject on air.

He was alarmed. 'How would you guide and control the discussion?'

'Director, isn't this the time for Reform and Opening Up? Why don't we give it a go?' I tried to draw justification from the newly fashionable vocabulary of openness and innovation.

'Reform is not revolution, opening up is not freedom. We are the mouthpiece of the Party, we can't broadcast whatever we like.' As he spoke, he gestured as if to slit his throat. Seeing that I wouldn't give up, he finally suggested that I pre-record a programme on the topic. This would mean that the script and any taped interviews could be carefully vetted in advance at the studio and the final, edited programme sent to the monitoring department before it was broadcast. Because all pre-recorded programmes had to pass through so many stages of editing and examination they were considered absolutely safe. With live broadcasts there were far fewer checks in place. Everything was dependent on the presenter's technique and ability to steer a discussion away from problematic areas. Directors would often listen to these programmes with pounding hearts, since mistakes could lose them their jobs, or even their freedom.

I was disappointed not to be able to take calls on air. It would take me two if not three times as long to make a pre-recorded programme in this way, but at least I would be able to make one that was relatively free of Party 'dye'. I set to work recording a series of telephone interviews.

Contrary to my expectations, when it was broadcast the public response was muted. There was even one very hostile letter of criticism, anonymous of course:

Before, radio programmes were nothing but strings of slogans and bureaucratic jargon. A slightly different tone had finally been achieved, with something of a human touch, so why this regression? The topic is worth examining, but the presenter is shirking responsibility with her cold, distant manner. Nobody wants to listen to someone declaiming wisdom from afar. Since this is a topic for discussion, why aren't people allowed to speak freely? Why doesn't the presenter have the courage to take calls from the audience?

The distant effect this disgruntled listener had described was the result of the lengthy editing process. The monitors, long used to working in a certain way, had cut out all the parts of the script where I had tried to introduce a more personal tone into my commentary. They were like the cooks in a big hotel: they only made one kind of dish and adjusted all voices to their accustomed 'flavour'.

Old Chen saw that I was feeling hurt and resentful.

'Xinran, there is no point in being angry. Put it behind you. When you walk though the gates of this radio station, your courage is impounded. You either become an important person or a coward. No matter what other people say or what you yourself think, none of it is any use: you can only be one of these two things. You had better face the fact.'

'Well, what are you then?' I asked.

'I'm both. To myself I'm very important, to others I'm a coward. But categories are always more complex underneath. You were discussing the relationship between love, tradition and morality. How can we draw a distinction between these three things? Each culture, each sensibility perceives them differently. Women who have been brought up in a very traditional manner blush if they see a man's chest. In the nightclubs there are young women who flaunt themselves half naked.'

'Isn't that an exaggeration?'

'Exaggeration? The real world of women is full of even greater contrasts. It you want to deepen your understanding of women you should try to find a way to get out of this radio station and observe life. Sitting in an office and a studio all day is no good.'

Old Chen had inspired me. He was right. I had to see more of ordinary women's lives and let my views mature. But, at a time when travel was restricted, even for journalists, it was not easy. I started to make opportunities whenever I could, collecting information about women on business trips, visits to friends and family, and when I went on holiday. I wove this information into my programmes and noted what reactions it elicited from my listeners.

One day, I was hurrying to the radio station from the university where I was a guest professor. The university campus was a hive of activity at lunchtime, and I had to push my bicycle through crowds of students. Suddenly, I heard several young women having a conversation that seemed to be to do with me:

'She says Chinese women are very traditional. I don't agree. Chinese women have a history, but they have a future too. How many women now are traditional? What's traditional anyway?

Padded coats that fasten at the side? Wearing your hair in a bun? Embroidered shoes? Covering your face in front of a man?'

'I think the tradition she is talking about must be a concept, precepts passed down from the ancestors, or something like that. I didn't listen to the programme yesterday so I'm not sure.'

'I never listen to women's programmes, I only listen to the ones with music.'

'I've heard it, I like going to sleep listening to her programme. She plays nice music and her voice is soothing. But I don't like the way she harps on about women's gentleness. Surely she can't mean that men are savage?'

'I think she does, a bit. She must be the sort of woman who acts like a spoiled princess in her husband's arms.'

'Who knows? She could just as well be the kind of woman who makes her old man kneel at her feet so she can vent her anger on him.'

I was dumbstruck. I didn't know young girls talked like this. As I was in a hurry, I didn't stop to ask them about their opinions as I usually would, but resolved to spend some time talking to university students. Since I worked at the university occasionally as a guest professor, it was easy for me to set up interviews there without any bureaucratic hassle. It is always among students that revolutions start; these young people were cresting the wave of change in the modern Chinese consciousness.

Someone told me about a young woman who was a celebrated member of the 'in-crowd' at the university, well known for her initiative, modern ideas and opinions. Her name had a fine ring to it: Jin Shuai, 'golden general'. I invited her to meet me in a tea house.

Jin Shuai looked more like a PR executive than a student. Though her features were unremarkable, she commanded attention. She wore a well-cut navy suit that showed her figure to advantage, an elegant shirt and seductively high leather boots. Her long hair hung loose.

We sipped Dragon Well tea from small vermilion glazed cups.

'So, Xinran, are you as well read as people say?'

Jin Shuai immediately reversed our roles by asking the first question.

Keen to impress her, I listed some of the books on history and economics that I had read.

She was not impressed. 'What can those dusty old tomes teach you about human needs and desires? They just witter on about empty theories. If you want to read some books that are of use to you, try *Modern Commercial Management*, *The Study of Personal Relations*, or *The Life of an Entrepreneur*. At least these help you make money. Poor you, you've got all those important connections, not counting your thousands of listeners, and you still work day and night to earn a paltry salary. You've wasted so much time reading all those books that you've missed your opportunity.'

I grew defensive. 'No, everybody makes their own choices in life . . .'

'Hey, don't take it badly. Isn't it your job to answer listeners' questions? Let me ask you some more. What philosophy do women have? What is happiness for a woman? And what makes a good woman?' Jin Shuai drained her cup in one gulp.

I decided to hand the reins to Jin Shuai, hoping she would reveal her true thoughts. 'I want to hear what you think,' I said.

'Me? But I'm a science student, I've no idea about social science.' She had turned strangely modest, but I suspected I could use my interview skills to make her continue.

'But your opinions are not limited to the sciences,' I suggested.

'Yes, well, I do have a few opinions.'

'Not just a few. You are well known for your opinions.'

'Thank you.' For the first time, she spoke in the respectful tone I had previously thought all university students employed.

I seized the opportunity to ask her a question. 'You are clever, young and attractive. Do you consider yourself to be a good woman?'

'Me?' She appeared irresolute for a moment, then replied firmly, 'No.'

My curiosity was piqued. 'Why?' I asked.

'Waitress, two more Dragon Well teas please.' The confidence with which Jin Shuai placed her order displayed an ease born of wealth. 'I don't have the necessary gentleness and conscientiousness. Good Chinese women are conditioned to behave in a soft, meek manner, and they bring this behaviour to bed. As a result, their husbands say that they have no sex appeal, and the women submit to oppression, convinced the fault is their own. They must bear the pain of menstruation and childbirth, and work like men to keep the family when their husbands don't earn enough. The men pin pictures of beautiful women above the bed to arouse themselves, while their wives blame themselves for their care-worn bodies. Anyway, in men's eyes, there's no such thing as a good woman.'

I queried this. Jin Shuai needed no encouragement.

'When men's hormones are raging, they swear undying love. This has given rise to reams of poetry through the ages: love as deep as the oceans or what have you. But men who love like that only exist in stories. Real men make the excuse that they haven't met a woman worthy of such emotion. They are expert at using women's weaknesses to control them. A few words of love or praise can keep some women happy for a long time, but it's all an illusion.

'Look at those old couples who have relied on each other for decades. You'd think the man would be satisfied, wouldn't you, but give him the chance and he'll reject the old to marry the new. The reason he's bound to give is that his wife is no good. In the eyes of men who keep mistresses, there are still fewer good women. Those men simply see women as playthings. They despise their mistresses, or else they would have married them long ago.'

Jin Shuai paused, and grew solemn. 'Do you know what sort of woman men want?'

'I'm not an expert,' I replied truthfully.

Jin Shuai spoke with an air of authority. 'Men want a woman who is a virtuous wife, a good mother, and can do all the house-work like a maid. Outside the home, she should be attractive and cultivated, and be a credit to him. In bed, she must be a nymphomaniac. What is more, Chinese men also need their women to manage their finances and earn a lot of money, so they can mingle with the rich and powerful. Modern Chinese men sigh over the abolition of polygamy. That old man Gu Hongming at the end of the Qing dynasty said that 'one man is best suited to four women, as a teapot is best suited to four cups'. And modern Chinese men want another cup to fill with money too.

'So tell me, how many Chinese women can fulfil all these requirements? All women are bad by these standards.'

Two men at the table next to us turned to look at Jin Shuai from time to time. She continued undaunted.

'Have you heard the saying "Other people's wives are always better, but your own children are always best"?'

'Yes,' I said, relieved that I could finally claim to know something.

She mused, 'I once read a book about love where it said: "A hungry lion will eat a rabbit if there is nothing better, but once he has trampled the rabbit, he will abandon it to chase a zebra . . ." The tragic thing is that so many women accept men's judgement of them as "bad women".'

Feeling that Jin Shuai counted me among these women, I coloured slightly. She did not notice.

'Xinran, do you know that it is the really bad women who are the lucky ones? I believe the saying "Money makes men bad; badness makes women money." Don't think that we're all poor students here. Many of us young women live in style without a penny from our parents. Some girls couldn't even afford to eat meat in the canteen when they first came to university, but now they wear cashmere and jewels. They take taxis everywhere and stay in hotels. Don't get me wrong though, these girls aren't necessarily selling their bodies.'

Jin Shuai could see that I looked shocked and continued, smiling.

'Today, rich men are becoming more exacting in their requirements for female company. They want to parade a "personal secretary" or "escort" with learning. With China's current shortage of talent, where can so many "personal secretaries" be found, apart from in the universities? A woman with no certificates will only be able to attract some small businessman; the better educated you are, the more you have the chance to hook a big entrepreneur. A 'personal secretary' works for just one man, an "escort" works for many. There are three levels of companionship. The first level involves accompanying men to restaurants, nightclubs and karaoke bars. The second level takes it further to include accompanying them to other events such as the theatre, cinema and so on; we call this "selling art not self". Of course, letting those men fumble with your clothes is part of the deal. The third level involves being at a man's beck and call night and day, also for sex. If you're this sort of "personal secretary" you don't sleep in the university dormitory, except in the unlikely event of your boss going home. Even then, the man mostly lets you stay on in the hotel room he has rented, to make it easier for him to find you when he returns. As a "personal secretary" all your meals, clothes, lodging and travel are taken care of. Nobody dares to cross you when you're so close to the boss. You're under one man but over a thousand! If you're clever, you can soon get some real power, and if you're really sharp, you'll never have to worry about money.'

She poured herself more tea.

'Don't they say "Times make the man"? The "personal secretary" in China is a creation of Deng Xiaoping's Reform and Opening Up policy. As soon as China opened up, everyone started chasing money; everybody wanted to be a boss. Many dream of wealth, but few succeed. Have you noticed that everyone's title is "general manager" or "director" on their business cards? Regardless of the size of the business, their companies inevitably have grandiose names.

'And how can all these men start a company without a secretary – wouldn't they lose face? But a secretary for only eight hours a day is not enough, someone has to be there to fix everything all the time. Add to this the law of sexual attraction, and opportunities abound for attractive young girls. Fashionably dressed young women rush about between the stuffy government departments and quicken the pace of economic development in China.

'Personal secretaries are also required by the foreigners fighting to stake a claim on our economy. They don't understand the first thing about China and its customs. If not for the help of their secretaries, the corrupt Chinese officials would have made mincemeat of them long ago. To be a foreigner's secretary, you also have to speak a foreign language.

'Most "personal secretaries" are quite realistic about their prospects. They know that their bosses will never abandon their families. Only a fool would take their sweet words for love.

There are some fools though, and I hardly need to tell you the result.'

I had listened to Jin Shuai's exposé of the world of 'escorts' and 'personal secretaries' open-mouthed. I did not feel that we came from the same century, let alone the same country. 'Does this really go on?' I stuttered.

Jin Shuai was astounded by my ignorance.

'Of course! Let me tell you a true story. I have a good friend, Ying'er, a lovely, considerate girl, tall and slender, with a sweet face and voice. Ying'er was a talented student at the art college. She could sing and play any kind of instrument, so she brought music, smiles and laughter everywhere. Both men and women liked her company. Two years ago, when Ying'er was in her second year, she met a Taiwanese company director called Wu at a dance hall. He was good-looking and smart; the real estate company he ran in Shanghai was doing well, so he wanted to open a branch in Nanjing. But when he arrived here, he found it hard to get to grips with all the commercial regulations. He spent thousands of US dollars, but was nowhere near setting up the branch after six months.

'Ying'er took pity on Wu. With her resourcefulness, pleasant manner and good contacts, she sorted out the red tape with the commercial bureau, the tax office, the city council and the bank. Soon, the branch office was in business. Wu was overcome with gratitude. He rented a suite in a four-star hotel for Ying'er, and covered all her expenses. Ying'er was a woman of the world, but she was won over by Wu's gentlemanly behaviour. He did not behave like the fat cats who think that money can buy everything. Ying'er decided to stop escorting other men and to throw herself into helping Wu with his Nanjing business.

'One day, at about three o'clock in the morning, Ying'er rang me, sounding extremely happy:

'"This time it's the real thing. But don't panic, I haven't told him how I feel. I know he has a wife. He said she was a good woman. He showed me their wedding photographs: they're well matched. I don't want to tear his family apart, it's enough that he's good to me. He's so loving; when I feel down or lose my temper, he doesn't get angry. When I asked him why he was so patient, he said: 'How can a man call himself a man if he gets angry with a woman in pain?' Have you ever heard such tenderness? All right, I won't disturb you any longer, I just didn't want to keep anything from you. Good night, my dear."

'I couldn't get to sleep for ages, wondering if such ideal love between men and women could really exist. I hoped Ying'er would prove it, and give me a bit of hope.

'I didn't see Ying'er for the next few months as she withdrew into the bliss of love. When we met again, I was shocked at her thin, drawn appearance. She told me that Wu's wife had written to him, ordering him to choose between divorce and leaving Ying'er. Naively, Ying'er had thought Wu would choose her since he had seemed unable to live without her. Besides, the Wu fortune was so large that dividing it wouldn't affect his business too much. However, confronted by his wife, who came over from Taiwan, Wu announced that he could let neither wife nor fortune go, and ordered Ying'er to get out of his life. He and his wife gave Ying'er 10,000 dollars as a token of gratitude for her help with their affairs in Nanjing.

'Ying'er was devastated, and asked for time alone with Wu to ask three questions. She asked if his decision was final. Wu said it was. She asked if he had meant his earlier declarations of affection. He said he had. Finally, Ying'er asked him how his feelings could have changed. He replied brazenly that the world was in a constant state of flux, then announced that her quota of three questions was up.

'Ying'er returned to her life as an "escort", now firm in the conviction that true love did not exist. This year, less than two months after she graduated from university, she married an American. In the first letter she sent me from America, she wrote, "Never think of a man as a tree whose shade you can rest in. Women are just fertiliser, rotting away to make the tree strong . . . There is no real love. The couples who appear loving stay together for personal gain, whether for money, power or influence."'

'What a pity that Ying'er realised this too late.'

Jin Shuai fell silent, moved by her friend's fate.

'Jin Shuai, do you plan to get married?' I asked curiously.

'I haven't thought much about it. I can't figure love out. We have a professor who abuses his power to determine exam marks. He calls up pretty students for "a heart-to-heart talk"; they talk their way to a hotel room. This is an open secret, everybody except his wife knows. She talks contentedly about how her husband spoils her: he buys her everything she wants and does all the housework, saying he can't bear for her to do it. Can you believe the lecherous professor and devoted husband are the same man?

'They say, "Women value emotions, men value the flesh." If this generalisation is true, why marry? Women who stay with their unfaithful husbands are foolish.'

I said that women were often slaves to their emotions, and told Jin Shuai about a university lecturer I knew. Several years before, her husband, also an academic, had seen many people make a lot of money by starting their own businesses. He was chafing to leave his job and do the same. The woman told him that he did not have the business or management skills to compete, and reminded him of his skills: teaching, research and writing. Her husband accused her of looking down on him, and set out to prove her wrong. His business was a spectacular failure: he drained the family savings and had nothing to show for it. The woman became the family's sole breadwinner.

Her unemployed husband refused to help her in the home. When she asked him to help with the housework, he would protest that he was a man, and couldn't be asked to do womanish things. The woman left early for work and came home late, staggering with exhaustion. Her husband, who never got out of bed before one o'clock in the afternoon, and spent all day watching television, claimed that he was much more exhausted from the stress of unemployment. He could not sleep well and had little appetite, so needed good, healthy food to build up his strength.

His wife spent all her spare time tutoring children for extra money, only to be criticised by her husband for running herself down. He did not give a thought to how the family was being fed and clothed. Unwilling to spend money on make-up or new clothes for herself, the lecturer never let her husband go without good suits and leather shoes. He was unappreciative of her efforts, and complained instead that his wife was not as well dressed and elegant as before, comparing her unfavourably to attractive younger women.

For all his education, he seemed like a peasant anxious to prove his power and position as a man.

The woman's university colleagues chided her for spoiling her husband. Some of her students also expressed their disapproval. They asked her why she was putting herself through so much for such an unworthy man. The woman replied helplessly, 'He used to love me very much.'

Jin Shuai was incensed by my story, but recognised that it was a very common situation.

'I think more than half of all Chinese families are made up of women who are overworked and men who sigh over their unfulfilled ambitions, blaming their wives and throwing tantrums. What's more, many Chinese men think that saying a few loving words to their wives is beneath their dignity. I just don't get it. What has happened to the self-respect of a man who can live off a weak woman with an easy conscience?'

'You are sounding like a feminist,' I teased her.

'I'm no feminist – I just haven't found any real men in China. Tell me, how many women have written to your show to say that they are happy with their men? And how many Chinese men have asked you to read out a letter saying how much they love their wife? Why do Chinese men think that to say the words "I love you" to their wives undermines their status as a man?'

The two men at the next table were pointing at where we were sitting. I wondered what they made of Jin Shuai's fierce expression.

'Well, that's something Western men say because of their culture.' I made an attempt to defend the fact that I had never received such a letter.

'What, you think it's a cultural difference? No, if a man doesn't have the courage to say those words to the woman he loves before the world, can you call him a man? As far as I'm concerned, there are no men in China.'

I was silent. Faced with a woman's heart that was young and yet frozen solid, what could I say? But Jin Shuai laughed.

'My friends say that China has finally come into line with the rest of the world when it comes to our topics of conversation. Since we no longer have to worry about not having enough food or clothes, we discuss the relationship between men and women instead. But I think the subject of men and women is even more complex in China. We have to contend with over fifty ethnic groups, countless political changes and prescriptions for the behaviour, bearing and dress of women. We even have over ten different words for wife.'

For a moment, Jin Shuai looked like a carefree, innocent girl. Her enthusiasm suited her better than the carapace of the PR girl and I liked her better.

'Hey, Xinran,' she said, 'can we talk about all the famous sayings associated with women. For example, "A good woman doesn't go with a second man." How many widows in China's history have not even considered remarrying in order to preserve the reputation of their families? How many women have "emasculated" their female nature for the sake of appearances? Oh, I know "emasculate" isn't a word used for women, but that's what it is. There are still women like that now in the countryside. And then there's the one about the fish . . .'

'What fish?' I had never heard this figure of speech and realised I must seem very ignorant in the eyes of the younger generation.

Jin Shuai sighed ostentatiously and tapped the table with her varnished fingernails. 'Oh, poor Xinran. You haven't even got the various categories of women straight. How can you possibly hope to understand men? Let me tell you. When men have been drinking, they come out with a set of definitions for women. Lovers are "swordfish", tasty but with sharp bones. "Personal secretaries" are "carp", the longer you "stew" them, the more flavour they have. Other men's wives are "Japanese puffer fish", trying a mouthful could be the end of you, but risking death is a source of pride.'

'And what about their own wives?'

'Salt cod.'

'Salt cod? Why?'

'Because salt cod keeps for a long time. When there is no other food, salt cod is cheap and convenient, and makes a meal with rice . . . All right, I've got to go to "work". You shouldn't have listened to me rabbiting on for so long. Why didn't you say anything?'

I was silent, preoccupied by the startling comparison of wives with salt cod.

'Don't forget to answer my three questions on your programme: What philosophy do women have? What is happiness for a woman? And what makes a good woman?'

Jin Shuai finished her tea, picked up her handbag and was gone.

I pondered Jin Shuai's questions for a long time, but I realised that I didn't know the answers. There seemed such a huge gap between her generation and mine. In the course of the next few years, I had the opportunity to meet many more university students. The temperaments, attitudes and lifestyles of the new generation of Chinese women who had grown up during the period of 'Reform and Opening Up' were entirely different from those of their parents. But although they had colourful theories on life, there was a deep layer of emptiness behind their thoughts.

Could they be blamed for this? I did not think so. There had been something missing from their upbringing that had made them like this. They had never had a normal, loving environment in which to grow up.

From the matriarchal societies in the far distant past, the position of Chinese women has always been at the lowest level. They were classed as objects, as a part of property, shared out along with food, tools and weapons. Later on, they were permitted to enter the men's world, but they could only exist at their feet – entirely reliant on the goodness or wickedness of a man. If you study Chinese architecture, you can see that many long years passed before a small minority of women could move from the side chambers of the family courtyard (where tools were kept and the servants slept) to chambers beside the main rooms (where the master of the house and his sons lived).

Chinese history is very long, but it has been a very short time since women have had the opportunity to become themselves and since men have started to get to know them.

In the 1930s, when Western women were already demanding sexual equality, Chinese women were only just starting to challenge male-dominated society, no longer willing for their feet to be bound, or to have their marriages arranged for them by the older generation. However, they did not know what women's responsibilities and rights were; they did not know how to win for themselves a world of their own. They searched ignorantly for answers in their own narrow space, and in a country where all education was prescribed by the Party. The effect that this has had on the younger generation is worrying. In order to survive in a harsh world, many young people have adopted the hardened carapace of Jin Shuai and suppressed their emotions.

4

The Scavenger Woman

By the wall of the radio station, not far from the security guards, there was a row of small shacks pieced together from scrap metal, roofing felt and plastic bags. The women who lived here supported themselves by collecting rubbish and then selling it. I often wondered where they were from, what had brought them together, and how they had come to end up there. In any case, it was wise of them to have chosen a relatively safe place for their shacks, just a shout away from the armed guards on the other side of the wall.

Among the scattered huts, the smallest of them stood out. The materials from which it was built were not different, but it had been carefully designed. The scrap-metal walls had been painted with a bright sunset, and the roofing felt had been folded into a castle-like turret. There were three small windows made from red, yellow and blue plastic bags, and a door made of coloured cardboard woven with strips of plastic sheeting, which would have no difficulty keeping out the wind and rain. I was moved by the care and attention to detail that had obviously gone into building this flimsy hut, and found the wind chimes made of broken glass tinkling gently over the door especially poignant.

The owner of this scrap castle was a thin, frail woman of over fifty. It was not only her shack that was unique; she too was set apart from the other scavenger women by her appearance. Most of the women had dishevelled hair and dirty faces, and were dreadfully ragged, but this woman kept herself neat, and her worn clothes were scrupulously clean and well mended. But for the bag she carried to collect rubbish, you would never imagine she was a scavenger. She seemed to keep to herself.

When I told my colleagues what I had observed of the scavenger woman, they piped up one after the other that they too had noticed her, not wanting me to feel that I was in any way unique. One of them even told me that the scavenger women were keen listeners to my programme. I could not tell if they were mocking me.

From the sidelines, Big Li, who reported on social issues, rapped his desk with a pen, a sign that he was about to give his younger colleagues a lecture.

'You shouldn't pity the scavengers. They are not poor at all. Their spirits transcend the mundane world in a way that ordinary people can't imagine. There is no room in their lives for material possessions, so their material desires are easily satisfied. And if you take money as a standard by which to judge people, you will find that some of those women are no worse off than people in other jobs.' He told us that he had seen a scavenger woman in an expensive nightclub, covered in jewels and drinking French brandy at a hundred yuan a glass.

'What nonsense!' retorted Mengxing, who worked on the music programme. To her, the difference in their ages alone meant that she never believed anything Big Li said.

Normally the most cautious of men, Big Li unexpectedly got the bit between his teeth and offered to make a bet with Mengxing. Journalists love stirring things up, so everyone else enthusiastically started pitching in with suggestions about what the stake should be. They decided on a bicycle.

To carry out the bet, Big Li lied to his wife saying that he would be doing some evening reports, and Mengxing told her boyfriend that she had to go out and research contemporary music. Every night, for several days in succession, the two of them went to the nightclub Big Li claimed was frequented by the scavenger.

Mengxing lost. Sipping whisky, the scavenger had told Mengxing that her income from selling rubbish was 900 yuan a month. Big Li said that Mengxing had been in shock for hours. Mengxing earned about 400 yuan per month, and she was considered one of the favoured employees of her grade. From then on, Mengxing was no longer particular about the artistic value of a job; as long as she could earn money, she would take on absolutely anything. Everyone in the office said that the loss of her bicycle had brought on this new pragmatism.

Despite having noticed the tidy woman who lived in the scrap castle, I had not paid much more attention to the manner in which the scavengers passed their days. Frankly, part of me shied away from them. However, after Mengxing's encounter, every time I saw people scavenging I would try to guess if they were really 'fat cats'. Perhaps the scavenger women's shacks were just their workplaces, and their homes were ultra-modern flats.

It was the pregnancy of my colleague Xiao Yao that prompted me to get to know the scavenger woman. As soon as Xiao Yao found out she was going to have a baby, she started to look for a nanny. I could understand her starting her search nine months in advance: finding someone reliable to look after a child and do the housework was no easy task.

My own nanny was a kind, honest and diligent nineteen-year-old country girl, who had fled alone to the big city to escape a forced marriage. She had some native intelligence, but it had never been given the help of education. This placed all sorts of obstacles in her way: she could not tell one banknote from another, or understand the traffic lights. At home she could be reduced to floods of tears because she could not get the lid off the electric rice cooker, or would mistake gourmet pickled eggs for rotten eggs and throw them in the bin. Once, she pointed to a litter bin by the side of the road, telling me in all seriousness that she had put my letters in that 'postbox'. Every day I would leave careful instructions about what she should and should not do, and would telephone regularly from the office to check that everything was all right. Fortunately, nothing ever went terribly wrong and she and PanPan had a very loving relationship. There was one time, however, when I had been unable to stop myself being angry. It was winter and I arrived home after my programme to find PanPan, then only eighteen months old, sitting in the stairwell of the fifth floor, dressed only in a thin pair of pyjamas. He was so chilled by the bitter cold that he could only cry in faint moans. I hastily gathered him in my arms and woke the sleeping nanny, reproaching myself for not being able to give my child the time or care a mother should.

I never discussed my own childcare difficulties with my colleagues, but I heard plenty of horror stories from other people. The newspapers were full of them. Careless maids had let children fall from fourth-floor windowsills to their deaths; others, ignorant and foolish, had put children in washing machines for a wash, or shut them in the fridge during a game of hide-and-seek. There were cases of children being kidnapped for money, or beaten.

Few couples were prepared to ask their parents for help with childcare, as that would involve living under the same roof. Most were prepared to have their lives made a bit more difficult in order to avoid the critical eyes of the older generation. Chinese mothers-in-law, especially the traditional or less educated ones, were legendary for terrorising their sons' wives, having cowered under their own mothers-in-law in their time. On the other hand, a woman giving up her job to be a full-time mother was impracticable, because it was next to impossible to support a family on an average single income. House-husbands were unheard of.

Listening to Xiao Yao's pleas for help to find a trustworthy, affectionate and cheap nanny, Old Chen responded flippantly, 'There are so many women around picking up scrap, why don't you ask one of the poor ones to work for you? You wouldn't have to worry about her running off, and you wouldn't need to pay her a lot either.'

People say that men are good at seeing the big picture, and women are good on detail. Like all generalisations, I have never believed this to be true, but Old Chen's throwaway remarks amazed me with the kind of genius-bordering-on-idiocy that you sometimes find in men. I was not the only one who felt this way. Several of my female colleagues were also beside themselves with excitement: 'Yes! Why didn't we think of that before?'

Confirmation of Chairman Mao's famous words – 'A single spark can start a prairie fire' – swiftly followed. Choosing a scavenger as a nanny became a subject of fevered conversation among my female colleagues for several days. Since all their children were of different ages, they thought they might find someone they could share. They made detailed plans about how to supervise and assess her, and what kind of rules to set.

Soon after, I was asked to attend a 'women's meeting' in the small meeting room next to the women's toilets. No sooner had I sat down and asked uneasily if they had not called the wrong person, than they announced that I had been unanimously chosen as their representative to pick a nanny from among the scavenger women living by the radio station. In a militant manner that brooked no argument, they set forth the criteria that had led them to choose me as their representative. This was the first time my female colleagues had displayed any approval of me. They said that I appeared sincere, that I had the human touch and common sense, and that I was thorough, thoughtful and methodical. Despite suspecting them of ulterior motives, I was touched by their estimation of me.

Over the next few days, I started inventing excuses to go over to the scavenger women's huts. But the results of my observations were disappointing: looking at the women rooting around for salvageable rubbish, it was difficult to imagine them as caring, reasonable people, let alone think of inviting them into the home. They wiped their snot on to anything within reach, and those who had children tucked them under their arms to leave their hands free for picking rubbish. With only a piece of paper to shield them, they relieved themselves by the roadside.

The only scavenger woman worth considering was the owner of the scrap castle. In her daily activity, she seemed to display kindness, cleanliness and warmth. After several false starts, I worked up enough courage to stop her on her way home.

'Hello! My name is Xinran, I work at the radio station. Excuse me, but may I have a word with you?'

'Hello. I know you. You're the presenter of *Words on the Night Breeze*. I listen to your programme every night. What can I do for you?'

'It's like this . . .' I, the radio presenter who could talk endlessly in front of the microphone, suddenly grew so incoherent that I could barely follow my own babbling speech.

The scavenger lady was quick to grasp what I had in mind. She replied calmly, but decisively. 'Please thank your colleagues for their good opinion of me, but it would be very hard for me to accept their generous offer. I like to live an unfettered life.' She swept away all the persuasive talents my colleagues had seen in me with one quiet sentence.

When I reported back to my colleagues, they could not believe their ears. 'The great radio presenter can't even talk a scavenger round . . .'

There was nothing I could have done. The look in the scavenger lady's eyes prevented all argument. I felt that there was more than simple refusal in her expression, but did not know what.

From then on, observing the scrap castle and its owner became part of my daily routine. One evening in the second month of autumn, I finally got another chance to get close to the little hut. After I had finished my programme, I walked past the scavengers' shacks as usual. When I passed the scrap castle, the faint sound of singing drifted out – it was the Russian folk song 'Grasslands'. I grew intensely curious. After the Cultural Revolution, China had been through another Cold War with Russia, so not many people knew this song; even fewer knew it well enough to sing it. My mother had studied Russian at university and taught me the song. How had the scavenger woman come to know it?

I drew closer to the scrap castle. The singing suddenly stopped, and the specially designed window opened silently. The scavenger lady, dressed in a home-made nightdress, asked, 'What is it? Do you need something?'

'I'm . . . I'm sorry, I just wanted to listen to you singing, you sing really well!'

'Really? Xinran, do you like that song?'

'Yes, yes! I like it a lot. I'm very fond of both the words and the tune, especially late at night. It's like a perfectly composed picture.'

'Can you sing it?'

'A little, not well. I can't seem to convey its flavour.'

'You radio people are funny. You make words live, but can't sing. What's the flavour of a song then? Sweet? Sharp? Bitter?'

'Excuse me, but how should I address you?'

'You all call us scavenger women, don't you? I think that's a good way to address us, so just call me Scavenger Woman. Scavenger Woman is just right for me.'

'Isn't that a little inappropriate?'

'Don't worry about it, Xinran. Just call me Scavenger Woman "A", "B" or "C". It doesn't matter. So you were just listening to me singing to myself. Was there nothing else you wanted?'

'No, I was just passing on my way home after the programme. When I heard you singing that Russian folk song, I thought it was a bit out of the ordinary. Excuse me, but may I ask you how it is that you know it?'

'My husband taught me the song; he studied in Russia.'

The Scavenger Woman did not say much more, or invite me inside her castle, but I did not mind, for the Russian song had given me a small key to her memories.

After our conversation that night, the Scavenger Woman did not show any particular warmth when she saw me again. My mind was buzzing with questions: Her husband had been a student abroad, so how had she drifted into this life as a scavenger? Her speech and gestures were so refined – what sort of family did she come from? What kind of education had she had? Did she have children? If so, where were they?

Not long after that, as New Year was approaching, I went on a reporting trip to Beijing. A friend at Radio Beijing suggested a visit to the Lufthansa Centre, a shopping mall that sold famous foreign branded goods. I spotted a box of Russian liqueur chocolates. It was expensive, but I decided to buy it anyway. My friend tutted at my ignorance: the best liqueur chocolates were Swiss, who had ever heard of Russian liqueur chocolates? But I wanted to buy them for the Scavenger Woman. I felt sure that someone who could sing a Russian folk song so well would appreciate them.

On my return from Beijing, I could not stop myself from going straight to the scrap castle instead of heading home first. Before I knocked on the Scavenger Woman's door, I hesitated. The Chinese say, 'In this world, there is no love without a reason, there is no hate without a cause.' How could I explain the thought behind my gift to her, when I could not explain it to myself?

The Scavenger Woman took the box respectfully in both hands, deeply moved. Normally impassive, she was clearly shaken by the sight of the chocolates. She told me that her husband had loved this type of liqueur chocolates – just as I had guessed, people of that generation thought the best things were Soviet – and that she had not seen them for more than thirty years.

Calm gradually returned to her face, and at last she asked why I had given her such an expensive gift.

'Because we are both women, and I want to hear your story,' I said with a frankness that surprised myself.

'. . . All right then!' The Scavenger Woman seemed to have come to a momentous decision. 'But not here, there are no walls here. Nobody, least of all a woman, would allow everyone to see the scars on their breast.'

We walked to a small hill in the botanical gardens, where only the trees and I could hear the Scavenger Woman's tale.

Her story was fragmented. She did not expand on causes or consequences, and I got the strong impression that she was still unwilling to put her experiences fully on display. Her words only opened the box that she enclosed herself in, but did not lift the veil from her face.

As a young man, the Scavenger Woman's husband had studied in Moscow for three years, and entered politics not long after he came back. This coincided with the terrible events of the Great Leap Forward. Under the care of the Party, which pulled strings and built bridges for him, he married the Scavenger Woman. Just as her whole family was rejoicing over the birth of their second child, her husband died suddenly of a heart attack. By the end of the following year, her younger child had died of scarlet fever. The pain of losing her husband and child made the Scavenger Woman lose the courage to carry on living. One day she took her remaining child to the bank of the Yangtze River to seek a reunion with her husband and baby in her next life.

On the bank of the Yangtze, she was just getting ready to bid life farewell when her son asked innocently, 'Are we going to see Papa?'

The Scavenger Woman was shocked: how could a five-year-old know what was in her heart? She asked her son, 'What do you think?'

He answered loudly, 'Of course we're going to see Papa! But I didn't bring my toy car to show him!'

She started crying, and did not ask her son any other questions. She realised that he was very much aware of what she was feeling. He understood that his father was no longer in the same world as they were, but like all young children, had no clear understanding of the difference between life and death. Her tears revived her maternal feelings and sense of duty. She cried with the child in her arms, letting the rushing of the river wash away her weakness and give her strength. Then she picked up her suicide note and took her son back home.

Her child asked her, 'Aren't we going to see Papa then?'

She replied, 'Papa's too far away, and you are too little to go there. Mama will help you to grow up, so you can take more, and better, things to him.'

After that, the Scavenger Woman did all that a single mother could to give her son the best of everything. She said he had gone on to achieve great success.

But why did her son, who must be married and established in a career by now, allow his mother, who had toiled for him all his life, to be reduced to the condition of a scavenger? 'Where is your child? Why . . . ?' I asked falteringly.

The Scavenger Woman did not give a direct reply. She only said that no one could describe a mother's heart. She hinted firmly that I was to enquire no further.

The New Year was over and Spring Festival was approaching. This is the most important festival of the year for the Chinese, and many people use it as an opportunity to solidify their business contacts. Every year, officials in the media do particularly well out of the festival. Irrespective of rank, they receive stacks of presents and dozens of invitations to social events. Even though I was only a humble presenter at the time, with no official power, I was still sought after by wealthy and influential people because of the popularity of my programme. Their attention was not a recognition of my own achievements, but of the importance of my listeners. All officials in China know the ancient teaching passed down from the Tang dynasty: 'Water supports a boat, it can also capsize it.' Ordinary people like my listeners were the water, and the officials were the boat.

Among the bright red-and-gold invitations I received was one from a newly appointed high flyer in the city council. Rumour had it that this young man was capable of great things; he had hopes of becoming one of the chosen few who went on to become cadres at provincial level. I very much wanted to know what special qualities this man – who was only a few years older than me – had, to be able to negotiate his way through the labyrinth of Chinese politics. I decided to attend his reception dinner; the invitation specified a Western-style self-service buffet, which would be something new.

The dinner was held at the politician's home, which, while not a mansion, was very impressive. The sitting room alone could have made four or five bedsits for single people like me. Because I had arrived rather late, the room was already filled with the chatter of the crowd and the clink of glasses. My hostess carefully introduced me to several important people in order of their rank. An irreverent thought flashed into my mind: when these exalted personages went to the toilet, did they have to go in hierarchical order? If so, the lower ranks must suffer terribly.

The Western buffet was sumptuous, and seemed authentic enough, if the pictures I had seen in magazines were anything to go by. To demonstrate that she was giving the women from the media special treatment, the zealous hostess, in a show of intimacy, called the few female news journalists to her bedroom, and brought out a box of liqueur chocolates she had put aside specially for us.

I was thunderstruck: the chocolates was identical to the ones I had given the Scavenger Woman. The hostess opened the box. Inside the lid were the lyrics to the Russian folk song 'Grasslands' that I had copied out by hand for the Scavenger Woman as a gesture of goodwill for the new year.

This powerful family was as far removed from the Scavenger Woman's scrap castle as the heavens from the earth. How had the chocolates arrived here? My brain was feverish with questions and my pulse quickened. I had no desire to stay any longer at the banquet, so made a hurried excuse and set off for the scrap castle, running like a woman possessed.

The Scavenger Woman was not there. I waited for a long time until she returned late that night. As soon as she saw me she burst out excitedly, 'New Year and Spring Festival are the busy season for collecting rubbish. In all the litter bins, big or small, there is a lot of food still in its packaging, and useful everyday things that people have thrown out. Honestly, the age we live in . . . People have forgotten what hard times are like.'

I could contain myself no longer, and interrupted her to ask baldly, 'Why have I just seen the box of chocolates I gave you in the house of an up-and-coming politician? Did someone steal them? What's been going on?'

The Scavenger Woman listened to this torrent of questions with a complex expression on her face. She was shaking visibly, but with a great effort she brought herself under control and replied, 'After Spring Festival we can fix a time, and I'll tell you.'

After that, she shut her door and paid no further attention to me. I stood there stunned. The wind chimes tinkling in the freezing wind finally roused me from my trance, and I started for home.

Spring Festival seemed to drag on endlessly. I was filled with remorse. Living alone in that flimsy shack battered by the wind and rain, with no friends or family, the last thing the Scavenger Woman had needed was the burden of my insensitive questions. I thought about going to visit her, but I knew that her words had been final: after Spring Festival it would have to be.

On my first day back at work after the holiday, I hurried to the office very early. When I passed the scrap castle, I saw that the door was padlocked. The Scavenger Woman always left very early too. This was not surprising: who would want to sleep late in a tiny shack that gave protection from neither heat nor cold? At the entrance to the radio station, the gatekeeper called out to say that someone had left a letter for me the day before. Many listeners took the trouble to deliver their letters personally. They seemed to think this was more secure, and more likely to get my attention. I thanked the gatekeeper, but took no particular notice of the letter, dropping it in my in-tray as I was passing.

That day I nipped outside four or five times to check on the scrap castle, but the door was always locked and the Scavenger Woman was nowhere to be seen. I was beginning to feel slightly put out that she had not kept her word, but was determined to wait for her. I wanted to apologise, and to clear up the incident over the chocolates. I decided to stay at the office until the late shift, and read my letters.

At about 8.20 in the evening, I went out once more, but the door to the scrap castle was still locked. I wondered why she was still out. Were the pickings so great? Back in my office, I continued reading my letters. The next letter I opened was written in a delicate, beautiful hand. The writer was obviously a highly educated woman, one who had received the very best education. I was rooted to the spot by what I read.

Dear Xinran,

Thank you. Thank you for your programme – I listen every day. Thank you for your sincerity – it has been many years since I have had a friend. Thank you for the box of Russian liqueur chocolates – it reminded me that I am a woman who once had a husband.

I gave the chocolates to our son. I thought he would enjoy them as much as his father once did.

It is very difficult for a son to live with his mother, and very difficult for his wife. I do not want to disrupt my son's life, or give him a hard time trying to keep the balance between his wife and his mother. However, I find it impossible to escape my female nature and the lifelong habits of a mother. I live as I do in order to be close to my son, to catch a glimpse of him as he goes to work early every morning, Please don't tell him this. He thinks that I have been living in the countryside all this time.

Xinran, I'm sorry, but I'm leaving. I am a teacher of foreign languages, and I should return to the countryside to teach more children. As you once said on your programme, old people should have a space of their own in which to weave a beautiful old age for themselves.

Please forgive my coldness to you. I have given all the warmth in me to my son, his father continues in him.

Wishing you a happy and peaceful Spring Festival,

Scavenger Woman

The Rubbish Hut

I could understand why the Scavenger Woman had left. She had allowed me to see into her heart and her shame would not let her face me again. I felt sorry that I had driven her away from her carefully constructed world but also sorry that she had burned herself up to give light to her children, only to resign herself to being cast aside. Her sole faith was in her identity as a mother.

I kept the Scavenger Woman's secret, and never told her son how she had watched over him. But I never went to his house again, since the Scavenger Woman, whose memory I treasured, had never even crossed its threshold. Although he appeared so wealthy, she was the one who was truly rich.

5

The Mothers Who Endured an Earthquake

When my colleague Xiao Yao had her baby, I arranged to visit her in hospital with several other women from the office. Mengxing was very excited, as she had never been to a maternity ward. Director Zhang from the External Affairs Office warned her not to go: in China, women who have not given birth are believed to bring bad luck to newborn children. Mengxing dismissed this as an old wives' tale, and went to the hospital ahead of us.

We arrived at the hospital laden with food for Xiao Yao: brown sugar and ginseng for her blood, pigs' trotters and fish to help her breastfeed, and chicken and fruit to build up her constitution. As we entered the room, we saw Mengxing chatting to Xiao Yao. She was eating one of the boiled eggs dyed red to symbolise happiness at the birth of a new child.

Xiao Yao's parents and parents-in-law were there too, and the room was filled with gifts. Xiao Yao looked happy and surprisingly fresh after her ordeal. I guessed that having given birth to a boy was one reason for her glow of well-being.

For countless generations in China, the following saying has held true: 'There are thirty-six virtues, but to be without heirs is an evil that negates them all.' A woman who has had a son is irreproachable.

When Xiao Yao was in labour, she had been in a ward with seven other women. Xiao Yao asked her husband several times to move her to a private room, but he had refused. On receiving the news that she had given birth to a son, her husband had immediately arranged for her to be moved to a single room.

The room was cramped but brightly lit. Each of us found a place to perch, and my colleagues began talking animatedly. I am no good at such conversations because I don't enjoy talking about my own life, which is a tale of incomplete families. As a child, I was separated from my father and mother; as an adult, I had no real family of my own – only my son. Listening quietly, I folded a piece of wrapping paper into an origami rabbit.

Over my colleagues' conversation, I heard voices from the corridor.

A man spoke in a low but determined voice. 'Please change your mind. It will be far too dangerous.'

'I'm not afraid. I want to experience the birth,' replied a woman.

'You may not be afraid, but I am. I don't want my child to be motherless.'

'If I don't give birth to it naturally, how can I call myself a mother?' The woman sounded impatient.

'But you know that in your condition you can't –'

'The doctors didn't say it was one hundred per cent impossible!' the woman interrupted him, 'I just want to do it myself . . .' Their voices faded as they walked away.

As I was leaving, Xiao Yao's mother-in-law furtively slipped me a piece of red cloth and asked me to burn it to 'drive away the evil influences brought by Mengxing'. I dared not disobey. When I left the hospital I tossed the cloth into the stove of a roadside food stall, but did not tell Mengxing, for she hated to acknowledge defeat.

Three months later, I received an invitation to a funeral dinner from a family I did not know. Listeners often invited me to family events, but they were usually weddings. Strangers are seldom invited to funeral dinners, so I was puzzled. The dinner was being held in a restaurant rather than in a funeral parlour or crematorium, and the invitation asked guests to bring a boy's name with them. I had never encountered these practices before.

I decided to go, and brought the name 'Tianshi' (Heaven's Key) with me. The host received the guests with a month-old baby in his arms; his wife had died in childbirth. When he found out who I was, he asked me tearfully why his wife had refused to have a

66

Caesarean knowing it would endanger her life. Was the experience of giving birth naturally so important that it was more important than life?

I wondered to myself if this could have been the couple I had overheard in the hospital. I was shocked by this unknown woman's decision, but on some deep level I understood her desire to have this unique experience. Her bereaved husband could not and did not. He asked me if I could tell him how he could understand women.

I do not know if his baby boy took the name Tianshi, but as I left the funeral dinner I hoped he would be a heaven-sent key to unlock the door to women's minds for his father.

I only truly understood what it means to be a mother, however, when, in 1992, I visited the industrial city of Tangshan, which had been rebuilt after its complete destruction in the terrifying earthquake of 28 July 1976 when 300,000 people lost their lives.

As the broadcasting station in Nanjing was an important one in China, I often had to travel the country to attend regional conferences on the development of radio and television programming. The sole purpose of these conferences was to parrot Party policy rather than engage in any genuine debate. To make up for the lack of intellectual stimulation, the organisers frequently arranged for the participants to travel the surrounding countryside during the conferences. This gave me many opportunities to interview women in different areas of China.

During one such conference in Tianjin, I took the opportunity to visit nearby Tangshan. The Tangshan earthquake of 1976 was notorious for exemplifying the complete breakdown in communication in China at that time. In 1976, the Chinese government was coping with the deaths of three crucial figures: Mao Zedong, Prime Minister Zhouenglai and the military leader Zhu De. Their preoccupation with this crisis, together with the inadequacy of Chinese technology, meant that they were completely unaware that the earthquake had happened. It wasn't until a man from Tangshan went all the way to Beijing that the news filtered through. Even then, people thought he was a lunatic. The Xinhua local news agency, which covered Tangshan, found out about the earthquake, not from government central office, but from the foreign press, who had received reports from the more sophisticated earthquake monitoring centres of other countries.

While I was in Tangshan I heard about an unusual orphanage founded and run by mothers who had lost their children during the earthquake. I was told they financed it out of the compensation money they had received. I telephoned to arrange a visit. The orphanage had been built with the help of the local army garrison, and was situated in a suburb, next to an army sanatorium. I heard children's voices as I approached the low wooden fence and shrubs that surrounded it. This was an orphanage without officials; some called it a family without men. A few mothers and several dozen children lived there.

I found the children exercising in the courtyard, and the mothers making dumplings in the kitchen. The women greeted me with floury hands, telling me how much they liked my programme. Still in their aprons, they took me on a tour of the orphanage.

Each mother lived with five or six children in one large room, simply furnished, but homely. Dwellings of this kind are common in northern China: half the room is occupied by a *kang*, a bed-cum-stove made out of bricks or earth. In the winter, a fire can be lit under the *kang* to keep it warm and at night everyone in the family sleeps on it. Individual quilts demarcate sleeping areas. In the daytime, the quilts are rolled up on one side and a small table is set up on the *kang* to form a living and dining area for the family. The other half of the room is filled with wardrobes, a settee and chairs for receiving guests.

Unlike normal homes, the rooms in the orphanage had been decorated in a riot of colour, according to the children's interests. Every room had its own style of decoration, but three things were present in all the rooms. The first was a frame containing pictures of all the children who had lived at the orphanage. The second was a crude painting of an eye brimming over with tears, with two words written on the pupil – 'the future'. The third was a book in which each child's history was recorded.

The women were very proud of the children, and regaled me with tales about their exploits, but it was the stories of the women that I was keenest to hear.

On my first visit, I managed to interview only one mother, Mrs Chen. She had been an army dependant, and had had three children. I talked to her as I helped her boil dumplings for the children, addressing her as 'auntie' as she was of my parents' generation.

'Auntie Chen, can I ask you about what happened the day of the earthquake? I'm sorry, I know the memories must be very painful . . .'

'That's all right – not a day goes by when I don't think of that day. I don't think anyone who survived it can ever forget. Everything was so unreal . . . That morning, before it was light, a strange sound woke me, a rumbling and hooting, like a train was being driven into our house. I thought I was dreaming – dreams are so strange – but just as I was about to cry out, half the bedroom caved in, along with my husband in his bed. The children's bedroom on the other side of the house suddenly appeared before me, like a stage set. My elder son was staring, mouth open; my daughter was crying and calling out, stretching her arms towards me; and my little son was still sleeping sweetly.

'Everything happened so quickly . . . the scene before me suddenly dropped away like a curtain falling. I was terrified, but I thought I was having a nightmare. I pinched myself hard, but didn't wake up. In desperation, I stabbed my leg with a pair of scissors. Feeling the pain and seeing the blood, I realised this was no dream. My husband and children had fallen into an abyss.

'I shouted like a madwoman, but no one heard me. The sound of walls collapsing and furniture smashing filled the air. I stood, trailing my bleeding leg, facing the yawning pit that had been the other half of my house. My husband and my beautiful children had vanished before my eyes. I wanted to cry, but there were no tears. I simply did not want to go on living.'

Her eyes were filled with tears.

'I'm sorry, Auntie Chen . . .' I stammered, overcome.

She shook her head. 'It's been nearly twenty years, but nearly every day at dawn, I hear a train rumbling and hooting, along with the cries of my children. Sometimes I'm so frightened of those sounds, I go to bed very early with the children and put an alarm clock under my pillow to wake me before three. When it rings, I sit up until it gets light, sometimes I go back to sleep after four. But after a few days of this, I crave those nightmarish sounds again, because my children's voices are in there too.'

'Does it make you feel better to have so many children around you now?'

'Much better, especially at night. I watch them sleeping and feel comforted in a way I can't explain. I hold their hands to my face as I sit by them. I kiss them and thank them for keeping me alive.'

'The children will thank you when they grow up – it's a cycle of love.'

'That's right, from old to young and back. All right, the dumplings are done, I must call the children in. Will you have a little too?'

I excused myself, saying I would be back tomorrow. My heart was too full to speak to anyone else. I left feeling emotionally and physically drained.

That night, I heard in my dreams the rumbling noise and children's cries that Auntie Chen had described, and woke drenched in cold sweat. Sunlight was streaming through the net curtains, and the sound of children on their way to school filtered through. Relief washed over me.

That day's meeting finished early. I politely refused an invitation to dinner from some friends in Tianjin and hurried to catch the train to Tangshan. At the orphanage, I spoke to a woman called Mrs Yang, who was in charge of the children's meals. She was supervising the children's dinner when I arrived.

'Look how the children are enjoying their food,' she said.

'That must be because you're a good cook.'

'Not necessarily. Children enjoy certain things, like food in special shapes. It may just be steamed bread shaped like a bunny or a puppy, but they'll eat more of it that way. They also like sweet things, so they enjoy sweet-and-sour dishes or Cantonese roast pork. They like food that is easy to chew, like meatballs or vegetable balls. Children always think what their friends have is nicer, so I let them choose their food and swap it as they wish. It stimulates their interest in food. My daughter was exactly the same; if you gave her one portion of the same thing on several different plates, she got so excited.' She shook her head fondly.

I spoke hesitantly, 'I heard that your daughter . . .'

'I will tell you my daughter's story, if you like, but I won't do it here. I don't want the children to see me cry. It's such a comfort to see them eating and laughing so happily, they really make me . . .' She stopped, her voice suddenly thick with tears.

I prompted her gently. 'Auntie Yang?'

'Not here, let's go to my room.'

'Your room?'

'Yes, I'm the only one to have a room of my own, because my other job is taking care of the children's health records and personal belongings. We can't let the children near those things.'

Mrs Yang's room was very small; one wall was almost completely covered with a photograph that had been so overenlarged that it looked like a painting in pixels of colour. It showed a young girl with lively eyes, lips parted as if about to speak.

Gazing at the picture, Mrs Yang said, 'This is my daughter. The photo was taken when she graduated from primary school. It's the only picture I have of her.'

'She's very pretty.'

'Yes. Even in nursery school, she was always acting and making speeches.'

'She must have been very clever.'

'I think so – she was never top of the class, but she never gave me any cause for worry.' Mrs Yang stroked the photograph as she spoke. 'It's been nearly twenty years since she left me. I know she didn't want to go. She was fourteen. She knew about life and death: she didn't want to die.'

'I heard that she survived the earthquake?'

'Yes, but it would have been better for her to have been crushed to death at once. She waited fourteen days – fourteen days and two hours, knowing death was approaching. And she was only fourteen . . .' Mrs Yang broke down.

Unable to keep my own tears back, I said, 'Auntie Yang, I'm sorry,' and put my hand on her shoulder.

She sobbed for a few minutes. 'I'm . . . I'm all right. Xinran, you can't imagine what a wretched scene that was. I will never forget the expression on her face.' She gazed at the photograph again with loving eyes. 'Her mouth was slightly open, just like this . . .'

Distressed by her tears, I asked, 'Auntie Yang, you've been busy all day, you're tired, let's talk next time, all right?'

Mrs Yang composed herself. 'No, I've heard you're very busy. You've come all this way just to hear our stories; I can't let you leave with nothing.'

'It doesn't matter, I have time,' I reassured her.

She was resolute. 'No, no. I'll tell you now.' She took a deep breath. 'My husband had died a year before, and my daughter and I lived in a fifth-floor flat allocated by the work unit. We had only one room, and shared a common kitchen and bathroom. It wasn't a big room, but we didn't find it cramped. Because I hate extremes of heat and cold, my half of the room was by the inner wall, and my daughter's was by the outer wall. That morning, I was woken suddenly by rumbling, banging and a violent shaking. My daughter called out, and tried to get out of bed to come over to me. I tried to stand, but couldn't stay upright. Everything was tilting, the wall was leaning towards me. Suddenly, the wall by my daughter disappeared, and we were exposed on the edge of the fifth floor. It was very warm, so we were only in our underclothes. My daughter screamed and wrapped her arms around her chest, but before she could react more fully, she was thrown over the edge by another falling wall.

'I screamed her name as I held on to some clothes hooks on the wall. It was only after the swaying had stopped and I could stand still on the sloping floor that I realised this was an earthquake. I looked frantically for a way to get downstairs, and staggered off, shouting my daughter's name.

'I hadn't realised that I wasn't dressed. All the other survivors were wearing very little too. Some were even naked, but nobody thought about these things. We were all running around wildly in the half-light, weeping and shouting for our relatives.

'In the cacophony, I screamed myself hoarse asking everyone in sight about my daughter. Some of the people I approached asked me if I had seen their relatives. Everyone was wild-eyed and yelling, nobody took anything in. As people gradually realised the full horror of the situation, a grieving silence fell. You could have heard a pin drop. I was afraid to move, in case I made the earth start shaking again. We stood surveying the scene before us:

collapsed buildings, broken water pipes, yawning holes in the ground, corpses everywhere, lying on the ground, hanging over roof beams and out of houses. A pall of dust and smoke was rising. There was no sun or moon, nobody knew what time it was. We wondered if we were still in the land of the living.'

I encouraged Mrs Yang to have a drink of water.

'Water? Ah, yes . . . I'm not sure how long it took, but I began to feel thirsty because I had shouted my throat raw. Someone echoed my thoughts in a weak voice, "Water . . ." reminding everyone to turn to the immediate matter of survival. A middle-aged man stepped out of the crowd, and said, "If we want to live, we must help each other and get organised." We murmured in agreement.

'It was starting to get light, and everything before us became more distinct, and more horrible. Suddenly someone shouted, "Look over there, someone's alive!" In the wan light, we saw a girl wedged in mid-air between the ruined walls of two buildings. Although her hair hung over her face, and her lower body was trapped and hidden from view, I knew from the colour and style of her bra, and from the struggling movement of her torso that she was my daughter. "Xiao Ping!" I shouted. I called her name over and over again, wild with joy and grief. She continued writhing desperately, and I realised that she could not hear or see me. I pushed my way forward through the crowd, gesturing towards her and sobbing hoarsely that she was my daughter. Rubble blocked my path. People started to help, trying to scale the wall my daughter was trapped in, but it was at least two storeys high, and they had no tools. I shouted Xiao Ping's name over and over again. She still had not heard me.

'A few women, then some men joined in shouting to help me. Soon, almost everyone was calling, "Xiao Ping! Xiao Ping!"

'Xiao Ping finally heard us. She raised her head, and used her free hand – her left – to push her hair off her face. I knew she was looking for me. She looked confused; she couldn't find me in the crowd of naked or near-naked bodies. A man next to me started pushing everyone around me aside. None of us understood what he was doing at first, but soon it became clear that he was trying to clear a big space around me so Xiao Ping could see me. It worked; Xiao Ping shouted "Mama!" and waved to me with her free hand.

'I shouted back, but my voice was hoarse and faint. I raised my arms and waved to her instead. I don't know how long we spent calling and waving. Finally, somebody made me sit down. A big empty space was still left around me, so Xiao Ping could see me. She was tired too, her head was lolling and she was gasping for breath. In retrospect, I wonder why she never screamed for me to save her. She never said anything like "Mama, save me", not a word.'

'When did you start counting the fourteen days and two hours you spoke of?'

'Someone shouted to Xiao Ping, "It's 5.30 in the morning, there'll be someone coming to rescue you soon!" He wanted to comfort her, to help her hold on. But seconds, minutes and hours passed, and nobody had come to the rescue.'

'That was because it took time for people to find out what had happened,' I said, remembering how long it had taken for a news report to appear.

Mrs Yang nodded. 'What kind of a country was this in 1976? A big city lay in ruins and three hundred thousand people had died, yet no one knew. How backward China was! I think that if we had been more advanced, many people might not have died. Xiao Ping might have survived.'

'When did the rescuers arrive?'

'I can't say for sure. I can only remember that the army came first. The soldiers were all sweaty from running, but not one paused for breath before they split up and went to the rescue. Equipped with ropes and pitons, two soldiers started to climb up the wall in which Xiao Ping was trapped. It looked like it might collapse at any moment and crush them all. I could hardly breathe as I saw them edge closer and closer to her . . .' She fell silent for a few minutes.

'When Xiao Ping saw that someone was coming to rescue her, she burst into tears. The first soldier to reach her took off his uniform jacket to cover her. She only had one arm free, so he had to wrap half the jacket around her like a Tibetan robe. The other soldier held a water bottle to her mouth. The two soldiers started pulling away the bricks and stones around Xiao Ping, and soon freed her right arm, which was bruised and bloody. For some reason, they suddenly stopped digging. I shouted to them, asking what the matter was, but they couldn't have heard me. After a while, they climbed down and walked over to me. Gesturing with bloodied hands, they told me that the lower half of Xiao Ping's body was wedged between the reinforced concrete slabs of the wall, which they couldn't dig away by hand. I asked them why their hands were all bloody. They put their hands behind their backs and said that they were not allowed to use tools to dig people free, for fear of hurting them.

'After it was all over, I found out that some soldiers' fingernails and fingertips had been worn away by digging, but they had bound their hands in cloth and carried on. Some soldiers shouted madly as they dug, because they could hear moans and cries for help deep within the rubble. How much could they do by hand? The heavy rescue equipment couldn't get to the city because the roads were destroyed. How many people died waiting for rescue?' She sighed, and wiped the tears from her eyes.

'Xiao Ping must have been very strong.'

'Yes. She used to howl over a scratch from a branch, and blanch at the sight of blood. But in those last fourteen days she was so strong, she even comforted me, saying, "Mama, I'm numb, so it doesn't hurt a bit!" When her body was finally freed, I saw that her legs had been crushed to a pulp. The person who laid her out for the funeral said that her pelvis had broken under the pressure. I hope she really had lost feeling in her lower body in those fourteen days, when she was exposed to the elements. I counted every minute. Throughout that time people tried all sorts of different methods to rescue her, working round the clock, but nothing worked.

'Finally, the soldiers helped me to climb the wall up to Xiao Ping, and piled up a makeshift seat for me so I could sit holding her in my arms for long periods at a time. Her small, weak body was icy cold, though it was summer.

'For the first few days, Xiao Ping could still talk to me, and waved her hands about as she told stories. After the fourth day, she grew weaker and weaker, until she could barely lift her head.

Although food and medicine were brought to her every day, and someone came to nurse her, the bottom half of her body must have been bleeding all the time, and gangrene must have been setting in. More and more people were concerned about her fate, but there was nothing anyone could do. The whole of Tangshan lay in ruins: there just weren't enough emergency workers or equipment to go round, and the roads to the city were impassable. My poor daughter . . .'

'Auntie Yang,' I murmured. We were both crying.

'In the last few days, I think Xiao Ping might have realised that there was no hope for her, though people made all sorts of excuses to keep her spirits up. She lay helplessly in my arms, unable to move. On the morning of the fourteenth day, she forced her torso upright and said to me, "Mama, I feel like the medicines you've been giving me are taking effect. There's some strength in me, look!"

'When they saw her sit up, the people around who had been watching her attentively for fourteen days all started clapping and cheering. I thought a miracle had happened too. When Xiao Ping saw how excited everyone was, she seemed to get a new surge of strength. Her face, which had been deadly pale, flushed bright red and she spoke to her well-wishers in a clear, loud voice, thanking them and answering questions. Somebody suggested that she sing a song, and the crowd clapped in approval. At first, Xiao Ping was shy, but people cheered her on: "Sing a song, Xiao Ping! Xiao Ping, sing a song!" At last, she nodded weakly, and started singing: "The red star is shining with a marvellous light, the red star is shining in my heart . . ."

'Everyone knew this song back then, and many people started to sing along with Xiao Ping. The sound of singing amid the desolation was like the flowering of hope. For the first time in many days, people were smiling. After a few verses, Xiao Ping's voice faltered, and she slowly sank back into my arms.'

Mrs Yang fell silent for a long time. Finally, she roused herself and continued. 'Xiao Ping never woke again. I thought she was sleeping, but when I realised my mistake, it was too late. She had no last words; her last experience of this world was of people singing and smiling around her. When the doctor told me that she was dead, I was calm – those fourteen days and two hours had wrung me dry. It was only four days later, when they finally dug out Xiao Ping's body, which had started to smell, that I began to weep. Her body was in such a state . . . my own flesh and blood . . . I hurt, how I hurt!'

I sobbed with her, 'I'm sorry, Auntie Yang, I'm sorry.'

'Poor child, in her fourteen years she only saw three films, *Tunnel Warfare*, *Mine Warfare* and *The Battle of North and South*, and eight model operas. She never laid eyes on a pretty dress or a pair of high-heel shoes . . .'

'That is a great sadness in Chinese history. I came out of those times too, and had virtually no experience of youth or beauty.'

Mrs Yang sighed. 'Some people say the earthquake was divine retribution for the events of the Cultural Revolution. But who were the gods taking revenge on? I have never done anything to offend them or anything immoral. Why did they destroy my daughter?'

'Oh, Auntie Yang, don't say that! Xiao Ping's death wasn't retribution. Don't think that, whatever you do. If, in the place where she is now, Xiao Ping knew you were in so much pain, it would make her worry. You ought to live as best and as happily as you can – that's the best reward for Xiao Ping's sacrifice, don't you agree?'

'Yes, that's true . . . but I . . . oh well, let's not talk about that. You're busy, go and get on with your things, don't pay any attention to my silly talk.'

'Thank you, Auntie Yang.' I pressed her hand. 'I think you see a lot of happiness and laughter in the children here. I'm sure that as they grow up the children will be a continuation of Xiao Ping's soul, and the wonderful things she left to the world.' I looked up at Xiao Ping's photograph and felt as if she was imploring me not to leave her mother alone. It was as if she was speaking to me with my son PanPan's voice.

Several days later, I returned to Tangshan to interview the head of the orphanage, Warden Ding.

Warden Ding had been an administrative officer in the army for more than ten years. Her husband had left the army due to ill health, and she had moved with her family from south-west China back to Tangshan about a year before the earthquake. She had lost her daughter in the disaster, and her son had lost both his legs. Later, her husband had died from a heart attack. She had brought up her crippled son with the help of the government. He had taught himself accountancy, and had volunteered to help with the accounts when several mothers were discussing setting up the orphanage. Not long after my visit, he died of an infection in his wounds.

To avoid bringing back painful memories for Warden Ding, I tried to interview her son instead. However, he said that he had been too young at the time, and could not remember the earthquake. He told me his mother had never told him the true reason for his sister's death. He had only heard vaguely that she had not died in the earthquake, but had killed herself afterwards. He wanted very much to ask his mother about this, but every time he broached the subject, his mother would shush him.

There was nothing for it but to ask Warden Ding if she was willing to be interviewed. She agreed, but suggested that I wait until the National Day holiday to come back and interview her. When I asked why, she said, 'It won't take me long to tell you my story, but it will throw me off balance for several days after. I will need time to recover.' National Day that year fell before a weekend, so we had three days off in a row. This was a long holiday for China, where holidays were not routine.

The evening before the holiday, when I had just arrived in Tangshan, Warden Ding telephoned to invite me to meet her.

I went over to the orphanage, and sought to reassure her by saying that we could stop the interview at any time if she found it too difficult.

She smiled faintly. 'Xinran, thank you for the kind thought, but don't forget I am a soldier who has seen action in Korea.'

I nodded. 'I heard that you didn't lose a single member of your family in the earthquake?'

'That's right, but survival was disaster for all of us.'

'Am I right in thinking that your husband died of grief at your daughter's misfortune?'

'Yes, and I almost died too. It was the thought of my crippled son that held me back. I thought of myself as a necessary part of him, only then could I live on.'

In a faltering voice, I prompted, 'Your daughter committed suicide because . . .'

'To this day, only three people know why: my husband, my daughter and myself.'

'Oh?'

'Yes. You must have heard many times about how much destruction the earthquake caused – I don't need to go over it again. In fact, words cannot fully describe that scene. You only know what it feels like to be at the end of the world if you experience it yourself. In a situation like that, you think of your family first.

'The aftershocks had not yet died away when my husband and I managed to leave the building we had lived in, which was on the point of collapse. We discovered that the room where our children slept had been torn apart, but they were nowhere to be seen. My heart contracted with fear. Because there was a military airport near us, we were quickly rescued by the garrison. They soon dug my son out, but his legs had already been crushed, so they were amputated above the knee, as you see today. It's lucky he was rescued in good time, otherwise, on such a hot day, his wounds would have turned gangrenous and put his life in danger. After two days had passed and my daughter had still not been found, I was close to losing my mind. I saw injured, maimed and dead people dug out and carried away every day; almost never a whole person with nothing missing and no injuries.

'When I had almost given up hope, someone told me that many injured people had been taken to the airport runways. As long as there was a thread of hope, I had to go and have a look.

'But when I made it to the airport I was speechless with shock: the long runways were packed solid with groaning bodies, laid out in four or five rows. Only then did it really sink in that the earthquake had not just shaken our building, it had destroyed an entire city of hundreds of thousands of people. Filled with dread, I started to try to identify my daughter from among the rows of dead and injured people; they must all have been alive when they arrived, but some had died before there was time to administer first aid. It was difficult to identify anyone: hardly any of them were wearing clothes; some of the women's faces were covered by their hair; some people were covered in mud. After half a day, I had gone over less than half a runway. When dusk fell, I went to the tents the garrison had provided for us. I planned to continue my search the next morning.

'Many people were sleeping in the tent I was in. There was no distinction between the sexes, and no distinction between rich and poor either. People collapsed in any empty space they could find, exhausted from rushing about desperately, searching without eating or drinking, living on hope.

'Just as I was nodding off, the voices of two men drifted over from close by:

' "What are you up to? Still not sleeping?"

' "I'm thinking about that girl . . ."

' "Still?"

' "I'm not thinking about *that*. I was just wondering if she mightn't die after being dumped in that place."

' "Damn, I hadn't thought of that!"

' "What we did was bad enough, what if she dies?"

' "What do you mean by that? Do you want to go and check? If so, we'd better go quick. Then there'll still be a space for us when we get back, otherwise we'll get soaked by the rain if we sleep outside."

'I looked around to see who was talking, and was shocked to see a length of multicoloured string trailing from one of the men's shorts. It looked like the string my daughter used to tie her hair back. I didn't want to believe that it was my daughter they were talking about, but what if it was? I rushed over to the men and asked where the multicoloured string had come from. They wouldn't give me a proper answer, which made me even more suspicious. I shouted at them ferociously, asking them where the girl they had been talking about was; frightened, they mumbled something about a ditch by a distant runway, and then they fled. I could not ask them for any more details, let alone catch them; all I wanted was to know if the girl was my daughter.

'I ran off in the direction the men had indicated. When I had reached the edge of a ditch, I heard faint groans, but could not see who it was in the dark. Just then, two soldiers on patrol came over to me; they had electric torches and were guarding the injured people on the runways. I asked them to shine their torches into the ditch. In the weak torchlight, we saw a naked girl. At that moment my feelings were thoroughly confused; I both hoped she was and was not my daughter. When the two soldiers helped me carry her on to the runway, I realised that she was indeed my daughter.

' "Xiao Ying, Xiao Ying!" I shouted her name, but she looked at me in confusion, without the slightest reaction.

' "Xiao Ying, it's Mama!" Suddenly, I noticed that the lower part of her body was sticky and wet, but there was no time to think any more of it as I hurriedly dressed her in clothes the soldiers lent us. Strangely, Xiao Ying pulled the trousers down again.

'When I asked her why she had done that, she just closed her eyes and hummed. She was so tired, she soon fell asleep. I lay dazed for a long time before I too, fell asleep.

'At daybreak, the roaring of a plane woke me. When I saw Xiao Ying lying next to me, I was dumbstruck: she was pulling down her trousers with an idiot grin on her face, and her legs and groin were all bloody. Just then, I remembered the words of those two men. Had they taken advantage of the disaster to rape Xiao Ying? I dared not believe it. And my daughter, a radiant, vivacious girl, had lost her mind.

'The doctor said that Xiao Ying had had too great a shock, and told my husband and me that Xiao Ying had definitely been gang-raped. That was all I heard before I blacked out. When I came to, my husband was holding my hand, his face wet with tears. We looked at each other speechlessly and wept: our daughter had been brutalised and gone mad, our son's legs were gone . . .'

Warden Ding fell silent.

'May I ask if you sent Xiao Ying for treatment?' I asked quietly.

'We did, but we didn't understand that she would still feel the terror even if she recovered. Two and a half years later, just as her memory was starting to get back to normal, the day before we were planning to take her home to start a new life, she hanged herself in her hospital room.

In the letter she left for us she said:

Dear Mama and Papa,

I'm sorry, I can't go on living. You shouldn't have saved me. There is nothing in the memories that are coming back but everything falling apart, and the cruelty and violence of those men. That is all that is left for me in this world, and I can't live with those memories every day. Remembering is too painful, I'm leaving.

Your daughter, Xiao Ying.

'How old was Xiao Ying then?' I asked.

'She was sixteen, her brother was eleven.' Warden Ding paused. 'My husband tore his hair out with grief, saying that he was the one who had hurt the child, but of course it wasn't his fault. That night, he did not come to bed until very late. I was exhausted, and went to sleep, but when I woke up, his body was cold, and his face was frozen in sadness. The death certificate issued by the doctor states that he died of a heart attack from extreme exhaustion.'

I found it hard to breathe. 'Warden Ding, it's very hard to imagine how you could bear this.'

She nodded resignedly.

'And you didn't want your son to know?'

'He had already borne damage to his body; how could he bear the same damage to his mind and his emotions?'

'But you bravely carried on.'

'I made it, but I wasn't really brave. I am one of those who are strong in front of other people, a so-called tower of strength among women, but when I'm alone I cry all night: for my daughter, my husband, my son, and for myself. Sometimes, I can't breathe for missing them. Some people say that time heals everything, but it hasn't healed me.'

On the train home, I cried all the way. I cried again when I took up my pen to write down the experiences of these mothers. I find it very difficult to imagine their courage. They are still living. Time has carried them to the present, but in every minute, every second that has passed, they have been struggling with scenes left to them by death; and every day and every night they bear the painful memories of losing their children. This is not pain which can be removed by the will of an individual human being: the smallest domestic object – a needle and thread, a chopstick and bowl – can carry them back to the smiling faces and voices of dead souls. But they have to stay alive; they must walk out of their memories and return to reality. Only now do I realise why there was a picture of an eye in every room of the orphanage – that big eye, brimming over with tears, that eye with 'the future' written on the pupil. They did not lock their mother's kindness away in their memories of their children; they did not immerse themselves in tears of suffering and wait for pity. With the greatness of mothers, they made new families for children who had lost their parents. To me those women proved the unimaginable strength of Chinese women. As a mother, I can imagine the loss they must have felt, but I do not know if I would have been able to give so freely in the midst of pain like theirs.

When I presented a programme based on these interviews, I received more than seven hundred letters in five days. Some people asked me to send their respects to the mothers at the orphanage, and to thank them. Some people sent money, asking me to buy presents for the children. They shared the emotions the programme had roused in them: one woman said she felt grateful for her children; a girl said that she wanted to hug her mother for the first time; a boy who had left home several months before said that he had decided to return to his parents and beg their forgiveness. Every desk in the office was covered with these letters, and a big cardboard box by the door was filled with presents for the children and mothers. In it were things from Old Chen, Big Li, Mengxing, Xiao Yao, Old Zhang . . . and many other colleagues.

6

What Chinese Women Believe

I hadn't forgotten the university student Jin Shuai's three questions: What philosophy do women have? What is happiness for a woman? And what makes a good woman? In the course of the research for my programmes, I tried to answer them.

I thought it would be interesting to ask my older and more experienced colleagues Big Li and Old Chen their opinions about the philosophies that guide women's lives. Obviously, at a time when a belief in the Party always came first, I had to be careful how I phrased this question. 'Of course, women believe in the Party above everything else,' I began, 'but do they have any other beliefs?'

Old Chen was eager to discuss the subject. 'Chinese women have religious faith,' he said, 'but they seem to be able to believe in several religions at the same time. Women who believe in the spiritual and physical exercises of qigong are always changing the type of qigong they practise and the Master they follow; their gods come and go too. You can't blame them: the hardships of life make them long for a way out. As Chairman Mao said, "poverty gives rise to a desire for change." Now we believe in Mao Zedong and Communism, but before we believed in Heaven, in the Celestial Emperor, in Buddha, in Jesus and in Mohammed. Despite our long history, we have no native faith. The emperors and rulers were considered deities, but they changed constantly and people became accustomed to worshipping different gods. As the saying goes, "For a hundred people there are a hundred beliefs." In fact, you could say that there is no real belief at all. Women are much more pragmatic than men, so their attitude is to cover all the bases. They can't make out which god has power or which spirit is useful, so they'll believe in every one of them, just to be on the safe side.'

I knew that what he said was true, but wondered how people managed to reconcile the mutually antagonistic doctrines of different religions. Old Chen seemed to have guessed my thoughts: 'I think that hardly any women understand what religion is. Most are just trying to keep up with other people, afraid to be at a disadvantage.'

Big Li agreed with Old Chen. He pointed out how, especially since religious freedom was declared in 1983, one household could have several altars dedicated to different gods. Most people who prayed only did so to ask for wealth or other benefits. He told us about his neighbours: one grandparent was a Buddhist and the other was a Taoist, so they were constantly arguing. Away from the joss sticks, the Christian granddaughter had set up a cross; the grandparents constantly scolded her for this, saying she was cursing them to an early death. The girl's mother believed in some form of qigong and the father believed in the God of Wealth. They too were always quarrelling: the woman said that the man's desire for money had damaged her spiritual standing, and the man accused the woman's evil influences of attacking his wealth. The little money this family had was spent on religious rituals or holy pictures, but they had grown neither richer nor happier.

Big Li also told us of a woman manager he knew who was said to be very religious. In public speeches, she would hail the Communist Party as China's only hope; once off the podium, she would preach Buddhism, telling people that they would be rewarded in their next life according to their deeds in this one. When the wind changed, she would spread word of some form of miraculous qigong. Someone in her work unit said that she would wear a Communist Party badge on her coat, fasten a picture of Buddha to her vest and pin a portrait of Great Master Zhang of the Zangmigong sect to her bra. Seeing my look of incredulity, Big Li assured me that this woman was often mentioned in the newspapers. She was a Model Worker every year, and had been selected as an Outstanding Party Member many times.

'Her secret religiousness can't be too good in the eyes of the Party,' I said a touch irreverently.

Old Chen rapped the table and said sternly, 'Xinran, be careful. Talk like that could lose you your head.'

'Do we still have to be scared?'

'Don't be naive! In the fifties the Party called on us to "let a hundred flowers bloom, let a hundred schools of thought contend". What happened then? Those who answered the call were all imprisoned or sent to poor mountain villages. Some of them had only expressed their thoughts in their diaries, but they too suffered public criticisms and imprisonment.'

Old Chen was basically a kind man. 'You shouldn't talk about faith and religion too much,' he warned. 'You'll only be asking for trouble.'

Over the next few years, I interviewed a number of women about their beliefs and confirmed the fact that they were indeed able to believe in a whole variety of religions at the same time. In Zhengzhou, I met a retired woman cadre who managed to reconcile a devotion to the Communist Party with a strong faith in *Fangxiang Gong* (Scent and Fragrance qigong) – a kind of qigong where the idea is to cause the master to emit a fragrance by which you inhale his goodness and build up the strength of your body. Before that she had believed in keep-fit exercises and herbal remedies. When I asked her if she believed in Buddhism, she told me to keep my voice down but acknowledged that, yes, she did. The old people in her family had always said that it was better to believe in everything than nothing at all. She also told me that, at the end of the year, she believed in Jesus who was Father Christmas and came to your house to help you. When I expressed surprise that Jesus was the same person as Father Christmas, she told me I was too young to know and asked me not to tell anyone about our conversation: 'We say, "At home, believe in your own gods and do what you like; outside, believe in the Party and be careful what you do." But I wouldn't like anyone to know what I have just said. I don't want people to give me a hard time again now I'm old.'

'Don't worry, I won't tell anyone that you are my source,' I reassured her.

The woman looked doubtful. 'That's what you say, but in times like these, who can be trusted?'

The practice of qigong was gaining considerable ground in China at that time. People believed entirely in the masters who practised it and I was wary of their power. In 1995, I met a lecturer at Beijing University who was a fervent adherent of a new kind of qigong called *Falun Gong* – or should I say its founder, Li Hongzhi. Li Hongzhi taught that the world was divided into three levels: the level of the gatekeeper – himself; the level belonging to spirits of unusual virtue – the Christian God, Buddha, etc.; and the third level where ordinary people lived. 'Master Li is the god who will save humanity from the rubbish dump that this globe has become before it blows up,' she told me. 'He doesn't rely on magic to save people, rather he gives them spiritual exercises to increase the virtues of truth, goodness and tolerance, and make them fit to ascend to Heaven.' She said that she also believed in the Christian God and seemed troubled when I asked how she could do this if Li Hongzhi taught that, to practise *Falun Gong* one should have no other gods or spirits in one's heart.

And what of younger people? I once met two young girls of twenty or so in front of the Taiping South Road Protestant Church in Nanjing. One of them was fashionably dressed, and wore her long glossy hair loose. The other girl was not so well dressed, and wore her hair in a ponytail. I guessed the elegant girl came to church because it was fashionable, and that her friend had come out of curiosity, but I was wrong.

I asked them if they came to church often.

Looking at her friend, the well-dressed girl replied, 'It's my first time, I was dragged along by her.'

The girl with the ponytail chipped in, 'It's only the second time for me.'

'Did you come by yourself the first time? Or did someone else bring you?' I asked.

'I came with my granny, she's a Christian,' she replied.

'Isn't your mum one too?' her friend asked her.

'Well, my mum says she's Christian, but she's never been to church.'

I asked them both, 'Do you believe in Christianity?'

The well-dressed girl replied, 'I've never believed in it, I've just heard it's really interesting.'

'What do you mean by "interesting"?' I probed.

'So many people in the world believe in Jesus and Christianity, I think there must be something in it.'

'Well, there are many people in the world who believe in Islam and Buddhism, what about them?' I asked.

She shrugged. 'I don't know.'

Her friend with the ponytail said, 'Anyway, women have to believe in something when they get to forty.'

I was astonished at this reasoning. 'Oh? Why?'

'Look at the people praying in the churches and lighting joss sticks in the temples. They're all middle-aged women.'

'What do you think is the reason for this?'

The well-dressed girl cut in cryptically, 'Men labour hard for money, women labour hard because that's their fate.'

Her friend said, 'My granny says she didn't believe in God when she was young, but after she started to do so, many things didn't worry her the way they used to. And my mum says that after she started believing in God she stopped fighting with my dad. It's true, they used to quarrel fiercely, but now if my dad loses his temper, my mum goes up to the cross to pray, and my dad keeps quiet.'

'Women can't achieve anything big, anyway. Praying to some god is always better than playing mah-jong,' said the well-dressed girl.

I was amazed by her flippant remark. 'Can playing mah-jong and religion be spoken of in the same breath?'

The girl with the ponytail said, 'It's not a question of that. My mum says people who don't believe in anything live life one day at a time. If they had money they could have a good time, but they don't have enough to travel, or even to go out for a drink. So they stay at home and play mah-jong. At least they might win a bit of money.'

'What about religious women?' I asked.

'People who believe in a religion are different,' said the well-dressed girl, tossing her head.

Her friend confirmed this. 'Very different. Religious women

read the scriptures, attend religious activities and help other people out.'

'So, once you turn forty, will you believe in a religion?' I asked them both.

The well-dressed girl shrugged non-committally, but her friend replied firmly, 'If I'm rich, I won't believe. If I'm still this poor, I'll believe.'

'So what religion are you going to believe in?' I asked.

'That'll depend on what religion is in fashion then,' she replied.

The girls left me then, and I stood agape outside the church.

7

The Woman Who Loved Women

My colleagues had a saying: 'Journalists get more and more timid over time.' As I gained experience of how broadcasting worked and tried to push the boundaries of my programme, I began to understand what they meant by this. At any moment it was possible for a journalist to make a mistake that would endanger their career, if not their freedom. They lived within a carefully circumscribed set of rules which, if broken, entailed serious consequences. The first time I presented a radio programme, my supervisor looked so anxious I thought he was about to faint. It was only later, when I became a department head myself, that I discovered how, under Chinese radio and broadcasting regulations, if a broadcast was cut off for more than thirty seconds, the person in charge of that shift would have his or her name circulated throughout the country – a disciplinary action that could seriously affect future promotion. Even the smallest mistakes could mean a reduction in that month's bonus (which was a lot more than the salary); big mistakes often led to demotion, if not dismissal.

Two or three times a week the journalists at the broadcasting station had to attend a political study class. The sessions covered Deng Xiaoping's views on the policy of Reform and Opening Up and Jiang Zemin's theory of politics serving the economy. The principles and political significance of the news were drummed into us over and over again, and no session was complete without some condemnation of colleagues for various transgressions: not announcing leaders' names in the right hierarchical order on a programme, failing to grasp the essentials of Party propaganda in a commentary, lack of respect for one's elders, non-disclosure of a love affair to the Party, behaving with 'impropriety'; all these and other such faults were criticised. During these sessions, I felt as if China was still in the grip of the Cultural Revolution: politics still ruling every aspect of daily life, with certain groups of people subjected to censure and judgement so that others felt they were achieving something.

I found it very difficult to retain all this political information in my head, but made sure that I frequently reminded myself of the most important precept: 'The Party leads in everything.' The time came when my understanding of this principle was put to the test.

The success of my programme had brought me considerable acclaim. People were calling me the first female presenter to 'lift the veil' of Chinese women, the first women's issues journalist to delve into the true reality of their lives. The radio station had promoted me and I had received a considerable amount of financial sponsorship. I had also, finally, been able to make a 'hotline' programme and take listeners calls on air.

All live-broadcasting studios consisted of two rooms, one containing the presenter's broadcasting console, music and notes, the other a control room. Calls to my hotline came via the broadcast controller, who operated the time delay mechanism. This gave her about ten seconds to decide if a call was unsuitable to be broadcast and to cut if off without the listeners realising.

One evening, I was on the point of winding down my programme with some gentle music – which I usually did for about ten minutes at the end – when I took one last call:

'Xinran, hello, I'm calling from Ma'anshan. Thank you for your programme. It gives me a lot to think about, and helps me and many other women. Today I'd like to ask you what you think of homosexuality. Why do so many people discriminate against homosexual people? Why has China made homosexuality illegal? Why don't people understand that homosexuals have the same rights and choices in life as anyone else? . . .'

As the caller continued with her stream of questions, I broke into a cold sweat. Homosexuality was a forbidden subject under media regulations; I wondered desperately why the controller had not cut the call off at once.

There was no way that I could avoid answering this question: thousands of people were waiting for my answer and I couldn't let them know that it was considered a forbidden subject. Nor could I say that time was running out: there were ten minutes of the programme left. I turned some music up while I desperately went through everything I had ever read about homosexuality and tried to think of a way that I could deal with the subject diplomatically. The woman had just asked a penetrating question, which must have lingered in listeners' minds:

'Homosexuality has its own history, from ancient Rome in the West and the Tang and Song dynasties in China, until today. There are philosophical arguments that state that whatever exists does so for a reason, so why is homosexuality considered unreasonable in China?'

At that moment I saw through the glass partition the controller answer the internal telephone. She blanched and immediately cut the caller off mid sentence, regardless of the strict rule against doing this. Seconds later, the duty director burst into the control room, and said to me through the intercom, 'Be careful, Xinran!'

I let the music play on for more than a minute before I turned to the microphone. 'Good evening, friends by the radio, you're listening to *Words on the Night Breeze*. My name is Xinran, and I'm discussing live the world of women with you. From ten to twelve every night, you can tune in to women's stories, listen to their hearts and learn about their lives.' I did my best to fill airtime while I ordered my thoughts.

'Just now, we took a call from a listener who knows a great deal about society and history, and understands the experiences of a group of women with an unconventional lifestyle.

'To the best of my knowledge, homosexuality is, as the caller said, not just the product of one modern society: there are records of it in Western and Eastern history. It is said that, during the wars of conquest in ancient Rome, the rulers even encouraged their soldiers to engage in homosexuality. Then, however, it was perhaps more a question of the utility of homosexuality, rather than their approval of it. Homosexual relations helped the soldiers cope with the war and the longing for their families. In a cruel twist, the emotional attachments formed between the soldiers gave them additional impetus to avenge dead or wounded lovers.

'In China, homosexuality was not confined to the Tang and Song; there are records of it as early as the North Wei dynasty. These records all stem from the imperial court. But homosexuality has never dominated society – perhaps because mankind has a natural need for the love between a man and a woman, and a need to procreate. As the wise men and sages of classical China said, "Everything competes for its place, and Fate chooses."

'We all agree that everybody has the right to choose their lifestyle, and a right to their sexual needs. However, humanity is constantly in a state of transition. All countries, regions and ethnic groups are journeying towards the future of mankind as best they can, in search of the perfect system. None of us can yet reach a final conclusion about the rights and wrongs of this journey and, until we have reached perfection, we need guidance. We also need tolerance and understanding.

'I don't think heredity alone makes homosexuality, nor do I believe that the family environment can be solely responsible. Curiosity is even less credible as a single reason for homosexuality. I believe its sources are many and varied. We all have different experiences of life, and we make similar but different choices. Recognising difference means that we should not expect others to agree with our opinions on homosexuality, for such expectations can lead to prejudice of another kind.

'To our homosexual friends who have experienced prejudice, I would like to say "Sorry" on behalf of the careless people you have encountered. We all need understanding in this world.'

I turned the volume of the music up, switched off the microphone and took a deep breath. Suddenly, I realised that the control room on the other side of the glass partition was crowded with the most senior staff in the station. The station head and the director of programming rushed into the studio, grasped my hands and shook them vigorously.

'Thank you, thank you, Xinran! You replied very, very well!' The station head's palms were wet with perspiration.

'You saved our skins!' the director of programming stuttered, his hands trembling.

'Enough talk, let's go and eat! We can put it on the office account,' said Old Wu, the head of administration. I was overwhelmed by the attention.

Later, I found out what had happened. The broadcast controller told me that she had been worrying about her son's university entrance exams, so had not paid attention to the call until the duty director telephoned her in panic. Old Wu had been listening to the programme at home as he did every day. Realising that the programme had entered a minefield, he immediately called the director of programming, who hurriedly called the station head: to be aware of the situation and fail to report it would have made for an even more grievous error. They all hurried to the studio, listening to my programme on the way. By the time they arrived in the control room, the crisis had resolved itself.

The first time I even heard of homosexuality was at university. Because I had a good complexion, the female students nicknamed me 'Egg' or 'Snowball', and often stroked my cheeks and arms admiringly. Observing this, a male instructor teased, 'Watch out for a homosexual assault!'

I knew the word 'assault' in terms of physical aggression, but I had no idea what the instructor was talking about. He explained, 'Homosexuality is a woman loving a woman or a man loving a man. It's against the law.'

'What? Is it against the law for mothers to love their daughters, or fathers to love their sons?' I countered.

The instructor shook his head. 'Those are blood relationships, not sexual love. Oh, it's no use talking to you. I might as well be "playing music to a buffalo". Forget it, forget it.'

Later, I heard about homosexuality at a reunion of some of my mother's former colleagues. Apparently, my mother had once worked with two women who had shared a single room. When conditions improved, and the work unit allocated them a room each, they had turned the offer down. They behaved like sisters so nobody gave the matter much thought at the time. Their contemporaries were busy with courtship, marriage and children, then with grandchildren. Ground into a state of mental and physical exhaustion by the demands of their families, in their old age they remembered the two women and envied their life of ease and relaxation together. All the gossip and speculation that no one had bothered with in their youth emerged, and the group of former colleagues concluded that the two women were homosexual.

Listening to the elderly women drawing their conclusions, I thought of how free of cares those two women were: they probably had no feelings of bitterness against men, and certainly no all-consuming worries about their children. Perhaps homosexuality was not wicked after all, I thought, perhaps it was just another path in life. I did not understand why it was against the law, but there seemed to be no one I could ask about this subject.

Once, I was brave enough to ask the head of a gynaecology department.

She looked at me in astonishment. 'What made you think of asking about this?'

'Why, is it bad to ask? I just want to find out what makes these women different from other women.'

'Apart from differences in mindset and sexual behaviour, they are no different from ordinary women,' the gynaecologist said, brushing lightly over the subject.

I pressed her. 'If a woman's mindset and sexual behaviour are different from that of women in general, does she still count as a normal woman?' The gynaecologist either did not know how to elaborate or was not prepared to do so.

The third time I encountered the issue of homosexuality was when I was sent to cover a city-wide public order campaign for the radio station.

When the organiser of the operation saw me, he exclaimed, 'How could the radio station have sent a woman? It must be a mistake! Oh well, since you're here you may as well stay. But I'm afraid you'll have to do a follow-up report, not an on-the-spot one.'

His colleagues roared with laughter, but I was none the wiser. Once the operation began, the reason for their mirth became clear: they were carrying out surprise inspections of male public toilets –

which stank to high heaven – and arresting men who were engaged in homosexual behaviour.

I had my doubts about the campaign: weren't there enough thieves and other criminals to apprehend? And surely there wouldn't be that many men having sex in the toilets at the same time? Unbelievably, more than a hundred men were arrested that night. When the operation was almost over, I asked one of the public order personnel dazedly, 'Are there people responsible for maintaining order in women's toilets too?'

'How are we supposed to check on women? You're joking, right?' he replied, shaking his head in wonder at my naivety.

The caller who asked about homosexuality on my hotline programme was the first person to give me a true understanding of the issue.

About a week after she had called, I returned home on an adrenalin high from presenting my programme. At about two in the morning, when I was finally beginning to feel sleepy, the telephone suddenly rang.

'Xinran, do you remember me?' a woman's voice said. 'You must: I asked you such a difficult question on the radio the other day.'

Angry and irritated, I wondered how the woman had got my home telephone number. Surely common sense should have stopped whoever it was at the station from giving out my private number. It was too late to do anything about it now.

I fumed silently as the woman said, 'Hey, I know what you're thinking. Don't blame your duty editor for giving me your number. I said I was a relative from Beijing and that my bag had been stolen as I got off the train – with my telephone book in it. I needed you to come and collect me. Not bad, eh?'

'Not bad, not bad,' I repeated coldly. 'Is there something I can do for you? I remember you, you're from Ma'anshan, right?'

'Yes, I knew you wouldn't forget me. Are you tired?'

I was exhausted. 'Um, a bit. What do you want?'

She seemed to have got the hint. 'All right, you're tired. I won't say anything now. I'll ring you again tomorrow after your programme.' With that, she hung up.

By the following night, I had almost forgotten about the call, but after I had been home for less than an hour, the telephone rang.

'Xinran, I'm a bit earlier today, right? Please don't worry. I won't say much. I only wanted to tell you that I'm very grateful to you for apologising to homosexuals for the prejudice they have encountered. Okay, that's all for now, good night!'

Again, she hung up before I could say anything. I consoled myself: she meant well and seemed considerate enough.

The woman rang me at the same time every night for three weeks. She told me what she thought of my programme that evening, suggested books and music that I might find useful for it, or simply gave me common-sense advice on life in general. She only spoke for a couple of minutes each time, and never gave me a chance to talk. She did not tell me her name.

One day, as I was leaving the radio station at about one in the morning, I found a neighbour waiting for me at the gate. This was very strange. He told me my nanny had asked him to come as she was scared out of her wits. A strange woman had been calling the house telling her to 'Leave Xinran!'

I felt very uneasy.

At exactly the same time that night, as it had for the last three weeks, the telephone rang. Before the caller could say anything, I blurted out, 'Was it you who phoned earlier?'

'Yes, I spoke to your nanny and told her she ought to leave you,' she said, quite calm and self-possessed.

'Why did you do that?' I asked angrily.

'Why not? She shouldn't have you all to herself – you should belong to more women.'

'Listen,' I replied, 'I'm happy to exchange ideas or talk about life in general with you. But if you interfere with my life, then I can have nothing more to do with you. I don't interfere with other people's lives, other people can't interfere with mine.'

She was silent for a moment, then said in a pleading tone, 'I'll do as you say, but you can't abandon our love.'

The idea that this woman might be in love with me made me feel very anxious. I didn't answer the telephone for several days and I thought to myself that, like obsessed fans of pop stars, her infatuation would probably come to an end; there was no need to worry.

One afternoon, the station head summoned me to his office and said, 'A female presenter from Radio Ma'anshan named Taohong has attempted suicide. Her father sent me her suicide note. It says that she loves you very deeply, but that you have rejected her.'

I was speechless. This woman named Taohong had to be my mystery caller. I had no idea that she, too, was a radio presenter – and I had certainly not thought that ignoring her calls would lead to this.

The station head suggested that I lie low for a bit. Apparently, the first thing Taohong had said when she regained consciousness was, 'I must see Xinran!'

A few days later, while I was in a meeting with the planning department, a presenter came in to tell me that I had a visitor. When he escorted me to the reception room, I found a young woman dressed in stylish men's clothes. Her hair was close-cropped, so from behind it would have been impossible to tell that she was a woman. Before the presenter who had fetched me could introduce us, she came up and clutched my arms with both hands, saying emotionally, 'Don't say anything, let me take it all in. I knew immediately that you were my Xinran!'

'*Your* Xinran?' the presenter asked.

'Yes, my Xinran! I'm Taohong, your Taohong!'

My colleague slipped away. He knew of Taohong's story, so I guessed he had gone to fetch help.

Taohong's eyes were fixed on me as she continued speaking, 'You're even lovelier than I imagined, so feminine, so soft. I'm meeting you at last! Come, come, sit down. Let me take a good look at you. It's been more than half a year . . . I didn't come once in all that time. I wanted to get to know and understand you through your programme, and through the image of you in my heart.

'What you say is true, women are the creative force in the universe. They give the world beauty, feeling and sensitivity. They are pure and clean. Women are the best of all creatures . . .'

My colleague had returned with three or four other presenters, and they all sat down not far from us, chatting as they kept an eye on me.

'Look what I've brought you. These books are full of drawings of women. See how beautiful their bodies are. Look at this picture, that expression, see how alluring that mouth is. I brought them especially for you; you can keep them and look at them in your own time. I've also brought you this . . . to bring you sexual pleasure. And this too. When I rub your body with it, you'll feel as if you are approaching paradise!'

My colleagues were sneaking glances over at the objects that Taohong was laying out in front of me. I felt sick with embarrassment. I had always maintained that sex without emotion was bestial; I had not even known that contraptions existed to arouse sexual sensations in this mechanical way.

Taohong was still in full flow: 'With the help of modern tools, we can achieve things our ancestors wished for but couldn't have. Unlike them, we can take our feelings as far as we want to . . .'

I tried to distract her by pointing to a pile of papers she was holding, which looked like publicity material of some sort. 'Taohong, what's this? You haven't said anything about this.'

'Oh, I knew you would ask about these. These are the guiding principles of the Chinese Homosexual Association. Have you heard of it? We planned a conference a year and a half ago. The hotels, the agenda and everything were ready, but the government cracked down on it. It didn't really matter though. We had already achieved almost everything we wanted to: during several dinners before the conference, we had defined our principles, passed resolutions and discussed our physical needs, and how to get more out of sex . . .'

I remembered the conference Taohong was talking about. I had almost gone to Beijing to report on it. The day before I was due to set off, someone in the Nanjing Public Security Bureau called to tell me that they were sending staff to assist the Beijing police in putting a stop to the conference. They were going to search and close down a big hotel, and arrest several key members of the Homosexual Association. I immediately called several psychologists and doctors whom I knew had been invited to the conference to warn them not to go; I was afraid that things would end in bloodshed.

Fortunately, as Taohong now told me, the break-up of the conference did not lead to violence. In order to prevent the situation from turning nasty, the police had deliberately leaked information about the operation, so the Homosexual Association had aborted the conference. Both sides had accomplished the greater part of their aims: the government had the situation under control, and the association had still managed to meet while planning the conference. The Chinese were getting more sophisticated in their political manoeuvring.

A wave of nausea washed over me when I read the eye-catching title of one of the leaflets Taohong was clutching: 'Oral Sex Techniques, Part Four: Use of the Upper Jaw'. I found such bald discussions on sex very difficult to accept. Taohong noticed the look of revulsion on my face, and said in a patient tone, 'Don't feel you have to look now. Try it later and you'll discover the pleasures of sex.'

My colleagues sniggered quietly.

'Let's go for a walk,' I said, desperate to escape my colleagues' tittering.

'Really? Of course, we should have gone for a stroll in the streets earlier. We'll make a good couple.'

We left the broadcasting station and Taohong asked where we were going. I told her not to ask – she'd know when we arrived. She grew even more animated, saying that this was just the kind of adventure she liked, full of mystery; she adored me all the more for it.

I took her to the Cock-Crow Temple, an old Nanjing temple whose bells could be heard from a great distance. When I felt troubled or in low spirits, I sometimes came to sit in the temple's Pagoda of the Healing Buddha. Listening to the bells as I gazed at blue sky and white clouds lifted my gloom and gave me new resolve, confidence and contentment. I thought Taohong's spirit might be touched too by the sound of the bells. At the temple gate, Taohong paused and asked anxiously, 'If I walk through it, will it purify me? Will it remove certain qualities?'

'Anything it removes is bound to be meaningless. Emotion and meaning can't be swept away by purification. That's what I think,' I said.

The instant Taohong stepped through the gate, the temple bells sounded. She mused, 'My heart was touched for a moment. Why?'

I did not know how to reply to her question.

Standing in the Pagoda of the Healing Buddha, neither of us spoke for a long time. When the bells sounded again, I asked Taohong two questions: When had she started to love women? And who had been her first lover?

Taohong's story flooded out:

Taohong's father had been very ashamed of not having a son. After giving birth to her, her mother had developed cancer of the womb and could not have any more children; she later died of the cancer. Her father was distraught that his family line had been 'cut off', but there was nothing he could do. He therefore regarded Taohong as a son and had brought her up as a boy in every respect, from her clothes and her hairstyle to the games she played. Taohong had never gone to public toilets, because she couldn't decide whether to go to the men's or the women's toilet. She was proud of her masculine behaviour and had no love for women at all at the time.

The year Taohong turned fourteen, however, the events of one summer night changed her and her view of men and women completely. It was the summer before she was to enter senior school. She had been told that senior school was the most terrible time: the course of her life would be determined by it, achievement there would lead to future success. She was determined to enjoy the summer to the full before buckling down to study hard for three years, and she spent many evenings out with her friends.

That particular night, it was about eleven o'clock by the time she set off for home. She didn't have far to go, and it wasn't an isolated route. Just a few paces from home, a gang of four men leaped out of the shadows and grabbed her.

They took her, blindfolded and gagged, to what seemed to be a tool shed on a building site. Her blindfold was removed, but she remained gagged. There were three more men in the room, making the gang seven altogether. They told Taohong that they wanted to see what she really was, a man or a woman, and began removing her clothes. They were momentarily struck dumb by the sight of her young woman's body but then their faces flushed red, and all seven of them threw themselves on her. Taohong lost consciousness.

When she came round, she found herself lying naked and bloody on a workbench. The men lay snoring on the ground; some of them still had their trousers around their ankles. Taohong sat in a blind panic for some time before she finally shifted herself awkwardly off the bench. Trembling and swaying, she slowly gathered her clothes from the floor. As she was moving about, she trod on one of the men's hands; his cry of pain woke the other men. They watched, paralysed by guilt, as Taohong picked her clothing up and put it on, piece by piece.

Taohong did not say a word in the thirty minutes it took her to dress with difficulty.

From then on, she hated all men, even her father. To her, they were all filthy, lustful, bestial and brutal. She had only had two periods at the time.

She continued dressing as a boy, for no reason that she could explain, and never told anyone what had happened. The gang rape had made it quite clear to Taohong that she was a woman. She started to wonder what women were like. She did not believe that she had feminine beauty, but she wanted to see it.

Her first attempt to do so was with the prettiest girl in class in the first year of senior school. She told her classmate that she was afraid to be alone while her father was away on business, and asked if she would stay the night with her.

Before they went to bed, Taohong told her classmate that she slept naked. The girl was a little uneasy about doing the same, but Taohong said she would give her a massage, so she agreed to undress. Taohong was astonished by the soft smoothness and pliability of the girl's body, especially her breasts and hips. The slightest contact with it sent the blood rushing to Taohong's head, and thrills all over her. Just as Taohong was rubbing the girl until she gasped for breath, Taohong's father came in.

With unexpected calm, Taohong pulled a quilt over their naked bodies and asked, 'Why are you back, didn't you say you were off on business?' Her father backed out without a word, stupefied.

Later, when I interviewed Taohong's father on the telephone, he told me that, from that day on, he knew Taohong had grown up, and, moreover, had become part of a special group. He could not bring himself to ask Taohong why she was homosexual, but often put the question to her dead mother when he swept her tomb during the Festival of Pure Brightness every year.

From then on, Taohong often brought girls home 'for a massage'. She thought women were exquisite beings, but there was no love in her feelings for them.

She fell in love for the first time during the preparations for the homosexual conference she had told me about. Taohong was allocated a hotel room with a woman fourteen years her senior. The woman was graceful, quiet and very friendly. She asked Taohong why she was attending the conference, and learned that Taohong liked women. She told Taohong that sexual love was the most exalted mental state, and that that of women was the most precious of all. When the conference was aborted, she took Taohong to another hotel with her for a course of 'sexual training'. Taohong experienced sexual stimulation and pleasure that she had never known before. This woman also gave Taohong guidance about sexual health and how to use sex tools. She told her a lot about the history of homosexuality, in China and outside it.

Taohong said she fell in love with this woman because she was the first person to share ideas and knowledge with her, to protect her and give her physical pleasure. But the woman told Taohong that she did not and could not love her; she could not forget, let alone replace, her former lover, a female university lecturer, who had died many years before in a car accident. Taohong was very moved; she said she had known that love was more pure and holy than sex since she had been a child.

After Taohong had answered my two questions, we left the Cock-Crow Temple. As we walked Taohong told me she had been in search of a woman with whom she might be able to share the same kind of relationship as with her first lover. She read widely, and had passed the exam to be a presenter in Radio Ma'anshan eight months ago. She presented a hotline programme on film and television. She told me that one of her listeners had written to her to suggest that she listened to *Words on the Night Breeze*. She had tuned in every day for six months, and had pinned her hopes on me as someone who could be her new lover.

I told Taohong a saying that I often repeated on air, 'If you can't make someone happy, don't give them hope,' and said frankly,

'Taohong, thank you. I am very happy to have met you, but I do not belong to you, and I cannot be your lover. Believe me, someone is waiting for you out there. Carry on reading and expanding your horizons, and you will find her. Don't make her wait for you.'

Taohong was subdued. 'Well, can I consider you my second ex-lover?' she asked slowly.

'No, you can't,' I said, 'because there was no love between us. Love must be mutual; loving or being loved in isolation is not sufficient.'

'How should I think of you then?' Taohong was beginning to come round to my point of view.

'Think of me an older sister,' I said. 'The ties of kinship are the strongest.'

Taohong said she would think about it, and we parted.

When, a few days later, I received a call from a listener who preferred to remain anonymous, I could tell immediately that it was Taohong. 'Sister Xinran,' she said. 'I wish that everyone had your sincerity, your goodness and your knowledge. Will you accept me as a younger sister?'

8

The Woman Whose Marriage Was Arranged by the Revolution

There is a saying in Chinese: 'The spear hits the bird that sticks its head out.' I had not been a radio presenter for long before the number of letters I received from listeners, the promotions and awards that were given to me earned me snide remarks from my colleagues. The Chinese say, 'If you stand up straight, why fear a crooked shadow?', so I tried to remain cheerful in the face of any envy. In the end, it was the voices of Chinese women themselves that brought my colleagues closer to me.

The radio station had bought for me four long-playing telephone answering machines, each with tapes that lasted four hours. Every evening after eight, these machines would be available to women who wanted to offer an opinion on the programme, ask for help or tell me their story. My greeting on the machines invited them to unburden themselves so they could walk towards their futures with lighter loads, and assured them that they need not identify themselves or tell me where they were from. Each morning, when I arrived at the office, I found more and more of my colleagues – editors, reporters and presenters – waiting to hear the stories that came spooling out of the tape recorders, told in voices coloured by embarrassment, anxiety and fear.

One day, we heard:

'Hello, is anybody there? Is Xinran there? Oh, good. It's just a tape.'

The woman paused for several seconds.

'Xinran, good evening. I'm afraid I'm not really one of your regular listeners; I'm not from your province, and I only started listening to your programme recently. My colleagues were discussing you and your programme the other day, they said you had installed special telephones where listeners could leave messages – and where every woman could tell her story anonymously. They said you broadcast these stories the next day for your listeners to discuss freely on the hotline, hoping to help women understand each other, help men understand women, and bring families closer together.

'For the last few days, I've been listening to your programme every day. The reception isn't very good, but I like the programme a lot. I hadn't thought there would be so many women's stories, similar yet different. I'm sure you're not allowed to broadcast all of them. Even so, I think many women will be grateful to you. Your phone lines give women the opportunity to talk about things they have not dared to or have not been able to talk about since they were very young. You must know what a great relief it is for women to have a space to express themselves without fearing blame or negative reactions. It's an emotional need, no less important than our physical needs.'

There was another long pause.

'Xinran, I seem to lack the courage to tell my own story. I want very much to tell people about what kind of family I live in. I also want to hear my own story, because I have never dared look back at the past before, afraid that my memories might destroy my faith in life. I once read that time heals everything, but more than forty years haven't taken away my hatred or regret; they have only numbed me.'

She sighed faintly.

'In the eyes of others I have everything a woman could want. My husband has an important post in the provincial government; my son, who is nearly forty, is a manager in the city branch of a national bank; my daughter works in the national insurance company and I work in the office of the city government. I live quietly and peacefully; I don't have to worry about money or my children's future like most people, and I needn't worry about being made redundant either.

'At home, we have more than enough of everything we need. My son has a big flat of his own, and my daughter, who says that she remains single on principle, lives with us. The three of us live in a big flat of nearly two hundred square metres, with designer furniture and the latest electrical appliances – even the toilet bowl and seat are imported. Most days, someone comes in to do the cleaning and brings fresh flowers. However, my home is merely a display case for household objects: there is no real communication in the family, no smiles or laughter. When we are alone with each other, all you hear are the noises of animal existence: eating, drinking and going to the toilet. Only when there are visitors is there a breath of humanity. In this family, I have neither a wife's rights nor a mother's position. My husband says I'm like a faded grey cloth, not good enough to make trousers out of, to cover the bed, or even to be used as a dishcloth. All I am good for is wiping mud off feet. To him, my only function is to serve as evidence of his "simplicity, diligence and upright character" so he can move on to higher office.

'These were his very words to me, Xinran – he said them to my face.'

The woman broke off, sobbing. 'He told me that in such an indifferent manner! I thought of leaving him countless times. I wanted to rediscover my love of music and rhythm, to fulfil my longing for a true family, to be my old free self – to rediscover what it meant to be a woman. But my husband said that if I left him, he would make life so difficult for me that I'd wish I were dead. He would not stand for me jeopardising his career, or making him a target for gossip. I knew he would be as good as his word: over the years, not one of his political enemies has escaped his revenge. The women who rejected his advances have all been trapped in the worst jobs, unable to leave or transfer for a very long time. Even some of their husbands were ruined. I cannot escape.

'You may wonder why I believe I don't have the position of a mother. The children were taken away from me soon after they were born and sent to the army nursery because the Party said they might affect the "commander's" – their father's – work; it was the same for most soldiers' children back then. Whereas other families could see their children once a week, we were often away, so we saw our children only once or twice a year. Our few meetings were often interrupted by visitors or telephone calls, so the children would be very unhappy. Sometimes they even returned to the nursery ahead of time. Father and Mother were only names to them. They were more attached to the nurses who had cared for them for so long.

'When they got a little older, their father's position brought them many special rights that other children didn't have. This can influence growing children for the worse, giving them a lifelong feeling of superiority and the habit of contempt for others. They regarded me as an object of contempt too. Because they picked up how to deal with people and get things done from their father, they saw his kind of behaviour as a means to realise their ambitions. I tried to teach them how to be good, using my ideas and experiences, hoping maternal love and care would change them. But they measured a person's worth in terms of status in the world, and their father's success proved that he was the one worth emulating. If my own husband did not see me as worthy of respect or love, what chance did I have with my children? They did not believe that I had once been worth something.'

She sighed helplessly.

'Forty years ago, I was an innocent, romantic girl, and had just graduated from a small town girls' senior school. I was much luckier than other girls of my age; my parents had studied abroad and were open-minded. I had never worried about marriage like my classmates. Most of them had had their marriages arranged for them in the cradle; the rest were betrothed in junior middle school. If the man was very keen or family tradition dictated it, the girls had to leave junior middle school to be married. We thought the unluckiest were the girls who became junior wives, or concubines. Most of the girls who dropped out of school to be married were in this position, married off to men who wanted to "try something fresh". Many films now depict concubines as the apple of the husband's eye; they show them making use of their position to throw their weight about in the family, but this is far from the truth. Any man who could marry several wives was bound to be the son of a large, important family, with many rules and household traditions. These families had more than ten ways of greeting people and paying respects, for example. Even a slight deviation from these rules would cause the family to "lose face".

An apology was not enough – the junior wives would be punished for any perceived misdemeanours. They would be slapped by the senior wife, forbidden to eat for two days, made to do hard physical labour or forced to kneel on a washboard. Imagine how my classmates from a modern, Western-style school bore all this! There was nothing they could do; they had known from their earliest youth that their parents had the final say in choosing their marriage partner.

'Many girls envied me for being able to leave the house and go to school. At that time, women obeyed the "Three Submissions and the Four Virtues": submission to your father, then your husband and, after his death, your son; the virtues of fidelity, physical charm, propriety in speech and action, diligence in housework. For thousands of years, women had been taught to respect the aged, be dutiful to their husbands, tend the stove and do the needlework, all without setting foot outside the house. For a woman to study, read and write, discuss affairs of state like a man, and even advise men, was heresy to most Chinese at that time. My classmates and I appreciated our freedom and good fortune, but were also at a loss because we had no role models.

'Although we all came from liberal families who understood the importance of study, society around us and the inertia of tradition made it hard for any one of us to fix on an independent course in life.

'I was very grateful to my parents, who had never made demands on me or made me follow the traditional Chinese rules for women. Not only was I allowed to go to school – albeit a girls' school – I was also allowed to eat at the same table as my parents' friends and discuss politics and current affairs. I could attend any meeting and choose any sports or activities I liked. The odd "good-hearted person" in the town admonished me for my modern ways, but throughout my childhood and time as a student I was very happy. Most importantly, I was free.' She muttered quietly to herself, 'Free . . .

'I drank in everything around me. Nothing restrained my choices. I longed for some grand undertaking on a spectacular scale; I wanted to startle the world with a brilliant feat, and dreamed of being a beauty accompanied by a hero. When I read a book on the Revolution called *The Red Star*, I found a world I had only previously known from history books. Was this the future I longed for? I was beside myself with excitement, and decided to join the revolution. Surprisingly, my parents took quite a different stance from their usual liberal one. They forbade me to go, telling me that my decision was neither sensible nor based on fact. They said that immature ideas were bound to be bitter and sour because they were unripe. I took their words as a personal criticism, and reacted very badly. Spurred on by youthful obstinacy, I decided to show them I was no ordinary girl.

'Over the next forty years, their words often sounded in my ears. I understood that my parents had not just been talking about me; they had been alluding to the future of China.

'One night in midsummer, I packed two sets of clothes and a few books, and left my happy, peaceful family, just like a heroine in a novel. I remember to this day my thoughts as I walked out of the gate: Father, Mother, I'm sorry. I'm determined to be written about in books, and to make you proud.

'Later, my parents did indeed see my name in many books and reports, but only as a wife, nothing more. I don't know why, but my mother always used to ask me: Are you happy? Right up to her death, I never replied directly to this question. I didn't know how to reply, but I believe my mother knew the answer.'

She stayed silent for several seconds, then continued in a confused tone, 'Was I happy?' She muttered to herself, 'What is happiness . . . am I happy?

'I was very happy when I first arrived in the area liberated by the Party. Everything was so new and strange: in the fields, peasants and soldiers were indistinguishable; on the parade ground, the civilian guard stood side by side with the soldiers. Men and women wore the same clothes and did the same things; the leaders were not distinguished by symbols of rank. Everyone was talking about the future of China; every day there were criticisms and condemnations of the old system. Reports of injury and death in combat were all around us. In this atmosphere, the female students were treated like princesses, valued for the lightness of spirit and beauty we brought. The men who roared and fought ferociously on the battlefield were meek as lambs beside us in classes.

'I stayed only three months in the liberated area. After that I was assigned to a team working on land reform on the north bank of the Yellow River. My work unit, a cultural troupe working under the general headquarters, brought the Communist Party's policies to the people through music, dancing and all kinds of other cultural activities. This was a poor area; apart from the Chinese trumpet played at weddings and funerals, they had never had any cultural life, so we were warmly welcomed.

'I was one of the few girls in my troupe who could sing, dance, act and play music; my dancing in particular was the best. Every time we had a get-together with the senior officers, they would always vie to dance with me. I was outgoing and was always smiling and laughing, so everyone called me "the lark". I was a happy little bird then, without a care in the world.

'You know the saying: "The chicken in the coop has grain but the soup pot is near, the wild crane has none but its world is vast." A caged lark shares the same fate as the chicken. On the evening of my eighteenth birthday, the group threw a birthday party for me. Back then there was no birthday cake or champagne. All we had was a couple of biscuits saved by my companions from their rations, with a little sugar dissolved in water. Conditions were hard, but we enjoyed ourselves. I was dancing and singing when the regimental leader signalled for me to stop and follow him. Very unwillingly, I went with him to the office, where he asked me seriously, "Are you prepared to complete any mission the Party organisation gives you?"

' "Of course!" ' I replied unhesitatingly. I had always wanted to join the Party, but because my family background was not revolutionary, I knew I would have to work much harder than others to qualify.

' "Are you willing to fulfil any mission unconditionally, no matter what it is?"

'I was puzzled. The regimental leader had always been so straightforward, why was he so vague and shifty today? But I replied quickly, "Yes, I guarantee to accomplish the mission!"

'He didn't seem at all happy with my determination, but told me to set off on my "urgent mission" immediately, travelling through the night to the regional government compound. I wanted to say goodbye to my friends, but he said there was no need. Because it was wartime, I accepted this and left with the two soldiers sent specially to collect me. They remained silent throughout our two-hour journey, and I couldn't ask questions either, that was the rule.

'At the regional government compound, I was introduced to a senior officer dressed in army uniform. He looked me up and down, and said, "Not bad at all . . . Right, from today you are my secretary. You must study more from now on, work hard to reform yourself and strive to join the Party as soon as possible." Then he ordered someone to take me to a room to rest. The room was very comfortable; there was even a new quilt on the *kang*. It seemed that working for a leader really was different, but I was so exhausted that I didn't give the matter further thought before I fell asleep.

'Later that night, I was woken by a man climbing into the bed. Terrified, I was about to scream when he put his hand over my mouth and said in a low voice, "Shhh – don't disturb the other comrades" rest. This is your mission.'

' "Mission?"

' "Yes, from today this is your mission."

'The unfeeling voice belonged to the senior officer I had met earlier. I had no strength to defend myself, and didn't know how. I could only weep.

'The next day, the Party informed me that they were holding a simple wedding party that night to celebrate our marriage. That officer is my husband now.

'For a long time, I asked myself how this could have happened. How could I have been "married off by the revolution"? For the last forty years, I have lived numbly in humiliation. My husband's career is everything to him; women only fulfil a physical need for him, no more. He says, "If you don't use a woman, why bother with her?"

'My youth was cut short, my hopes crushed, and everything beautiful about me used up by a man.'

She fell silent.

'Sorry, Xinran, I've only been thinking of myself, talking away like this. Did your machine get it all? I know women talk too much, but I so seldom have the opportunity or any desire to speak; I live like an automaton. At last, I've been able to speak out without fear. I feel lighter. Thank you. And thank your radio station and your colleagues too. Goodbye.'

My colleagues and I stood rooted to the spot for a few moments after the woman said goodbye, moved, sobered and shocked by her tale. When I applied for permission to broadcast it, the authorities refused, commenting that it would damage the people's perception of our leaders.

9

My Mother

Old Chen had been one of those who had crowded around the tape recorder to hear the wife of the provincial leader tell her story. Later, he told me he had not been surprised by it. Many men who joined the revolution left wives and children behind in order to follow the Party. Once they had attained senior positions, the Party matched them with new wives because their first wives were trapped in areas under enemy occupation.

The majority of the new wives were students who believed fervently in the Communist Party and hero-worshipped the gun-toting men in it. Many of them came from wealthy families; all were cultivated young women. They could not have been more different from the first wives, who were mostly peasants. Their refinement excited the officers' desire for novelty, and their education made them good teachers and staff officers.

In 1950, after the Communist Party had taken control of most of China, the new government was faced with the problem of what to do about the original wives of their leaders. The first wives of many men who had become high-ranking officials now trailed into Beijing with their children in tow, hoping to find their husbands. The government was promoting women's liberation, sexual equality and monogamy, so this posed a dilemma. The officials had started new families with their new wives: which wife and children were to go and which were to stay? There was no law on which any decision could be based.

As far as which family would benefit their career and position in society went, the choice was obvious. However, the men were lost for words before their first wives, who had gone through years of hardship for them. These illiterate women, who could not even read the simplest Chinese characters, understood one thing: they belonged to the men who had lifted their veils and changed them from girls to wives.

Eventually, a government document was drawn up which recognised the political position of these women. They were granted a few special political rights and a lifelong guarantee of living expenses. Obeying orders they barely understood, the women went back to their villages with their children, who grew to resent both parents.

The villagers did not dare condemn or mock the abandoned women because they were under government protection. However, few of these simple, honest women made use of their special position or privileges to seek an easier life. They merely accepted the living allowance from the government – a small sum, which hardly increased with inflation – and brought up their children alone. Very few of them married again.

Old Chen said that one of these women had told him, 'Why should I rub salt in my wounds by using my privileges? People would only talk about my husband, and make me miss him even more.'

Later, I found out that, like the woman who had telephoned my programme, many of the new wives were unhappily married: would it have comforted the first wives to know this? Like my anonymous caller, many new wives had been allocated a husband whom they knew nothing about. Their education, their culture, their refinement and the Western-style romanticism they had learned to feel in their progressive schools were initially attractive to their husbands, but ultimately unacceptable. Their husbands had grown up in the fields and amid the brutality of war. They had been taught by the older generation that a woman should be controlled and shut away. The gap between the husbands' and the new wives' expectations was narrowed by the women's compliance, but the men soon lost interest and began to see their wives as mere tools.

When I visited my parents one weekend, I said to my mother that

I found it very difficult to distinguish between life in an emotionally barren marriage and being in prison. My mother replied lightly, 'How many people in China have a marriage based on love?' When I asked her why she said this, she made an excuse and left the room. I knew that my mother listened to my radio programme almost every day, but we seldom spoke about our feelings. All my life, I had longed to be held by her: she never once hugged or kissed me when I was a child; when I became an adult, any such display of affection between us was prevented by traditional Chinese reserve. Between 1945 and 1985 (when movement around the country became possible once again) many Chinese families were split up. We were no exception and I had spent very little time with my parents. I very much wanted to know more about my mother, the woman who had given me life, and who had given me countless questions about women. My growing confidence as a journalist helped me to start piecing together what I knew of her story.

My mother comes from a large capitalist family in Nanjing, a city that teems with life but is peaceful and harmonious, quite different from political Beijing, commercial Shanghai and raucous Guangzhou. Sun Yat-sen, the founder of modern China, chose to be laid to rest in Nanjing and the Guomindang once had their capital there.

Situated on the banks of the Yangtze River in south-east China, by the imposing Zijin mountain, the city is one of lakes and green places. Shady, tree-lined boulevards lead off in all directions, and the historic palaces, the city walls and the modern buildings by the river show the richness of Nanjing's cultural heritage. The Chinese say that people are shaped by the water and earth around them; from what I know of my mother's family, I believe this to be true.

My mother's family once owned a vast amount of property in Nanjing: everything south of a line extending from the West Gate of Nanjing to the city centre nearly three kilometres to the east had belonged to them. My maternal grandfather was the chairman of the hemp industry in three provinces – Jiangsu, Zhejiang and Anhui – as well as owning a number of other factories. In prosperous south China, shipping was the most important means of transport. He produced everything from tarpaulins for warships to anchor cables for small fishing boats.

My grandfather was an extremely able entrepreneur and manager, without much education. Nevertheless, he realised the importance of culture and education and he sent his seven children to the best schools, and set up a school himself in Nanjing. Although this was a time when general opinion held that 'lack of talent in a woman is a virtue', his daughters were given the fullest education.

From my uncles and aunts, I know that strict rules were enforced in my grandfather's house. At mealtimes, if someone made a sound while eating, allowed their left hand to stray from the rice bowl or broke some other rule, my grandfather would put his chopsticks down and leave. No one was permitted to continue eating after that; they stayed hungry until the next meal.

After the new government was established in 1949, my grandfather had to hand over property to the government to protect his family. Perhaps in rebellion against their strict upbringing, his children all became actively involved in the Communist Party's revolutionary movements, struggling against capitalists like their father.

My grandfather split his immense property holdings with the government on three separate occasions – in 1950, 1959 and 1963 – but these sacrifices did not protect him. At the beginning of the Cultural Revolution, he was singled out for persecution because he had been praised by two of Mao Zedong's deadly enemies. The first was Chiang Kai-shek, who had spoken of my grandfather in glowing terms because he had worked to develop national industry in the face of Japanese aggression. The second was a former crony of Mao's, Liu Shaoqi, who had commended my grandfather for donating a large amount of property to the country. Chiang had been driven out of China to Taiwan, and Liu had been imprisoned after his fall from favour.

My grandfather was already over seventy when he was imprisoned. He survived his ordeal with an astoundingly strong will. The Red Guards spat or blew their noses into the coarse food and weak tea they brought to their prisoners. An old man who shared a cell with my grandfather died of grief, anger and shame at this treatment, but my grandfather kept a smile on his face. He removed the mucus and spit and ate everything that could be eaten. The Red Guards came to admire him, and eventually brought him food that was slightly better than the others'.

When my grandfather was released at the end of the Cultural Revolution, a fellow inmate invited him to a meal of the Nanjing speciality, salt-pressed duck, to celebrate. When the delicacy was brought to the table, my grandfather's friend collapsed and died of a cerebral haemorrhage brought on by overexcitement.

My grandfather showed neither joy at his freedom nor misery at the deaths of his friends and the loss of his family and property; his feelings seemed to have been permanently numbed. It was only when he allowed me to read his diaries on a visit I made to China in March 2000 that I realised he had never once stopped feeling the vicissitudes of the times. His experience and understanding of life had left him feeling incapable of expressing himself through the shallow medium of speech, but, although the emotion in these diaries is never overt, his innermost feelings lie within them.

My mother joined the Communist Youth League at fourteen, and the army and the Party at sixteen. Before that, she had had a modest reputation in Nanjing for her academic achievements and singing and dancing talents. In the army, she continued to shine. She topped the class in training and tests, and was among the top in nationwide military competitions. Brilliant and beautiful, she was sought after by many senior Party and army figures, who vied for her hand at dances. Years later, my mother said that she had felt like a Cinderella who had fitted perfectly into the glass slipper of the revolution, which was fulfilling all her dreams. Basking in a haze of success, my mother was unaware of how her family background would come to haunt her.

In the early 1950s, the army carried out its first internal Stalinist-style purge. My mother was relegated to the 'Black' class of capitalist descendants and cast out of the charmed circle of top revolutionaries. She worked instead at a military factory, where, in collaboration with East German experts, she successfully produced a new machine tool to be used for making military equipment.

When a group photograph was taken to mark this achievement, my mother was told that she could not stand in the front row because of her family background, so she was squashed into the back row.

During the Sino-Soviet Split, my mother became a special target of investigation. Her capitalist background was the justification for testing her loyalty to the Party. Towards the end of the Cultural Revolution, she led a small technical team that designed a tool that would greatly increase efficiency in manufacturing. However, she was not allowed to take credit for the work. She was denied the accolade of Chief Designer because it was deemed impossible for someone with her background to be truly loyal to the Party.

For more than thirty years, my mother struggled for the same treatment and recognition that other colleagues with her abilities were accorded, but she failed almost every time. Nothing could change the fact that she was the daughter of a capitalist.

A family friend once told me that the best proof of my mother's strength of character was her decision to marry my father. When they married, my father was a highly regarded instructor in a military academy; he had taught my mother, and was admired by many of the female students. Though my mother had many suitors among the instructors, she chose my father, who was not handsome, but the most intellectually gifted of them all. My mother's colleagues believed that she had not married him for love, but to prove her worth.

My father's intellect did indeed seem to be my mother's private justification for marrying him. Whenever she spoke of him, she would say how terribly clever he was; he was a national expert in mechanics and computing, and could speak several foreign languages. She never described him as a good husband or a good father. For my brother and me, it was hard to reconcile my mother's view of my father with the muddle-headed man we barely saw as children and addressed as 'Uncle'.

There are countless incidents that illustrate my father's absent-mindedness; many make amusing anecdotes in retrospect. In the officers' mess, he had once tucked his dirty plate under his arm, then carried a large dictionary over to the tap and rinsed it before his colleagues' astonished eyes. Another time, while reading a book, he had walked through the open door of another family's flat, lain down on the sofa and fallen asleep. The puzzled family did not have the heart to wake him.

To prove that he was as competent in practical, everyday skills as my mother, my father had tried to cook a meal. He bought a set of scales, complete with twenty weights, so he could follow recipes accurately. While he was carefully weighing salt, the oil in the wok caught fire.

My mother told me that one day he had hurried through the crowds on Tiananmen Square to meet her by the People's Revolutionary Memorial. He told her excitedly that his work unit had just issued him with two bottles of sesame oil. It was only when he held up his hands to show her the oil that he realised the bottles had broken along the way and all he was clutching were a pair of bottle tops.

Sympathy is often mistaken for love, trapping people into unhappy marriages. Many Chinese couples who married between 1950 and 1980 fell into that trap. Buffeted by political movements and physical hardship, feeling the pressure of tradition, many men and women married with feelings of sympathy and perhaps of lust, but not of love. Only after marriage did they discover that what had attracted their pity ultimately repelled them, leaving their family lives emotionally barren.

My parents shared a 'Black' capitalist background – my paternal grandfather worked for the British company GEC in Shanghai for thirty-five years – so mutual sympathy must have played a role in their marriage. I think they came to depend on and feel affection for each other over the years.

Did they love each other? Were they happy? I have never dared to ask, loath to stir up years of unhappy memories for them, memories of forced separations, imprisonment and a divided family.

I was sent to live with my grandmother when I was a month old. In all, I lived with my mother for less than three years. I cannot remember a single birthday that the whole family spent together.

Every time I hear the whistle of a steam train, I think of my mother. The long shrill sound strikes me as helpless and hopeful in turn, reminding me of a day in the year I turned five. My grandmother had brought me to Beijing railway station, and she held me by the hand as we stood on the platform. The station was nowhere near as crowded as it is now, nor did it contain many visual distractions in the way of signboards and advertisements. Unaware of why we were there, all I remember was us waiting quietly as I fiddled with my grandmother's stiff fingers, trying to fold them together like the fluted edge of a Chinese dumpling.

A mournful lingering whistle seemed to push a very long train up beside us. When the train clanked to a stop, chuffing away, it seemed weary from carrying so many people so far, so fast.

A beautiful woman walked towards us, the case in her hand swaying in time with her step; everything flowed as in a dream. My grandmother took my hand and pointed at the woman, saying, 'There's your mother. Say "Mama", go on!'

'Auntie,' I said, addressing the beautiful lady as I did any other woman.

'This is your mother, say "Mama", not "Auntie",' my grandmother said, embarrassed.

Wide-eyed and silent, I stared at the woman. Her eyes filled with tears, but she forced her face into a sad, tired smile. My grandmother did not prompt me again; the two women stood frozen.

This particular memory has haunted me again and again. I felt the pain of it most keenly after I had become a mother myself, and experienced the atavistic, inescapable bond a mother has with her child. What could my mother have said, faced with a daughter who was calling her 'Auntie'?

Over the years my mother had had to suppress her feminine nature. Competing with men and fighting the stain of her family background to succeed in her career and in the Party, she had felt that children were a burden, and that her family had ruined her life. Once the belle of the ball in the army, she paid scant regard to her clothes or her appearance.

I once called my mother from England when I was finding life in a foreign culture particularly difficult. 'Don't worry,' she said. 'The most important thing is that you are taking time to discover what it is to be a woman.'

I was astonished. Well into her sixties by then, my mother was acknowledging the fact that she had suppressed an important part of herself, and was urging me not to make the same mistake.

The second time I returned to China after coming to England, I was amazed to see my mother wearing lipstick to meet my British friend. My father could barely contain his excitement at this re-emergence of her elegance; she had not worn make-up for over forty years.

10

The Woman Who Waited Forty-five Years

It is characteristic of the modern Chinese to have either a family with no feelings or feelings but no family. Living conditions force young people to make jobs and housing the pre-eminent conditions for their marriages. Their parents, living amid the upheaval of political change, made security and reliability the basis on which to build a family. For both generations, practical arrangements have always come first and any family feeling there is has developed later. What most women are searching and yearning for is a family that grows out of feeling. This is why you can read about so many tragic love stories in Chinese history – stories which bore neither flower nor fruit.

In 1994, my father went to a celebration marking the eighty-third anniversary of Qinghua University – one of the best universities in China. When he came back, he told me about the reunion of two of his former classmates, Jingyi and Gu Da, who had been in love with each other as students. After university, they had been posted to different parts of China to fulfil 'the needs of the Revolution', and had lost touch during the decade-long nightmare of the Cultural Revolution, which had prevented any communication. The woman, Jingyi, had waited and searched for her beloved for forty-five years. At this university reunion they met again for the first time, but Jingyi was not able to throw herself into her lover's arms: his wife was standing beside him. Jingyi had forced herself to smile, shake hands and greet them civilly, but she was obviously deeply shaken, since she had left the reunion early.

The other former classmates who witnessed this painful meeting had felt their eyes reddening and noses smarting with emotion. Jingyi and Gu Da had been the great love story of their class; everybody knew that they had loved each other deeply for four years at university. They recalled how Gu Da had found her candied haws in the middle of a Beijing snowstorm, and how she had forgone sleep to nurse him for ten nights when he had had pneumonia. My father was melancholic as he recounted this, and sighed over fate and the passing of time.

I asked my father if Jingyi had married. He told me that she had not, but had waited for her lover throughout. Some former classmates had said that she was foolish to be so infatuated with her past love: how could anyone have nurtured such hope through the years of violent political upheaval? In the face of their incredulity, she had just smiled and remained silent. I said to my father that she sounded like a water lily, rising pure out of the mire. Listening from the sidelines, my mother pitched in with a comment that a water lily withered more quickly than any other flower once broken. I wanted very much to know if Jingyi had been broken.

I found Jingyi's work unit and address in my father's list of university classmates, but no home telephone number or address. Her work unit was a military factory for experimental projects deep in the mountains, where living conditions were basic and to which transport was difficult to arrange. I made a long-distance call to the factory, but was told that she had not returned from Beijing. I was asked to confirm that she had left. I agreed to do this, and asked her colleagues to send someone to look for her as well. Over the next couple of weeks, I made enquiries among Jingyi's university friends for any contact she might have had with them or other friends and family, but found no trace of her. Her work unit called to let me know that she had rung from Beijing to ask for leave, but had not called again to confirm that permission had been granted. I wondered if she could be with her old love Gu Da, but when I called him at a large-scale military factory in Jiangxi in south-west China, he could only ask helplessly, 'What has happened, where is she?'

For several weeks, Jingyi became the only subject of conversation in my telephone calls to my family. We were all extremely anxious, but there was nothing else we could do. She was lost somewhere in China.

One evening, I took a call from a listener who identified herself as a member of staff at a hotel by Lake Taihu in Wuxi. She told me about a very odd female guest who was staying in the hotel. This guest never left the room and would not allow the cleaner to enter it. The hotel staff knew she was still alive only because she answered the telephone. The woman was worried, and hoped I could help this strange guest.

After the broadcast, I called the hotel and asked the switchboard to put me through to the reclusive woman. She answered the phone promptly, but was plainly unwilling to speak. She asked me how I had found out about her. When I replied that many people at the hotel were concerned about her, she asked me to convey her thanks to them. I was astonished that she was asking someone so far away to thank the people by her side. In my experience, shunning personal communication in this way signalled a loss of faith in life. She said she had not heard my programme and did not have any plans to listen to it.

Our first conversation was brief, but I persisted in calling her every evening after my programme, thinking of the calls as a lifeline. After several conversations, a note of acceptance crept into her voice, and she occasionally asked me about myself rather than just replying coldly to my questions.

Two weeks later, she did not answer when I called. Alarmed, I immediately called the hotel staff to ask them to knock on her door, and was relieved when they told me that she had replied from inside the room. For the next few days she did not take my calls, but I kept to my daily routine to demonstrate my concern.

As chance would have it, I was given an assignment in Wuxi not long after. Even though the subject of my report was to be the lives of Wuxi traffic policemen, I could take the opportunity to visit the woman who had shut herself away from the world.

I told the station head that I would set off for Wuxi as soon as I had finished the evening's programme. He was puzzled: 'Have you gone mad? If you dash off late at night you won't get to Wuxi until the early hours, and there will be no one to meet you.' Experience had taught me to keep explanation to a minimum.

The driver assigned to me for the trip to Wuxi hated driving in heavy daytime traffic, and was pleased when I asked him to drive me to the hotel by Lake Taihu at night. We arrived at four o'clock in the morning to find the hotel receptionists sleep-dazed and sluggish. The driver, who was impatient by nature, hectored them loudly. 'Excuse me, please wake up! This is Xinran. She has come straight here by car after finishing her programme at midnight, and has to start her reporting at eight in the morning. Can you please hurry through the formalities?'

'What, Xinran? Xinran who presents *Words on the Night Breeze*? I was listening to your programme only a few hours ago.'

'Yes, that's her. She's tired – help us out!'

'Are you really Xinran? Yes, yes! I saw your photo in the paper, how wonderful to meet you in person. Ah, I'm going to call my colleagues . . .' the receptionist said as she made to hurry off.

'Don't worry,' I stopped her hastily. 'I'll be staying here for a few days. Please don't disturb your colleagues' rest, I really am quite tired.'

'Oh, sorry, sorry, I'll open a room with a view of the lake for you right now.' The receptionist turned to the driver. 'You'll get the same treatment, don't worry about being left out.'

'Thank you for not taking offence,' he said.

'It doesn't matter, your tongue is sharp but your heart is soft, eh? Anyway, everything goes in one ear and out the other with me.'

As the receptionist walked me to my room, I asked her if she knew about the unusual woman who was staying in the hotel.

'I've heard that there is a lady visitor in Building Four who is rather strange,' she said. 'She may have been staying here for several weeks, but I can't say for sure. Tomorrow, when we have our regular staff meeting and change shifts, I'll ask the team leader for you.'

'Thank you, I'm putting you to a lot of trouble.'

'Oh no, you are the one putting yourself out for so many listeners, but how many of us can thank you in person?' The Chinese say that the hands of men and the words of women are to be feared, but it seemed I was experiencing the gentler side of this woman's tongue.

Once in my room, I decided not to sleep immediately but to have a wash and then plan my interviews for the next day. Just as I had undressed, the telephone rang.

'Hello, is that Xinran? I'm the duty operator on the hotel switchboard. The receptionist in the main building told me you'd just arrived. I'm sorry to disturb you, but I heard you were asking about a particular guest. She rang me this evening, not long after your programme was broadcast, and asked if I'd listened to it. I told her I had, and asked if she needed anything, but she just hung up. I can see her room from the duty room; I'm on the night shift this week and I see her sitting by the window looking out at the lake all night. Perhaps she sleeps during the day?'

'Sorry, may I interrupt you for a moment? Can I ask if you see her now? Is she still looking out at the lake?'

'Er . . . I'm just looking. Yes, she's there . . . I can see her very clearly – she never seems to draw the curtains.'

'Thank you so much. Can I ask what her room number is?'

'She's . . . she's in room 4209, on the second floor of Building Four.'

'Thank you, operator. Is there anything I can do for you?'

'No, nothing . . . Well, would you give me your autograph?'

'Of course – maybe I'll find some time to visit you tomorrow, all right?'

'Really? That would be great. Goodbye.'

'Goodbye.' As I was speaking I was getting dressed again, having decided to visit the woman guest immediately, as time was so precious.

Standing before her room door, I suddenly found myself at a loss, and dithered a few minutes before I finally knocked and called out, 'Hello, it's Xinran here. I have come here from the other end of our telephone conversation to see you. Please open the door.'

There was no reply, and the door remained firmly shut. I did not knock or speak again but stood waiting, certain that she had heard me in the stillness of the early morning. I was sure that she was standing right behind the door and that we could both sense each other. About ten minutes later, her voice drifted through the door.

'Xinran, are you still there?'

'Yes, I've been waiting for you to open the door,' I replied softly but firmly.

The door opened quietly, and an anxious, exhausted-looking woman beckoned me in. The room was neat and tidy and its only sign of occupation was a large travel bag by the wall. I was relieved to see packets of instant noodles in it – at least she was not fasting.

I sat down close to her, but remained silent, thinking that any words would only meet resistance. I would wait for her to talk, but until she was ready to do so, I would try to create a confiding atmosphere. We sat there listening to the gentle lapping of water against the shore, and my thoughts wandered to the lake and its surroundings.

Lake Taihu is the third largest freshwater lake in China, and lies to the south of Jiangsu Province and the north of Zhejiang Province. It is a renowned beauty spot in the Yangtze delta. Around the lake there are landscaped gardens full of pools and streams. Lake Taihu is also well known for the Biluo Spring Tea produced there. Legend goes that a beautiful girl named Biluo watered a sapling with her own blood and brewed tea for her dangerously ill lover from its tender leaves. She did this day after day until the young man finally recovered his health, but Biluo herself then sickened and died.

I mused over this and other tragic love stories to the soft rhythm of lapping water as I sat quietly beside the woman. Though the lamps were still lit, their light was no longer discernible in the dawn. The early-morning light had gradually infused our silence with a new quality.

The telephone broke our communion. The call was for me. It was a quarter to seven, and the driver had to take me to Wuxi for an appointment with the Traffic Police Propaganda Office at 8.30.

I shook the woman's hand to take leave of her, but did not say much, only 'Please eat a bit more for me, and have a rest.'

On the road to Wuxi I fell asleep in the back seat of the car. The kind-hearted driver did not disturb me when we arrived at our destination, but parked and went to look for the people from the Wuxi Traffic Police Propaganda Office himself. No one had arrived in the office yet, so I got an hour's uninterrupted sleep. When I awoke, I found the people I was meant to meet standing outside the car chatting as they waited for me. I was embarrassed, and had no explanation to offer. One of the traffic policemen teased me, 'Xinran, if you go to sleep wherever you go, you'll get fat.'

The day unfolded at the hectic pace routine to journalism: I gathered material from several different places, and discussed the content of the report I was doing. Fortunately, quite a bit of time was spent in the car, so I snatched several catnaps.

When I returned to the hotel in the evening, I found on my bed a list of all the hotel employees who wanted my autograph. I put it aside, had a shower and went to visit the woman in room 4209 again. Even if she did not want to speak, I thought that sitting with her would be of some help. She must have been standing behind the door waiting for me, for it opened as soon as I stopped before it.

The woman smiled at me with some effort, but remained silent. Once again, we sat before the window, looking out at the moonlit lake. The surface of the lake was calm, and we kept each other company in the peace of this atmosphere.

At dawn, I signalled to indicate that I had to leave for work, and she shook my hand weakly, but with great feeling. I returned to my room, hurriedly flipped through some preparatory notes I had brought with me and wrote a thank-you note to the switchboard operator. I had fallen into the habit of carrying cards with me to autograph for enthusiastic listeners I met by chance. I signed some of these cards for the hotel employees, and left them with the attendant on my floor.

My short reporting trip fell into a regular pattern: I conducted interviews in Wuxi by day, and spent my nights sitting silently with the woman looking out at Lake Taihu. Our silences seemed to become deeper and more charged with feeling by the day.

On the last evening, I told the woman that I would be leaving the next day, but would call. She said nothing, but smiled wanly and shook my hand weakly. She gave me a photograph that had been torn in half, showing what looked like her as a student in the 1940s. The girl in the photograph bloomed with youth and happiness. On the back of the photograph was part of a sentence in faded ink: 'water cannot . . .' Another sentence in darker ink seemed to have been added more recently: 'Women are like water, men are like mountains.' I guessed that the person in the missing half of the photograph was the cause of the woman's pain.

I left the hotel by Lake Taihu – but I didn't feel as if I had left.

Back in Nanjing, I went straight to visit my parents to give them the Wuxi specialities – clay figurines and spare ribs – that I had got for them. As my driver opened the car door for me, he said, 'Xinran, if you go on another tour like that, don't come looking for me. I was bored to death in the car: you only wanted to sleep. Thanks to you, I didn't have a soul to talk to!'

It was late when I arrived and my parents had gone to bed. I decided to slip into the guest room and see them in the morning. My mother called from the bedroom, 'Was everything all right?' and my father's thunderous snores told me all was well with them.

The next day, at the crack of dawn, my father, who was an early riser, woke me with one of his uncontrollable sneezing fits. He did this every morning – I had once counted twenty-four sneezes in a row. Drowsy and exhausted, I went back to sleep, but was soon woken again by loud knocking, and my father calling, 'Get up, quick, it's urgent!'

'What is it? What's happened?' I was flustered, for my retired parents' household was normally serene.

My father was standing outside my bedroom, holding the torn photograph in his hand. I had left it on the sitting-room table the previous night. He asked excitedly, 'Where did you get this photograph? This is her!'

'What? What do you mean?'

'This is Jingyi – that classmate of mine. The one who waited for her lover for forty-five years!' My father was full of contempt at my slowness.

'Really? Are you sure it's the same person? Could it be old age affecting your eyes? It's been forty-five years, and this is an old photograph.' I hardly dared believe him.

'I couldn't possibly be mistaken. She was the beauty of the class – all the boys liked her and many of them were after her.'

'Even you?'

'Shhh! Keep your voice down. If your mother hears, she'll get more funny ideas into her head. To tell you the truth, I really liked Jingyi, but I wasn't in her league,' my father said, with a sheepish look on his face.

'Not in her league? Impossible! You always boast about what a debonair figure you cut as a young man,' I teased him as I began repacking my bags.

'Why are you leaving so soon?' my father asked as he watched me.

'I'm going back to Wuxi right now. I made so much effort to find Jingyi before, and now I have done it by chance.'

My father replied ruefully, 'If I'd known earlier, I wouldn't have woken you up.'

One of the directors of the broadcasting station lived close to my parents so I rushed to his house to ask for emergency leave. I lied that a relative was visiting, and I had to show her around for a few days. I hate lying because I believe it shortens life, but I was even more afraid of the director knowing the truth. Having obtained his permission, I telephoned the stand-in presenter of my programme to ask if she would cover me for a few more days.

I missed the noon train to Wuxi and had to wait till evening, head spinning with questions about Jingyi, fretting and impatient. Time seemed to crawl.

At about the time my broadcast would have begun, ten o'clock or thereabouts, I returned to the hotel by Lake Taihu. The receptionist recognised me and asked, 'Oh, haven't you left after all?'

'No, that's right,' I said, not wanting to waste time on explanations.

Standing in front of the door of room 4209, the questions that had been thronging in my mind suddenly vanished, and I was hesitant once again. I raised my hand and let it fall twice before I finally knocked.

'Jingyi, it's me, Xinran,' I called out. I felt like crying; I had sat with her for so many nights, and not known a thing. I imagined her sitting in silence for forty-five years, and my chest tightened.

Before I could compose myself, the door opened.

She stood there amazed and asked, 'Hadn't you left? How do you know my name?'

I pulled her over to sit by the window again, but was not silent this time. I gently told her what I knew of her from my father. Jingyi wept as she listened, making no effort to wipe away her tears. I felt choked with questions, but only managed to ask: 'Are you thinking about Gu Da?' At this, she fainted.

I was very frightened, and telephoned the switchboard to call an ambulance.

The operator was hesitant. 'Xinran, it's the middle of the night . . .'

'People don't distinguish night from day when they are dying. Can you bear to watch this woman die in front of you?' I asked agitatedly.

'All right, don't worry. I'll call at once.'

The telephone operator was very efficient. Not long afterwards, I heard someone in the building shouting, 'Where's Xinran?'

I replied quickly, 'Here I am!'

When the ambulance driver saw me he was stunned. 'You're Xinran? But you're perfectly all right!'

'I'm fine.' I was confused, but guessed that the telephone operator had made use of my supposed public prominence to summon the ambulance.

I travelled with Jingyi to a military hospital. The medical staff would not allow me to be present when they examined her, so I could only look in on her through a tiny window in the door. She lay immobile in the whiteness of the room, and I grew increasingly anxious as I imagined the worst. I could not stop myself from exclaiming tearfully, 'Oh, Jingyi, wake up!'

A doctor patted me on the shoulder. 'Xinran, don't worry, she's fine. She's just weak. It looks like she's had a great upset, but the tests on her vital functions show no changes for the worse. That's quite good for her age. She'll be fine on a more nourishing diet.'

As I listened to this prognosis, I began to feel calmer, though I still felt Jingyi's anguish keenly. I muttered helplessly to the doctor, 'She must have suffered so much. I don't know how she got through more than fifteen thousand nights . . .'

The doctor allowed me to rest in the duty room. Head spinning with random thoughts, I fell into an exhausted sleep. I dreamed of women crying and struggling, and woke unrefreshed.

The next day I went to see Jingyi four or five times, but she was always asleep. The doctor said she would sleep for several days, because she was so exhausted.

I booked a dormitory bed in the hospital guesthouse. I did not have enough money for a private room – and besides, I hardly used it. Not wanting Jingyi to be alone, I stayed all night by her bedside and rested a little in the daytime. Over the course of several days, she remained unconscious, a slight twitching of the eyelids the only sign of movement.

At dusk on the fifth day, Jingyi finally came round. She seemed not to realise where she was, and began struggling to speak. I put a finger to her lips and softly told her what had happened. As she listened, she reached out to clasp my hand in gratitude, and managed her first words: 'Is your father well?'

The dam had been breached, and Jingyi's tale flowed forth as she lay against the white expanse of the hospital pillow that evening. She told me her story in a steady voice.

In 1946, Jingyi passed the entrance examination for Qinghua University. On the first day of registration, she saw Gu Da for the first time. Among the students, Gu Da was distinguished neither by good looks nor extraordinary achievement. When Jingyi saw him that first day, he was silently helping others with their luggage, and looked like a university porter. Jingyi and Gu Da were put in the same class, where many young men began to court Jingyi for her beauty and sweet nature. Unlike them, Gu Da often sat alone in a corner of the classroom or deep in the university gardens reading. Apart from noting that he was a bookworm, Jingyi did not pay much attention to him.

Jingyi was a cheerful girl, and often suggested lively activities that her classmates enjoyed. One clear winter day after heavy snowfall, the students went outside excitedly to build a snowman. Jingyi suggested making two snowmen instead, using candied haws for their noses. With the men and women in different groups, they would take turns kissing the snowmen blindfolded. The lucky ones would get to eat a candied haw and the others a mouthful of snow.

At that time, public transport or bicycles were not common. The only way to get candied haws for this game was to walk several hours through the snow to the centre of Beijing – then known as Beiping. The male students who normally vied for Jingyi's attention did not offer to do this, and several slunk away to their dormitories quietly. Jingyi was disappointed that they had no sense of fun, but did not press her suggestion further.

The next day, more snow fell, blanketing the earth thickly and most of the students spent the day reading in the classroom. About halfway through the evening study period, under the dim light of the lamps, a man covered in ice entered. He walked up to Jingyi and, with some effort, pulled two sticks of Beiping candied haws from his pocket. They had been frozen into a lump. Before anyone could see who this iceman was, he turned and left the classroom.

The astonished Jingyi had recognised Gu Da. As her delighted classmates were chattering about playing Jingyi's game the next day, she stood distractedly, looking from the candied haws to the falling snow outside, imagining Gu Da walking through it.

Gu Da did not take part in the game the following day. The classmates in his dormitory said that he was sleeping like the dead, as though he had drunk a magic potion. Jingyi was worried that he had made himself ill with exhaustion. But at evening study that day, she was relieved to see him arrive and sit in his corner reading as before. After the study period, Jingyi stopped on her way out and thanked him. Gu Da smiled shyly and said, 'It was nothing. I'm a man.'

Gu Da's artless reply touched Jingyi. It was the first time she had felt male solidity and strength; she began to feel like a heroine in a book, kept awake all night by her thoughts.

Jingyi began to observe Gu Da closely. His taciturn nature led her to all sorts of conjectures, and she mulled over his behaviour endlessly. Apart from the time he had brought her the candied haws, Gu Da seemed indifferent to her, quite unlike the other eager young men who pursued her. She began hoping for some attention from him, and started finding excuses to speak to him. He replied impassively, displaying no particular attentiveness in either his speech or manner. Rather than putting Jingyi off, Gu Da's reserve merely heightened her hopes.

Jingyi's liking for Gu Da exasperated many of her would-be suitors. They poked fun at Gu Da for his wooden demeanour, calling him a frog who dreamed of kissing a princess, and accusing him of toying with Jingyi's feelings. None of these remarks were made in Jingyi's presence, but a girl classmate later told her about them, saying, 'Gu Da must really be made of wood. He just replied, "The people involved know what's true and what's false." '

Jingyi admired Gu Da's calmness in the face of his classmate's taunts, feeling that it displayed the qualities of a true man. All the same, she could not help being annoyed that Gu Da had been lukewarm in his behaviour towards her for so long.

Just before the end-of-term examinations, Gu Da was absent from class for two days in a row; his dormitory mates claimed he was asleep. Jingyi did not believe that he was just sleeping, but she was not allowed to visit Gu Da in his dormitory because of the strict segregation between the sexes. On the third day, however, she slipped out of the classroom while the others were absorbed in studying, and went to Gu Da's dormitory. She pushed open the door quietly, and saw Gu Da lying asleep. His face was extremely flushed. When she gently picked up his hand to tuck it back under the quilt, she found it burning hot. Although this was a time when no physical contact was permitted between men and women who were not a married couple, she touched Gu Da's head and face with no hesitation. They too were feverish. Jingyi called his name loudly, but Gu Da did not reply.

Jingyi ran back to the classroom, shouting for help. Everyone was alarmed by her panic and dashed off in different directions to look for a lecturer or a doctor. Later, the doctor said that it was lucky Gu Da had been found in time: half a day longer without medical attention would have resulted in his death from acute pneumonia. At that time, there were no hospital facilities on the Qinghua campus. The doctor prescribed between ten and twenty doses of herbal medicine, and said that it would be best if a member of his family could nurse him, administering cold compresses and rubbing his hands and feet with ice.

Gu Da had never mentioned any family or friends in Beiping.

His home was in the south of China, but the railway was cut off then, so there was no way of contacting his family. In any case, they would not have been able to arrive in time to nurse him through the critical period. As he was getting ready to leave, the doctor found himself in a quandary: he was not confident that Gu Da would survive under the care of these inexperienced young people. In the midst of earnest discussion amongst the students, Jingyi walked up to the doctor and said quietly, 'I'll look after him. Gu Da is my fiancé.'

The Dean of Studies was a kind man. He arranged for the boys who lived in Gu Da's room to move to another dormitory so Gu Da could rest in peace and Jingyi could stay at his bedside. She was strictly forbidden to sleep in the dormitory.

For more than ten days Jingyi laid cold compresses on Gu Da's head, washed and fed him, and brewed herbal medicine for him. The light shone through the night in Gu Da's dormitory, and the bitter smell of Chinese medicine wafted out along with the faint sound of Jingyi's voice. She sang one southern Chinese song after another, thinking to revive Gu Da with tunes from his homeland. Their classmates, especially the boys, sighed at the thought of the delicate Jingyi tirelessly nursing Gu Da.

Under Jingyi's painstaking care, Gu Da recovered. The doctor said that he had walked out from the jaws of death.

Their love for each other was cemented – nobody could begrudge it after the sacrifices they had made. However, some people still said privately that pairing Jingyi with Gu Da was like casting a fresh flower into cow dung.

Over the next four years of university, Jingyi and Gu Da supported each other through their studies and daily lives. Every passing day was proof of their love – first love for them both, and unwavering in its strength. Ideologically committed, they entered the underground Communist Party together and dreamed of a new era and a new life, imagining the children they would have, and speaking of their golden wedding anniversary.

Their graduation coincided with the foundation of a new China, and their newly revealed political status gained them unusual respect in society. They were called to separate interviews with the army. They had both studied mechanical engineering, and the new

Motherland, which was still in its infancy, needed their knowledge for national defence. It was a solemn time: everything was charged with a sense of mission, and things happened very quickly. Jingyi's and Gu Da's experiences in the underground Party had taught them that they were duty-bound to accept every mission and carry it through to the end. Everything, including separation, had to be accepted unconditionally.

Jingyi was posted to a military base in the north-west and Gu Da to an army unit in Manchuria. Before they parted, they made plans for a reunion in the gardens of Qinghua University, where they could share their individual achievements, and then go to Beijing city centre for some candied haws. After that, they would apply for a marriage permit from the Party, travel to Gu Da's home by Lake Taihu in south China, and settle down to start a family. This agreement was firmly imprinted in Jingyi's mind.

Against all expectations, they were both confined to their military work units the following year, after the outbreak of the Korean War. In their third year of separation, Jingyi was temporarily transferred to a special army research and development unit in the central China plain, with no leave to visit friends or family. In their fourth year apart, Gu Da was transferred to an airforce base in east China. The changing addresses in Jingyi's box of love letters were evidence that Jingyi and Gu Da were indispensable to the urgent needs of the new China and its military industry.

Their reluctance to let each other go was evident in their letters, but it was becoming increasingly difficult to arrange a meeting. 'Duty to the Party' led to countless postponements of planned meetings, and often interrupted their correspondence. In the chaos of political movements in the late 1950s, Jingyi was interrogated because of problems in her family background, and sent to rural Shaanxi for 'training and reform'. At that time, even the important task of building the national defence was considered secondary to the class struggle. She lost all personal freedom and was unable to communicate or come and go as she pleased. She nearly lost her mind missing Gu Da, but the peasants responsible for overseeing her reform refused to help her. They could not defy Chairman Mao's orders by allowing Jingyi to leave: she might become a spy or have contact with counter-revolutionaries. Later, an honest cadre suggested a way out for her: she could change her status and gain her freedom by marrying a peasant. Still deeply in love with Gu Da, Jingyi found this thought intolerable.

Jingyi spent nine years labouring in the village in Shaanxi. The village stream was both its lifeline and an unofficial meeting place, where village gossip and news from further afield were exchanged. Jingyi saw the stream as her sole means of communication with Gu Da. Almost every night, she would sit by the stream and silently express her longing for him, hoping that the fast-flowing water would carry her feelings to where he was. But the stream brought Jingyi no news of the world beyond.

Over the years, the villagers gradually forgot there was anything special about Jingyi; she had grown to look like a typical peasant woman. Only one quality distinguished her: she was the only woman of her age still unmarried.

In the late 1960s, a county official came to the village to give Jingyi government orders to prepare for a transfer. Orders were to 'grasp revolution and press on with production'. The anti-Soviet campaign had begun.

As soon as Jingyi returned to her military base, she set out to accomplish two things. First, she had to prove that she was essentially unchanged. Her years labouring in the fields had aged her and altered her appearance greatly. Her colleagues did not dare to acknowledge her at first, and could not believe that she still possessed her former skills. They gave her tests and experiments, made her analyse problems and describe past events. After a week, they concluded that her mental brilliance was undiminished.

Second, but more important to Jingyi personally, she had to get in touch with Gu Da again. Her colleagues were moved by her devotion to him, and each of them made their own enquiries to help her. After three months of searching, all they had found out was that Gu Da had been imprisoned at the start of the Cultural Revolution as a reactionary and a suspected secret agent of the Guomindang. Enquiries at all the possible prisons he might have been sent to drew unsatisfactory replies: Gu Da seemed to have passed through all of them, but nobody knew where he had gone next. Jingyi was despairing, but not resigned. As long as there was no news of Gu Da's death, there was hope, which gave her life meaning.

In the ensuing years of the Cultural Revolution, Jingyi was more fortunate than most of her colleagues and former classmates. She was given special protection because of her skills; the military base leaders skilfully hid her from the Red Guards many times. She understood the great danger the leaders faced in protecting her and contributed several major scientific achievements to repay her debt to them.

Jingyi never stopped searching for Gu Da. She visited every village and town he might have been in, and even went to Lake Taihu, which they had dreamed about. With the help of friends, she took two weeks to travel the circumference of the lake looking for Gu Da, but there was no trace of him.

In the 1980s, after the Reform and Opening Up policy, the people had finally woken from the endless nightmare of political and social chaos, and were putting to rights everything that had been thrown into confusion. Jingyi was one of countless other people searching for lost family or friends through letters, telephone calls and personal enquiries. The passion of her search often went unappreciated by others: Gu Da was Jingyi's lover, not theirs. The Cultural Revolution had numbed the feelings of many, who had been taught by bitter experience to put basic physical needs and political safety before empathy or emotion.

When Jingyi received a copy of the list of the people who would attend the Qinghua anniversary celebration in 1994, she searched it eagerly for Gu Da's name, but it was not there. When she travelled to Beijing for the event, she brought with her dozens of form letters requesting help, to distribute among her old classmates.

On the first day of the celebration, people from all over China assembled on the Qinghua campus. The younger people greeted each other excitedly: time had not changed them greatly yet. The older ones seemed more hesitant; for most of them, it was not until they had walked into the room designated for their year and class that they could identify old classmates with any certainty.

Nobody had recognised Jingyi in the initial mêlée, and she too had been unable to identify anyone at first. A university attendant directed her to the room assigned to her year and class. As she walked in, she immediately saw a man with his back to her, a man whose form would never be unfamiliar to her, no matter how the hardships of life had changed it – Gu Da. Jingyi was overcome; she began trembling, her pulse raced and she grew faint. The young attendant supported her by the arm and asked with concern what the matter was; did she have a history of heart disease? She was unable to speak – she waved her hand to signal that she was fine, pointing at Gu Da at the same time.

She forced herself to walk towards him, but her heart was so full she felt she could hardly move. Just as she was about to call out to him, she heard him say, 'This is my wife Lin Zhen, my eldest daughter Nianhua, my second daughter Jinghua and my third daughter Yihua. Yes, yes, we've just arrived . . .'

Jingyi froze.

Gu Da turned around just then, and was paralysed by the sight of Jingyi. He gaped foolishly. Concerned, his wife asked him what was wrong. He replied in a trembling voice: 'This . . . this is Jingyi.'

'Jingyi? She can't be . . .' His wife had heard the name.

The three elderly people were overcome, and remained silent for a few moments as they grappled with their feelings. With tears in her eyes, Gu Da's wife finally told Jingyi that he had only married when he heard that she was dead. Then she made to get up and leave Jingyi and Gu Da alone, but Jingyi held her back.

'Please . . . please don't go. What we had was in the past, when we were young, but you have a complete family in the present. Please do not hurt this family; knowing Gu Da is happy will be a much greater comfort.'

Jingyi did not truly mean what she said, but she spoke with sincerity.

When the youngest daughter heard who Jingyi was, she said, 'The initial characters of my and my sisters' names form the sentence "Nian Jing Yi" – in remembrance of Jingyi. My parents say it's to remember you by. The Cultural Revolution threw so many people's lives into chaos. Please find it in yourself to forgive my parents.'

Jingyi suddenly felt calmer, and found the strength to stand up and shake Gu Da's wife's hand, saying, 'Thank you for remembering me, thank you for giving him such a happy family. From today I will be happier, because I have one less worry. Come, let's go in to the meeting together.'

Everyone took their cue from Jingyi, and walked towards the auditorium. Once they were seated in their assigned places, Jingyi slipped out and returned to her hotel, where she burned the letters asking for help that she had brought with her. Along with the paper, her long-cherished hopes and her momentary calm melted away.

Several days later, she pulled herself together to call her work unit and request a few more days' leave. Her colleague told her that there was a telegram for her from someone called Gu Jian, asking her to get in touch as soon as possible. Jingyi realised that, for reasons unknown to her, Gu Da had changed his name to Gu Jian – that was why her enquiries had been unsuccessful.

Jingyi took a train south to Lake Taihu, planning to find a house for herself like the one she and Gu Da once dreamed of. She had neither sufficient strength nor money to accomplish this, so she moved into the hotel by the lake instead. She did not want to see anyone, and survived on instant noodles soaked in hot water as she spent the days and nights thinking.

Jingyi had nearly finished telling her tale. She raised a hand weakly and drew a circle in the air.

'Forty-five years of constant yearning for him had made my tears form a pool of longing. Every day I waited by that pool with confidence and love. I believed that my lover would step out of the pool and take me in his arms – but when he did finally step out, another woman was at his side. Their footsteps disturbed the clear surface of my pool. The ripples destroyed the reflections of the sun and moon – and my hope was gone.

'To continue living, I needed to wash Gu Da and my feelings away. I had hoped Lake Taihu would help me, but forty-five years are too difficult to get rid of.'

I listened to the emptiness in Jingyi's voice, anguished and helpless. No empathy could be sufficient.

I had to get back to PanPan and my work, but did not want to leave Jingyi alone, so I telephoned my father that evening to ask if he and my mother could come to Wuxi to keep Jingyi company for a few days. They arrived the next day. As she was seeing me off from the hospital, my mother said, 'Jingyi really must have been very pretty when she was young.'

One week later, my parents returned to Nanjing. My father told me that, with Jingyi's permission, he had contacted her work unit. They had been looking for her, and immediately sent someone to Wuxi to nurse Jingyi when they heard the news. My father said that, unknown to Jingyi, he had given her colleague a sketchy account of her story over the telephone. The gruff man had broken down, and said, sobbing, 'We all know how much Jingyi suffered looking for her love, but nobody can describe the depth of her feelings.'

My father had found out why Gu Da had changed his name, and told Jingyi what he knew. The leader of the Red Guards in the second prison Gu Da was sent to had exactly the same name, so Gu Da was forced to take a new name. The Red Guards changed his name to Gu Jian on all his documents without any authority. Gu Jian had fought with the local authorities to change his name back, but they had merely said, 'So many wrongs were committed in the Cultural Revolution – who can put them all right?' Later, someone told Gu Da that Jingyi, for whom he had searched for years, had died over twenty years previously in a car crash, so he decided to let the name Gu Da die as well.

Jingyi said that women were like water and men like mountains – was this a valid comparison? I put this question to my listeners, and received almost two hundred replies in a week. Of these, more than ten came from my colleagues. Big Li wrote: 'Chinese men need women in order to form a picture of themselves – as mountains are reflected in streams. But streams flow from the mountains. Where then is the true picture?'

11

The Guomindang General's Daughter

The subjects discussed on my programme sometimes provoked enormous debate among my listeners and, to my surprise, I often found that my colleagues would want to continue the discussion the next day. The morning after I had presented a programme on the subject of disability, which had elicited particularly varied opinions, I found myself in the lift with Old Wu, the head of Administration. As the lift creaked and juddered to the sixteenth floor, he took the opportunity to talk to me about the previous night's programme. He was a regular listener of mine, and was eager to share his views and ideas with me. I was touched by his interest. Politics had dulled so much enthusiasm for life in China that it was rare to find middle-aged men like Old Wu who were still curious about things. It was also unusual for people who worked in the Chinese media to watch, listen to or read the medium they worked in: they knew it was merely the mouthpiece of the Party.

'I thought what you discussed on your programme last night was very interesting,' Old Wu said. 'Your callers all agreed that we should have compassion and understanding for the disabled. Compassion is easy enough, but I think understanding is not so easy. How many people can break away from their able-bodied mindset and understand disabled people on their own terms? And the experiences of people who are born with a disability must be distinguished from those of people who become disabled later in life. Of course . . . hey, what's up? Is the red light on?'

The lift had jerked to a halt and the alarm light was on, but nobody panicked – breakdowns were an everyday occurrence. Luckily, the lift had stopped at one of the floors rather than in between, and the repairman (one of the most popular people in the building) soon opened the door. As Old Wu got out of the lift he said one last thing to me, almost as if he were issuing an order: 'Xinran, find some time to have a chat with me soon. Don't just think about your listeners. Did you hear that?'

'Yes, I heard that,' I replied loudly as Old Wu walked away.

'So you've heard, Xinran?' A programme supervisor stopped me in the corridor.

'Heard what? I was talking to Director Wu,' I said.

'I thought you'd heard about the argument the editorial department had yesterday about your programme.'

Knowing how sharp my colleagues' tongues could be, I was defensive. 'What were they arguing about? The topic? Something the callers said? Was it something I said?'

'They were arguing over whether it was sadder to be born disabled or to become disabled later,' the programme supervisor replied airily as he walked off without a backward glance.

That morning, the editorial department seemed to have renewed the previous evening's argument. As I walked into the office, seven or eight people were engaged in a heated discussion; two of the technicians had joined in. They all felt strongly about the topic: some of them were flushed with excitement, others were gesticulating or drumming their desks with pencils.

I was wary of being dragged into the fray, having experienced the difficulties of addressing the issue of disability with my listeners, who had kept me in the studio long after the broadcast; I had only got home at three in the morning. As unobtrusively as possible, I scooped up the letters I had come to retrieve, and hurried out.

Just as I reached the door, Old Chen shouted, 'Xinran, don't go! You started this fire, so you should put it out.'

I murmured an excuse – 'I'll be back, the boss wants me to see him for a minute' – and scuttled to take refuge in the station head's office, only to find him waiting for me.

'Speak of the devil!' he exclaimed.

I tensed, fearing the worst.

'Here's a copy of the register of incoming phone calls. I think there might be the possibility of a really interesting interview there. Take a look and put some ideas together by this afternoon,' he said peremptorily.

There was a message for me in the telephone register: the daughter of a Guomindang lieutenant general was in a mental hospital and I was to contact a Dr Li. There were no details that hinted at a good story, but I knew the director was very astute; if he said there was a lead, he was probably right. He had a knack for seeing wider, newsworthy issues behind smaller ones. I had often thought that he would have thrived professionally in a free press environment.

I called Dr Li, who was brief. 'This woman is the daughter of a Guomindang general, she's mentally retarded, but she wasn't born that way. They say she won some big province-wide prize for essay-writing as a child in Jiangsu but now –' He broke off suddenly. 'I'm sorry, can I talk to you in person?'

I agreed immediately, and we arranged for me to visit the hospital at half past one that day.

After exchanging a few words of greeting, Dr Li took me to see the woman. A pale, blank face turned towards us as we entered the still white room.

'Shilin, this is Xinran. She's come to see you,' said Dr Li.

Shilin was silent, and her face remained expressionless.

Dr Li turned to me, 'She reacts to virtually nothing, but I think we should treat her with respect regardless. She wasn't born mentally deficient – she understood normal feelings and speech once.' He looked at his watch. 'Yesterday, some of Shilin's family members heard your programme and one of them asked me to make an appointment with you. I'm on duty now, but please wait here for a moment. Shilin's relatives should be along any minute.'

I had never been alone with a mentally disabled person before. I tried to talk to Shilin; she seemed to hear me speaking, but she did not react at all. Not sure what to do, I took my sketchpad out and began to draw her. She remained completely still, and paid no attention to what I was doing.

Shilin was very beautiful. I guessed she was around forty, but the skin around her eyes was clear and unlined. Her features were regular and well proportioned, and her straight nose drew attention to her long, narrow eyes, which turned up slightly at the corners, as if she was about to smile. Her lips were thin, like those of the women depicted in ancient Chinese paintings.

Before I had finished my sketch, Shilin's relatives arrived: her aunt and cousin – a mother and daughter. Shilin's aunt, Wang Yue, was a well-spoken woman, who bore herself with great propriety. Shilin's cousin, Wang Yu, was in her thirties and worked as an accountant for a magazine publisher.

Wang Yue said that the night before, the family had switched on the radio before going to bed. She told me that they listened to my programme every night because it helped them to fall asleep. I wondered to myself whether my programme was so stultifying, and did not know whether to be put out or amused.

Wang Yue's daughter had obviously noticed the ambiguous expression on my face; she nudged her mother, but Wang Yue ignored her. She told me that they had become very agitated listening to those of the previous night's callers who had thought that it was much more tragic to be born mentally handicapped than to become so later in life. Shilin's family disagreed completely, and had felt a good deal of animosity towards those callers, whom they had thought completely wrong.

Wang Yue spoke passionately. Could people forget the pain of losing something they once had? Surely it was more tragic to once have had knowledge and understanding, and lose them irrevocably than never to have known anything else? Wang Yue said the family had become so worked up over this matter that none of them had been able to sleep. They had decided to prove their case by telling me about Shilin's life. Shilin's expression remained wooden as Wang Yue recounted her story.

Shilin was the daughter of a Guomindang general, the youngest in her family. Unlike her two elder sisters and elder brother, Shilin grew up protected and indulged. When civil war broke out in China in 1945, her father was promoted to the rank of general in Chiang Kai-shek's army. Unlike the Communists, the

Guomindang had lost the support of the peasants. This was a disaster, for the peasants constituted over 98 per cent of the population. Despite being supplied with arms by Britain and the United States, the situation deteriorated rapidly for the Guomindang. Chiang Kai-shek's army of several million was soon routed and driven to Taiwan by the Communists. As the Guomindang fled eastwards, many of their leaders were not able to arrange for their families to escape in time. Shilin's had been such a family.

In the spring of 1949, Shilin was seven, and had been living with her grandmother in Beiping for two years. She was getting ready to return to her parents' home in Nanjing, to go to school there. Her mother had written to say that Shilin's father was going away on a campaign so she had to stay in Nanjing to look after the other children and could not travel to Beiping to fetch Shilin. Her grandmother was weak and in poor health and could not manage the journey, so it was agreed that Shilin's young aunt, Wang Yue, would take her back to Nanjing.

This was the time of the Guomindang–Communist battles that were to prove decisive. When Wang Yue and Shilin reached the bank of the Yangtze River, the ferry service, the only means of transport between north and south, had just been partially shut down. Piles of goods were massed on both banks.

As they waited, they heard that there was going to be a battle in Nanjing; the People's Liberation Army was about to cross the river. Despite this, there was nothing for it but to go on to Nanjing. When they arrived in the city, with a great tide of people, they found a red flag flying outside Shilin's house; a crowd of People's Liberation Army soldiers had moved in.

Wang Yue did not stop before the house. She hurried Shilin on and enquired in the shops and tea houses nearby for news of Shilin's family. Some people had seen the family cars being packed and boxes taken away, and had heard that the family had dismissed many of their servants. Others had heard that the whole family had vanished without trace the day before the Communists crossed the Yangtze. Nobody could give them any definite news, but it seemed that Shilin's family had fled to Taiwan without her.

Soon after, Wang Yue received the news that her mother had

died while the Communists were searching her house in Beiping – renamed Beijing by the new government – because of her relationship to Shilin's father. Returning to Beiping was now impossible. Not knowing what else to do, Wang Yue took Shilin to stay in a small guesthouse in Nanjing. One day, the kind-hearted landlord said to her, 'Didn't you say you could read and write? The new government is recruiting teachers for new schools – you should apply for a position.' Wang Yue only half believed him, but she applied anyway, and was taken on as a teacher.

Though Wang Yue was only twenty – a mere thirteen years older than Shilin – she had told Shilin to address her as 'mother' in order to conceal their identities. As 'mother and daughter', they were allocated a room by the new government-run school, which also helped them acquire some household items. Shilin was accepted as a pupil in the school.

Wang Yue made herself up and did her hair to make herself look old enough to be Shilin's mother. She reminded Shilin every morning not to mention her parents' names or anything about their old home under any circumstances. Though Shilin kept her aunt's warnings firmly in mind, she did not realise the full implications of letting anything slip. Children enjoy showing off to each other; once, playing jacks using tiny cloth beanbags, Shilin told her classmates that the little beanbags her father had given her to play jacks with had had little jewels sewn on them. One of her classmates mentioned this at home, and word spread among the adults.

At the time, everyone sought political advantage to consolidate his or her own position in the new Communist order. Before long, a representative from the local army garrison informed Wang Yue that she would have to give a full account of her 'late husband', Shilin's father.

One night, the headmaster of Wang Yue's school ran over to their room in a state of high agitation. 'Both of you must go now – they're going to arrest you. Run away as far as you can. Don't come back to Nanjing whatever you do. They say Shilin is the daughter of a Guomindang general, and you have committed the crime of sheltering a counter-revolutionary. I don't want to hear your explanations. In these times the less one knows the better. Go at once! Don't pack anything, they might even seal off the riverbank at any moment. Go, hurry! If you need anything in the future, come and look for me. I have to go. If the PLA catch me, my whole family will be in for it.'

Ready to weep with anxiety, Wang Yue took the half-asleep Shilin by the hand and walked out of Nanjing. Wang Yue had no idea where to go, but there was no possibility of asking anyone for help. She dared not imagine what would become of them if they were caught. They walked for nearly three hours; the sky was lightening but Nanjing still seemed to be right behind them. When Shilin could not walk any further, Wang Yue pulled her into some bushes by the roadside and sat down. The ground was wet with dew, and they were hungry and cold, but Shilin was so exhausted that she fell asleep immediately, leaning against her aunt. Tired and frightened, Wang Yue eventually cried herself to sleep as well.

Some time later, voices woke Wang Yue. A middle-aged couple and a tall young man were standing close by, looking concerned.

'Why are you sleeping here?' the middle-aged woman asked. 'It's cold and damp. Get up at once and find a house or some other place to sleep in, or you'll fall ill.'

'Thank you, but I, we, can't go any further – the child is too tired,' Wang Yue replied.

'Where are you going?' the woman asked, as she gestured to the young man to pick Shilin up.

'I don't know. I just want to get further away from Nanjing.' Wang Yue did not know what to say.

'Running away from a forced marriage, eh? Ah, it's hard when you've a child with you,' the woman said kindly. 'Wait a moment, I'll try to work something out with my husband. This is my son Guowei, and this is my husband.'

The middle-aged man standing to one side looked bookish and kindly. He spoke quickly, but with warmth. 'No need to talk it over. We're all in a hurry, so just come along with us. It's easier to travel in a group. Besides, how could we abandon a widow and orphan like you? Come, let me carry your bundle of things. Guowei can take charge of the little girl. Ting, give her a hand up.'

On the road, Wang Yue learned the older man was called Wang Duo and that he had been headmaster of a school in Nanjing. His wife, Liu Ting, had been educated in a progressive girls' school, so she had helped her husband with the teaching and the accounts at his school. Wang Duo was originally from Yangzhou, where his ancestors had taught the Confucian classics in a private academy. The school had been closed during the various wars and general chaos of the last decades, and had become a family dwelling. When Wang Duo married, the family profession and the house had passed on to him. He had wanted to set up a school, but found it difficult to realise his plans in the small town of Yangzhou. Because he wished his only son to have a good education, he had moved the family to Nanjing, where they stayed for ten years.

In the unsettled times, Wang Duo had faced difficulties setting up his school in Nanjing. He thought several times of returning to Yangzhou to write in peace, but Liu Ting, who wanted Guowei to complete his higher education in Nanjing, always talked him into staying on. Now that Guowei had completed senior school, they were returning to Yangzhou.

Wang Yue did not dare to tell the truth in return, but only spoke vaguely of some secret that was hard to put into words. At that time, educated people knew that knowledge was dangerous. After the fall of the Qing dynasty, China had fallen into a long period of anarchy and feudal rule. The chaos had been worst in the forty-five years prior to the new Communist government: governments and dynasties had seemed to change every day. No one knew the laws of the new republic yet, so the popular saying went: 'Keep silent on affairs of the state, speak little of family matters: one thing less is better than one thing more.' The Wang family did not press Wang Yue for details.

Yangzhou is a picturesque riverside town close to Nanjing. The local specialities of steamed vegetable dumplings, dried turnip and stewed tofu sheets with ginger are famous all over China. Girls from Yangzhou are renowned for their complexions and their beauty. Yangzhou's rural setting and its backdrop of mountains and water have attracted many members of the literati and of the government. The Beijing Opera master, Mei Lanfang, and the famous poet of the New Moon School, Xu Zhimo, are both from Yangzhou, as is Jiang Zemin, the current President of China.

Wang Duo and Liu Ting's house was a traditional courtyard

house in a western suburb of Yangzhou by Lake Shouxi. Centuries of dredging and the planting of gardens and woods had transformed the lake into one of the most beautiful in China.

In their absence, the house had been looked after by an old couple, so it was clean and tidy. Though everything about the house was old, there was a pleasant, scholarly air about it. Shortly after they arrived in Yangzhou, Wang Yue and Shilin both came down with high fevers. Liu Ting was very worried, and had hurriedly called the Chinese herbalist, who diagnosed shock and chills from exhaustion, and prescribed some herbal treatments, which Liu Ting brewed for them.

Wang Yue and Shilin recovered after a week or two, but Shilin was no longer her former lively self, and hid behind the grown-ups when the Wang family took her to see the neighbours' children. Wang Yue believed that Shilin was still suffering the after-effects of their flight from Nanjing, but would soon get over it.

Not long after, Liu Ting said to Wang Yue, 'My husband says you're a good hand with a pen. If you like, you can stay with us and help us with some clerical work. You can call us Uncle and Aunt, and Guowei Elder Brother. We will help you look after Shilin too.'

Wang Yue was overcome with gratitude, and accepted immediately.

The political climate in Yangzhou in the 1950s was much less fraught than in bigger towns. The people in Yangzhou were not overfond of politics, and the cultural tradition there was for everyone to live and work in peace. The sincerity and goodness of the Wang family helped Wang Yue to put the terror and insecurity of the past few months behind her.

Guowei started teaching at a newly built primary school, where he took Shilin every day. Back with children of the same age, Shilin gradually became less withdrawn and more like her old self.

Guowei liked his job, for the school had a lively, creative atmosphere, and did not distinguish between rich and poor. Guowei's commitment was rewarded by the school, which arranged for him to participate in many extra-curricular activities. When Guowei spoke enthusiastically about his work at home, his parents often warned him to be more circumspect. Wang Yue was a keen and faithful listener, showing interest and understanding for Guowei's passions. The couple fell in love, and were engaged during Wang Yue's third year in Yangzhou.

Wang Yue told the Wang family the truth about herself and Shilin on the day of the engagement. As Liu Ting listened, she took Wang Yue's hand, saying over and over again, 'You've had a hard time, you've had such a hard time.'

Wang Duo said, 'Shilin is your sister's child, and she's our child too. From tomorrow, you are the daughter of the Wang family, so Shilin is the granddaughter of the Wang family.'

Shilin already addressed Wang Duo and Liu Ting as her grandparents, and Wang Yue as her mother, but it was not so easy for her to address Guowei as her father. She was now ten, and it was particularly hard for her to change her manner of address to Guowei in front of her classmates. At Wang Yue and Guowei's wedding, however, she called Guowei 'Papa' without being prompted. Guowei was so pleased and surprised that he caught her up in his arms and hugged her tightly, until Liu Ting shouted, 'Put her down, you'll hurt her.'

Shilin was bright and diligent, and was guided by her family members, who were all teachers. She excelled at school, and skipped a grade, moving from the third to the fifth year. When she entered the sixth year, Shilin represented the school in the North Jiangsu Regional Essay Competition, and won first prize. She went on to win the bronze medal in an essay competition for the whole of Jiangsu Province. Wang Yue and Guowei were overjoyed by the news – hugging Shilin and paying no attention to the cries of their first baby in their excitement. Everyone in the family was bursting with pride, and their neighbours congratulated them on Shilin's brilliance.

The next day, as Guowei was writing couplets on lucky red paper to display for International Children's Day on 1 June, a girl pupil rushed over to him, gasping for breath:

'Mr Wang, come quickly. The boys are calling Shilin names and she is quarrelling with them. She's exhausted, but we girls don't dare help her – the boys say they'll hit anyone who does!'

As Guowei hurried towards the small school sports ground he heard the boys yelling at Shilin:

'You hypocrite!'

'Bastard child!'

'Bastards are always the clever ones!'

'Ask your mum who your father was. Was he a drunk she found in a ditch?'

Guowei rushed forward, pushing the boys around Shilin aside with his fists. He took Shilin in his arms and roared, 'Who says Shilin has no father? If anyone dares to say another word, they won't be able to open their mouths by the time I've finished with them! If you don't believe me, try it and see!'

Frightened, the bullies ran off in an instant. Shilin trembled in Guowei's arms, white as a sheet, sweat on her brow and blood on her lip where she had bitten it.

At home, Shilin developed a high fever, murmuring, 'I'm not a bastard, I have a mother and a father,' over and over again. Liu Ting and Wang Yue kept watch over her.

The doctor told the family that Shilin was suffering from shock: irregularities had appeared in her heartbeat. He said that if her temperature was not lowered as quickly as possible, she might become mentally deranged. He wondered how a twelve-year-old girl had received such a great shock.

Wang Duo said furiously, 'This country is getting worse by the day. How can little children do such a thing. What they did to her is murder in all but name.'

Guowei kept apologising to the family for not looking after Shilin, but everyone knew that he was not to blame. Later, Guowei found out how the scene in the sports ground had started. An older boy had wanted to embrace Shilin, but she had rejected him and told him to behave. Angry and ashamed, he had pointed at Shilin and shouted, 'Who do you think you are? Who is your father? There isn't so much as a shadow of Wang Guowei in your face. Go home and ask your mother who she slept with to get a bastard like you! Stop pretending to be decent and modest!' He ordered the younger boys standing about to join in calling Shilin names, threatening to beat up anyone who did not obey him. Guowei was livid: without the slightest regard for the dignity of his position as a teacher or any thought of the consequences, he sought the bully out and gave him a thorough beating.

Shilin recovered, but she said little, rarely went out, and often stayed at home alone. The middle-school entrance exams were approaching, so everyone thought that she was revising and did not want to be disturbed. Wang Yue was the only one who still felt uneasy. She felt that there was something not quite right about Shilin, but dared not share her conjectures with anyone, lest the family got into trouble. Political movements like the Anti-Rightist Movement were starting to spread in Yangzhou, and many ignorant, uneducated people thought this was the time to narrow the property gap by raiding the houses of the rich and dividing the spoils, a practice that had existed since the Ming dynasty. They started compiling lists of wealthy households, planning to cause trouble under the cover of revolution. The Wang family fell between stools, being neither wealthy nor ordinary, so they could never be sure when someone with a grudge against them might categorise them as a rich household.

Shilin did not perform as brilliantly in the middle-school entrance exams as she had been expected to before the incident in the sports ground, but her results were still good enough to gain her a place in one of the top schools. The school she chose was not far from home, which Wang Yue found reassuring.

Shilin remained silent and withdrawn at school, but she became more talkative at home. She started asking Wang Duo about the reasons behind the political movements taking place in China, and about the enmity between the Guomindang and the Communist Party. She often asked Wang Yue about her parents, but Wang Yue knew little about her sister because of the age gap between them. Wang Yue had been very young when her sister left home to go to school in the south, and had been only three or four when she married. Shilin thought that Wang Yue was being deliberately reticent because she did not want her to dwell on the past.

At the beginning of the Cultural Revolution, when extra-marital relationships were seen as a 'counter-revolutionary' crime, the Red Guards labelled Wang Yue a criminal for having had Shilin before marriage. Pregnant with her second child, Wang Yue was subjected to frequent public condemnations by the Red Guards. Through it all, she did not say a word. Wang Duo, Liu Ting and Guowei were then imprisoned and interrogated in turn, but all three maintained that they knew nothing about Wang Yue and Shilin's past. One of the Red Guards who conducted the brutal interrogations was the teenager who had tried to embrace Shilin, and had been beaten by Guowei. He humiliated them all mercilessly, and beat Guowei so hard his left foot was permanently crippled.

The Red Guards forced Shilin to watch from a window as they interrogated and tortured the Wang family. They pulled her hair and pinched her eyelids to keep her awake over several days and nights, as she watched Guowei's foot bleeding, Wang Yue clutching her belly, Wang Duo and Liu Ting trembling with fear, and Wang Yue's tiny son hiding in a corner and crying. Shilin's face remained expressionless throughout, but she was sweating and shivering. Just as the Red Guards were about to smash Guowei's right foot with sticks and cudgels, Shilin suddenly cried out in a high, inhuman voice, 'Don't hit him, don't hit him! They aren't my parents. My father's name is Zhang Zhongren, my mother's name is Wang Xing, they are in Taiwan!'

Everyone was shocked into silence for a moment, then the Wang family hurled themselves against the window and shouted, 'It's not true! She's gone mad, she doesn't know what she's talking about!'

Shilin watched them as they shouted their denials, then burst out laughing. 'I know I'm not a bastard, I have a mother and father of my own,' she said. Then she started foaming at the mouth, and collapsed.

The Red Guards pounced on the names Shilin had let slip; based on their confirmation of Shilin's parentage and other incriminating evidence they claimed to have established, the Wang family was imprisoned. Wang Duo had a weak constitution and was often ill – he died in prison. Liu Ting became paralysed on one side of her body from sleeping on the prison floor. Wang Yue gave birth to her second child, a daughter, in prison. She was named Wang Yu because the character for Yu (jade) is written by adding an extra dot to the character for Wang, symbolising an addition to the Wang family. They nicknamed her Xiao Yu (little Jade) because she was so small and weak. When they were released from prison ten years later, Guowei could only walk leaning on a stick.

In the late 1980s, Wang Yue and Guowei ran into one of the Red

Guards who had persecuted them. He admitted that, apart from Shilin's parents' names and a group photograph of the leaders of the Guomindang, the Red Guards' evidence against Shilin and the Wangs had been fabricated.

Shilin was mentally ill, but her condition varied: on some days she was much better than on others. The Red Guards sent her to a village in a mountainous area of Hubei to be 're-educated' by the peasants. She could not work in the fields because of her unstable mental condition, so she was allocated the relatively light job of cowherd. Soon, the men in the village started to invent excuses to climb up to the remote grassy slopes where Shilin had taken the cows to graze. They had discovered that all it took to send Shilin over the edge was the question: 'Who is your father?'

She would laugh and shout wildly, and then faint. While she was confused, the men raped her. If she struggled, they shouted over and over again, 'Who is your father, are you a bastard?' until Shilin was so unbalanced that she complied with their orders.

A good-hearted grandmother in the village found out what had been going on when she overheard a man quarrelling with his wife. She stood in the centre of the village cursing the men, 'You heartless beasts. Were you born of women? Don't you have mothers of your own? You will pay for this!' The grandmother took Shilin in to live with her, but she had lost all awareness of her surroundings.

In early 1989, Wang Yue and her family found Shilin in the village in Hubei and took her away to live with them. Shilin did not recognise them, and they barely recognised her after her years in the countryside. Wang Yue took Shilin for a full physical examination at the hospital. When she read the results, she fell ill. The report stated that Shilin's torso was scarred with bite-marks, part of one nipple had been chewed away and her vaginal labia were torn. The neck and lining of her womb had been severely damaged, and a broken branch had been extracted from it. The doctors could not establish how long the branch had been in her womb.

When Wang Yue recovered from her illness, she telephoned the Party officials in the Hubei village Shilin had lived in, and told them that she would be taking them to court for abusing Shilin.

The cadres pleaded with her: 'This is a very poor place. If all the men in the village are imprisoned, the children will go hungry.' Wang Yue decided not to prosecute. As she put the phone down, she thought, 'God will punish them.'

Though he feared that regaining her memory would cause Shilin great pain, Guowei had suggested trying to find some way of helping Shilin regain some awareness of her surroundings. Over seven or eight years, Wang Yue and Guowei had tried several courses of treatment for Shilin, none of which had had any result. The thought of asking Shilin about her father to trigger a reaction had crossed their minds, but they feared the consequences too much.

Wang Yue managed to establish contact with Shilin's sisters and brother in Taiwan, and they came to visit their long-lost sister. They could not connect the unresponsive, dead-eyed woman before them with the clever, lively girl their parents had described, but Shilin looked so much like their mother that there could be no doubt about her identity.

Wang Yue did not tell them the real reason for Shilin's condition. She was not afraid of being blamed for not looking after Shilin, but she knew that people who had not lived through the Cultural Revolution would be unable to imagine or grasp what had happened. Wang Yue had no desire to sow hatred, and shied away from having to recount the details of Shilin's story. She told them that Shilin had lost her mind after a car accident. When Shilin's brother and sisters asked if Shilin had suffered, Wang Yue reassured them that she had not, and had lost her memory soon after the accident.

Wang Yue had never stopped asking herself how much of her suffering Shilin had been conscious of before she lost her mind. I told her reluctantly that, like other people who lose their awareness in adulthood, Shilin must have done so as a result of extreme pain. Shilin's pain had built up in layers from the night she fled Nanjing through her confused childhood, and she had never had an outlet for it because she did not want to make the Wang family unhappy. The years of abuse in Hubei had crushed her consciousness.

*

When I returned to the radio station for my night broadcast after spending the afternoon at the hospital, the office was empty. I found a glass of fruit juice on my desk with a note from Mengxing, who had kept the juice for me, concerned that I would be exhausted. Mengxing had a reputation as a tough woman who never gave anyone anything, so I was very touched. The station director had also left me a note asking me to hand in my report on the interview with the Guomindang general's daughter the next day.

In the morning, I told the director about Shilin, but said that we could not broadcast her story. He was surprised. 'What's wrong? Usually you are pleading to be able to broadcast things.'

'Nothing's wrong,' I replied, 'but I can't bring myself to tell this story again or make a programme about it. It would be too difficult.'

'This is the first time I've ever heard you say anything is too difficult, so it really must have been a hard story to listen to. I hope you can manage to put it behind you.'

I never did manage to have a talk about understanding the disabled with Old Wu. He died of a liver ailment during a banquet that weekend. At his memorial service, I silently told him my thoughts, sure that he could hear me. After people leave this world, they live on in the memories of the living. Sometimes you can feel their presence, see their faces or hear their voices.

12

The Childhood I Cannot Leave Behind Me

I had begun my search for Chinese women's stories full of youthful enthusiasm but knowing very little. Now that I knew more, I had a more mature understanding – but I also felt more pain. At times a kind of numbness would come over me from all the suffering I had encountered, as if a callus were forming within me. Then I would hear another story and my feelings would be stirred up all over again.

Although my internal life was in turmoil, in career terms I was becoming more and more successful. I had been made Director of Programme Development and Planning, which meant that I was responsible for developing the future strategy of the whole broadcasting station. As my reputation and influence grew, I was able to meet women who would otherwise have been inaccessible to me: the wives of Party leaders, women in the military, in religious institutions, or in prison. One such meeting came about because of an encounter at a Public Security Bureau award ceremony. I had done some work organising public education activities for the PSB and, as a result, I was to be awarded the title of 'Flower of the Police Force'. The award didn't mean a great deal, but I was the only woman in the province to be honoured in this way and it was to prove extremely useful in my attempts to reach out to more women.

The Chinese will use any excuse to throw a banquet: we live according to the principle 'food is heaven', and eat and drink away untold wealth. Although only four people were receiving prizes, there were more than four hundred guests at the banquet. Very few women win honours or receive prizes in police circles, let alone those from outside the PSB, so I became the subject of much discussion that evening. I hated the crush and the endless questions, so I slipped into the service corridor to escape. When the bustling waiters in the corridor saw me, they shouted, 'Out of the way, move along, don't block the way!'

I pressed myself back against the wall. The discomfort of this place seemed better than the scrutiny of my fellow guests. A few moments later, Chief Constable Mei came by to thank the waiters, and was surprised to see me. He asked me what I thought I was doing.

I had known Chief Constable Mei for a while and trusted him, so I spoke frankly. He chuckled and said, 'There's no need for you to hide in this horrible, cramped space. Come, I'll take you to a better place.' He led me away.

The banqueting hall, which was famous throughout the city, had several adjoining parlours and meeting rooms that I had not been aware of. Chief Constable Mei led me into one of these rooms, telling me that the hall had the same layout as the Great Hall of the People in Beijing, which had been designed for the convenience of central government leaders when they came to inspect the city. I felt rather overwhelmed to be admitted to this inner sanctum, and was also worried that other people might put a malicious construction on us being alone together.

Noticing my hesitation, Mei said, 'You needn't worry about gossip. There's a sentry outside. Ah, I'm so tired . . .' He yawned and collapsed on to the sofa.

The police guard outside tapped on the door and asked quietly, 'Chief Constable, do you need anything?'

'That will be all,' Mei replied in a terse, cold tone. This was how all senior officials spoke to their underlings in China; it made me think about how this had created the habitual attitudes of superiority and inferiority among the Chinese.

Chief Constable Mei massaged his head with both hands as he sprawled on the sofa. 'Xinran, I've just come back from a trip to Hunan where I visited a number of prisons. I heard about a female inmate who might interest you. She's been in and out of prison several times on charges of sexual deviance and illegal cohabitation. Apparently, she has a very tragic family history. If you'd like to interview her, I could set things up and send a car for you.'

I nodded and thanked him. He shook his head wearily, saying, 'Chinese women really have a hard time of it. I've listened to your programme several times. It's sad, very moving. How much happiness can there be in the life of a woman who has lived through the last few decades? My wife says that women give their smiles to others and save their heartaches for themselves. She likes your programme a lot, but I don't want her to listen to it too much; she's very emotional, and one story can torture her for several days.' He paused. 'I wouldn't want her to die before me, I couldn't bear it.'

Chief Constable Mei was a big, tough man from Shandong. I had known him for many years, but never guessed that he could be so sensitive. Chinese men are brought up to believe that they should command respect, and many are unwilling to let others see their softer side. For the first time in our acquaintance, our conversation that evening was not about work, but about men, women and relationships.

Two weeks later, a PSB jeep took me to a women's prison in the mountains of west Hunan. The group of buildings looked like any other prison: the electric fence, the sentries and the searchlights mounted on the dark grey wall instantly created an atmosphere of fear and tension. The main gate, through which only the cars of the powerful could pass, was shut; we entered through the side gate.

Looking up at the huge building, I could guess from the sizes and shapes of the windows what was behind them. Behind the wide, high, broken windows, grey figures moved back and forth amid the thundering of machines. Prisoners usually work while they serve their sentence: mending cars, lorries or machine tools, or sewing and producing textiles. Some are set to hard labour, quarrying stone or working in mines. Through the mid-sized windows, uniforms, equipment and dashes of colour could be seen; these were offices and political study rooms. The smallest windows at the top of the buildings belonged to the convicts' dormitories and canteens.

The main building formed a horseshoe around a smaller building which housed the prison officers' sleeping quarters and control rooms. Two things about West Hunan Women's Prison struck me as different from other prisons: one was that the walls were covered with dark green moss and lichen because of the humid west Hunan weather; the other was the strangeness of seeing policewomen shouting at women prisoners. The lives, loves, sorrows and joys of the women in police uniforms could not be so very different from those of the women in prison clothes.

Chief Constable Mei's letter of introduction acted like an imperial edict; after reading it, the prison governor allocated me a private interview room for my meeting with Hua'er, the prisoner Mei had mentioned.

Hua'er was a slight woman of about my age. She shifted restlessly in her prison uniform, as if struggling with her powerlessness. Although her hair had been cut by inexperienced hands and was ragged and uneven, it reminded me of some of the bizarre styles hairdressing salons were turning out. She was beautiful, but her hard, closed expression was like a flaw in an exquisite piece of porcelain.

I did not ask for details of her sentence, nor why she had broken the law against cohabitation time after time. Instead, I asked her if she would tell me about her family.

'Who are you?' she retorted. 'What's so special about you that I should tell you?'

'Because you are the same as me – we are both women, and we have lived through the same times,' I said slowly and distinctly, looking into her eyes.

Hua'er was momentarily silenced by this.

Then she asked in a mocking tone, 'If that is so, do you think if I tell you my story you will be able to bear it?'

It was my turn to be lost for words. Her question had struck home: would I be able to bear it, indeed? Did I not still struggle to forget my own painful memories?

Hua'er sensed that she had hit home. Smugly, she asked the warden to open the door and let her go back to her cell. The warden shot me an enquiring look and I nodded unthinkingly. As

I stumbled back to the officers' quarters where I would sleep that night, I was already immersed in my memories. Try as I might, I have never been able to walk away from the nightmare of my childhood.

I was born in Beijing in 1958, when China was at its poorest, and a day's food ration consisted of a few soybeans. While other children of my age were cold and hungry, I ate imported chocolate in my grandmother's house in Beijing, surrounded by flowers and birdsong in the courtyard. But China was about to iron out the distinctions between the rich and poor in its unique political way. Children who had struggled to survive poverty and deprivation would spurn and insult me; soon the material riches I had once possessed were more than balanced out by spiritual privation. From then on, I understood that there are many things in life more important than chocolate.

When I was little, my grandmother combed and plaited my hair every day, making sure the braids were even and regular before tying ribbons into a bow on each end. I was extremely fond of my plaits, and tossed my head proudly to display them when walking or playing. At bedtime, I would not let my grandmother untie the ribbons, and would position my plaits carefully on either side of the pillow before going to sleep. Sometimes, when I got up in the morning to find my bows undone, I would ask sulkily who it was who had spoiled them.

My parents were stationed at a military base near the Great Wall. When I was 7, I went to live with them for the first time since I was born. Less than a fortnight after I arrived, our house was searched by the Red Guards. They suspected my father of being a 'reactionary technical authority' because he was a member of the Chinese Association of High-Level Mechanical Engineers and an expert on electrical mechanics. He was also thought to be a 'British imperialist running dog' because his father had worked for the British company GEC for thirty-five years. In addition, because our house contained many cultural artefacts, my father was charged with being a 'representative of feudalism, capitalism and revisionism'.

I remember Red Guards swarming all over the house and a great fire in our courtyard on to which were thrown my father's books, my grandparents' precious traditional furniture and my toys. My father had been arrested and taken away. Frightened and sad, I fell into a stupor as I watched the flames, hearing cries for help coming from within them. The fire burned away everything: the home I had only just come to call my own, my hitherto happy childhood, my hopes and my family's pride in its learning and riches. It burned regrets into me that will remain till my death.

In the light of the fire, a girl wearing a red armband walked over to me carrying a big pair of scissors. She caught hold of my plaits and said, 'This is a petit-bourgeois hairstyle.'

Before I had realised what she was talking about, she had cut my plaits off, and thrown them into the fire. I stood wide-eyed, watching dumbly as my plaits and their pretty bows turned to ashes. When the Red Guards left our house, the girl who had cut my plaits off said to me, 'From now on, you are forbidden to tie your hair back with ribbons. That is an imperialist hairstyle!'

After my father had been thrown into prison, my mother seldom had time to look after us. She always came home late, and when she was home she was always writing; what, I did not know. My brother and I could only buy food in our father's work unit canteen where they served a meagre diet of boiled turnips or cabbage. Cooking oil was a rare commodity then.

Once, my mother brought home some belly of pork, and stewed it for us through the night. The next morning, as she was about to leave for work, she said to me, 'When you come home, poke the coals to make them hotter and heat up the pork in the pot for lunch. Don't leave any for me. Both of you need the nourishment.'

When I got out of school at midday, I went to fetch my brother from the house of a neighbour who was looking after him. When I told him he was going to have something nice to eat, he was very happy, and sat obediently by the table watching me as I set to warming the food up.

Our stove was a tall brick range of the sort used by the northern Chinese and I was dwarfed by it. In order to be able to prod the coal with a poker, I had to stand on a stool. This was the first time I had done this alone. I did not realise that the poker would become red-hot from the fire within the range and when I had difficulty pulling it out with my right hand, I grasped it firmly with my left. The skin on my palm blistered and peeled off, and I screamed in pain.

My neighbour came running when she heard the noise. She called a doctor, but though he lived nearby, he told her that he did not dare to come because a certificate of special permission was required for him to make an emergency visit to a member of a household that was under investigation.

Another neighbour who came hurrying round was an old professor. He had somehow picked up the notion that soy sauce should be rubbed into burns and poured a whole bottle of it on to my hand; it stung so excruciatingly that I fell to the floor writhing in agony and passed out.

When I came round, I was lying in bed and my mother was sitting beside me, holding my bandaged left hand in both of hers, reproaching herself for asking me to use the stove alone.

To this day, I find it hard to understand how that doctor could have let our family's political status prevent him from coming to my aid.

As the 'daughter of a capitalist household', my mother was soon detained for investigation as well, and forbidden to return home. My brother and I were moved to living quarters for children whose parents were in prison.

At school, I was forbidden to take part in singing and dancing activities with the other girls because I was not to 'pollute' the arena of the revolution. Even though I was short-sighted, I was not allowed to sit in the front row in class because the best places were reserved for children born to peasants, workers or soldiers; they were deemed to have 'straight roots and red shoots'. Similarly, I was forbidden to stand in the front row during PE lessons, though I was the smallest in the class, because the places nearest the teacher were for the 'next generation of the revolution'.

Along with the other twelve 'polluted' children who ranged from two to fourteen years in age, my brother and I had to attend a political study class after school, and could not participate in after-school activities with children of our age. We were not allowed to watch films, not even the most fervently revolutionary ones, because we had to 'thoroughly recognise' the reactionary nature of our families. In the canteen, we were served food only after everyone else because my paternal grandfather had once 'helped the British and American imperialists take food from Chinese mouths and clothes off Chinese backs'.

Our days were regulated by two Red Guards barking orders:

'Out of bed!'

'Go to class!'

'Go to the canteen!'

'Study the Quotations of Chairman Mao!'

'Go to sleep!'

Without any family to protect us, we followed the same mechanical routine day after day, with none of the smiles, games or laughter of childhood. We did the housework ourselves, and the older children helped the younger ones to wash their clothes, faces and feet every day; we only had one shower a week. At night, we all – boys and girls together – slept squeezed together on straw bedding.

Our one small comfort lay in trips to the canteen. No one chatted or laughed there, but kind people sometimes slipped small parcels of food to us surreptitiously.

One day, I took my brother, who was not yet three years old, to stand at the end of the canteen queue, which was unusually long. It must have been a day of national celebration, for roast chicken was being sold for the first time, and the delicious smell wafted through the air. Our mouths watered; we had eaten nothing but leftovers for a long time, but we knew there would be no roast chicken for us.

My brother suddenly burst into tears, shouting that he wanted roast chicken. Afraid that the noise would annoy the Red Guards and that they would turn us out, leaving us with no food at all, I did my best to coax my brother to stop. But he continued crying, getting more and more upset; I was so petrified that I was on the verge of tears myself.

Just then, a motherly-looking woman walked past. She tore off some of her roast chicken, gave it to my brother and walked off without a word. My brother stopped crying, and was just about to start eating when a Red Guard ran up, snatched the chicken leg from his mouth, threw it on to the ground and trampled it to mush.

'You pups of imperialist running dogs, you're fit to eat chicken too, are you?' the Red Guard shouted.

My brother was too scared to move; he ate nothing that day – and he did not cry or make a fuss over roast chicken or any such luxury for a long time after that. Many years later, I asked my brother if he remembered that incident. I am glad to say that he did not, but I cannot forget it myself.

My brother and I lived in the home for almost five years. We were lucky compared to other children, some of whom lived there for nearly ten.

In the home, the children trusted and helped each other. All of us were equal there. But there was no place for us in the outside world. Wherever our little troupe went, people would recoil as if we had the plague. Mature adults would express their sympathy with silence, but children humiliated and insulted us. Our clothes were streaked with gobs of spit or phlegm, but we did not know how to defend ourselves, let alone how to fight back. Instead, self-loathing was branded into our hearts.

The first person to spit at me was my best friend. She said, 'My mother says your grandfather helped those horrible English people eat Chinese flesh and drink Chinese blood. He was the very, very worst of all bad people. You're his grandchild, so you can't be a good person either.' She spat at me, walked away and never spoke to me again.

One day, I was huddled at the back of the classroom, crying after being beaten up by the 'red' children. I thought I was alone, and was startled when one of my teachers came to stand behind me and patted my shoulder lightly. Through my tears, it was hard to read the expression on his face in the dim light of the lamps, but I could see that he was gesturing for me to follow him. I trusted him because I knew that he helped poor people outside the school.

He walked with me to a hut by the side of the playground where the school stored its junk. He opened the lock very quickly and ushered me in. The window was covered with newspapers, so it was very dim inside. The room was piled high with jumbled odds and ends, and smelled of mould and decay. I stiffened in distaste, but the teacher wriggled his way through the junk with the ease of long practice. I fought my way in after him.

In the inner room, I was amazed to find a neat, well-ordered library. Several hundred books were arranged on broken planks. For the first time, I understood the meaning of a famous line of poetry: 'In the darkest shadow of the willows, I suddenly came upon the bright flowers of a village.'

The teacher told me that this library was a secret that he was planning as a gift for future generations. No matter how revolutionary people were, he said, they could not live without books. Without books, we would not understand the world; without books, we could not develop; without books, nature could not serve humanity. The more he spoke, the more excited he became, but the more afraid I grew. I knew that it was these very books which the Cultural Revolution was fighting to destroy. The teacher gave me a key to the hut and told me that I could take refuge and read there at any time.

The hut was behind the only toilet in the school, so it was easy for me to go there without being noticed when the other children were taking part in activities I was barred from.

On my first few visits to the hut, I found the smell and the darkness stifling, so I poked a pea-sized hole into the newspapers over the window. I peered out at the children playing, dreaming that one day I might be allowed to join in.

When the bustle in the playground had made me too sad to go on looking out of the window, I started to read. There were not many elementary readers among the books in the library, so I had great difficulty with the obscure vocabulary. At first, the teacher would answer questions and explain things when he came to check up on me; later he brought me a dictionary, which I used diligently, though I still only understood about half of what I read.

The books on Chinese and foreign history fascinated me. They taught me about different ways of life: not only about the dramatic stories that everybody knew, but about ordinary people weaving their own history through their daily lives. From these books, I also learned that many questions remained unanswered.

I learned a great deal from the encyclopaedia, which saved me trouble and expense later in life, for I can now turn my hand to manual work and repairs on everything from bicycles to small electrical appliances. I used to dream of becoming a diplomat, a lawyer, a journalist or a writer. When I had the opportunity to choose a profession, I left my administrative job in the army after twelve years to become a journalist. The passive knowledge I had accumulated in my childhood helped me once again.

My dream of joining in with the other children in the playground never came true, but I gained comfort from reading about battles and bloodshed in that secret library. The records of war made me feel lucky to be living in peacetime, and helped me to forget the taunts that awaited me outside the hut.

The first person to show me how to see happiness and beauty in life by observing the people and things around me was Yin Da.

Yin Da was an orphan. He did not seem to know how he had lost his parents; all he knew was that he had grown up under the care of his neighbours in the village while living in a hut 1.5 metres long by 1.2 metres wide, containing only a bed which took up the whole room. He had eaten the rice of a hundred families and worn the clothes of a hundred households, and called all the villagers Mother and Father.

I remember Yin Da only having one set of clothes. In winter he simply wore a thick, padded cotton jacket over his summer clothes. Everyone around him was poor, so a padded jacket for the winter was comfort enough.

Though Yin Da must have been five or six years older than I was, we were in the same class at the army school. During the Cultural Revolution, virtually all institutions of education were frozen; only military schools and colleges were allowed to continue to train young people in matters of national defence. To show support for the peasants and workers from the town occupied by the military base, my school arranged for the local children to be educated alongside army children. Many of them were already fourteen or fifteen when they started primary school.

If Yin Da was around when I was being beaten up, spat at or called names by the children from 'Red' families, he would always stand up for me. Sometimes, when he saw me crying in a corner, he would tell the Red Guards that he was taking me to get to know the peasants and would lead me on a tour of the town. He would show me the houses of very poor people, and tell me what made these people happy, even though they earned much less than a hundred yuan a year.

At break time, Yin Da would take me up the hill behind the school to look at the trees and flowering plants there. There were many trees of the same kind in the world, he said, yet no two leaves were the same. He told me that life was precious and that water gave life by giving of itself.

He asked me what I liked about the town where the military base was. I said I did not know, there was nothing to like; it was a small, shabby, colourless place, filled only with the choking smoke of cooking fires, and people walking about in torn jackets and ragged shirts. Yin Da taught me to look at and think about each house in the town carefully, even the ones cobbled together from scrap. Who lived in these houses? What did they do inside? What did they do outside? Why was that door ajar? Was the family inside waiting for someone or had they forgotten to close the door? What consequences would their forgetfulness bring?

I followed Yin Da's advice to find interest in my surroundings and was no longer so saddened by the spitting and taunts I encountered every day. I would be wrapped up in my own thoughts, imagining the lives of the people in the houses. The contrast between imaginary and real worlds was to become a source of both comfort and sorrow for me.

At the end of the 1960s, relations between China and the Soviet Union broke down completely, and an armed conflict over China's northern border took place on Zhenbao island. Every town and city had to dig tunnels as air-raid shelters. In some big cities, the shelters were capable of accommodating the entire population. Simple equipment and food reserves would enable them to survive in the tunnels for several days. Everyone from old to young was set to digging these tunnels; even children as young as seven or eight were not excused.

The children in our school had to dig tunnels into the side of the hill behind the school. We were split into two groups, one working inside the tunnel and one outside. Though I was assigned to the group inside, I was set to work at the mouth of the tunnel because I was a girl, and relatively weak.

One day, about half an hour after we had started work, there was a great roaring sound: the tunnel had collapsed. Four boys were buried inside, including Yin Da, who had been the furthest in. By the time they had been dug out, four days after the accident, their bodies could only be told apart by their clothes.

The children and dependants of 'Black' families were not permitted a last look at the four boys, who had been posthumously recognised as heroes. From afar, my last glimpse of Yin Da was of his lifeless arm dangling from a stretcher.

Yin Da once taught me the theme song from the film *A Visitor to Ice Mountain*. It had a beautiful melody, and the lyrics remembered a lost friend. Years later, when China had begun to open up and reform, this film was shown again. Memories of Yin Da came flooding back.

> *My beautiful homeland lies at the foot of the Mountains of*
> * Heaven,*
> *When I left home, I was like a melon broken from the vine.*
> *The girl I loved lived under the white poplar trees.*
> *When I left, she was like a lute, left hanging on the wall.*
> *The vine is broken, but the melons are still sweet.*
> *When the lute player returns, the lute will sing again.*
> *When I parted from my friend,*
> *He was like a mountain made of snow – in one avalanche,*
> * gone forever.*
> *Ah, my dear friend,*
> *I will never see your mighty form or your kindly face again.*
> *Ah, my dear friend,*
> *You will never hear me play the lute, never hear me sing again.*

I don't know if Yin Da had sensed his fate in this melancholy song when he sang it to me, but he had left behind a melody for himself, through which I could remember him.

13

The Woman Whose Father Does Not Know Her

During my first night at West Hunan Women's Prison, I did not dare to close my eyes for fear of my recurring nightmares. Yet even with my eyes open, I could not block out images of my childhood. At dawn, I told myself I had to leave the past behind and find a way to get Hua'er to trust me so that I could share her story with other women. I asked the Warden if I could speak to Hua'er again in the interview room.

When she came in, the prickliness and defiance of the previous day had melted away, and her face was etched with pain. From her look of surprise, I guessed that I too looked different after a night of being tormented by memories.

Hua'er started our interview by telling me how her mother had chosen names for her and her sister and brothers. Her mother had said that all things in the natural world struggled for their place, but that trees, mountains and rocks were the strongest, so she had called her first daughter Shu (tree), her elder son Shan (mountain) and her younger son Shi (rock). A flowering tree will bring forth fruit, and flowers on a mountain or a rock beautify it, so Hua'er had been called Hua (flower).

'Everyone said that I was the most beautiful . . . perhaps because I was called Hua.'

I was struck by the poetry of these names, and thought to myself that Hua'er's mother must have been a very cultivated woman. I poured Hua'er a glass of hot water from the thermos flask on the table. She gripped it with both hands, staring at the steam rising from it, and muttered in a low tone, 'My parents are Japanese.'

I was taken aback by this. There had been no note of it in Hua'er's criminal record.

'They both taught at university, and we were given special treatment. Other families had to live in one room, but we had two rooms. My parents slept in the small room and we had the big room. My sister Shu often took my elder brother Shan and me to her friends' homes with her. Their parents were kind to us, they would give us snacks to nibble on, and ask us to speak Japanese for them. I was very young, but my Japanese was very good and I enjoyed teaching the adults little words and phrases. The other children grabbed all the food while I was doing this, but my sister always kept a bit for me. She protected me.'

Hua'er's face lit up.

'My father was proud of Shu because she did well in school. He said that she could help him become wiser. My mother also praised my sister for being a good girl because she kept an eye on my elder brother and me, giving my mother time to prepare lessons and look after my younger brother Shi, who was three years old. We were happiest when we were playing with our father. He dressed up as different people to make us laugh. Sometimes he was the Old Man Carrying the Mountain from the Japanese fairy tale, and he carried all four of us on his back. We pressed down on him until he gasped for breath, but he continued carrying us, shouting, "I'm . . . carrying . . . the mountain!"

'Sometimes he wrapped my mother's scarf round his head to be the Wolf Grandmother from the Chinese fairy story. Whenever he played hide-and-seek with us, I dived under the quilt, and shouted innocently, "Hua'er is not under the quilt!"

'He hid in the most ingenious places. Once he even hid in the large jar where grain was kept. When he came out, he was covered with maize, buckwheat and rice.' Hua'er laughed at the memory, and I joined in.

She took a sip of water, savouring it.

'We were very happy. But then, in 1966, the nightmare began.'

The leaping flames of the bonfire that had marked the end of my happy childhood appeared before my eyes. Hua'er's voice banished the image.

'One summer afternoon, my parents had gone to work, and I was doing my homework under my sister's supervision while my little brother sat playing with his toys. Suddenly, we heard the rhythmic shouting of slogans outside. Grown-ups were always shouting and yelling then, so we didn't think much of it. The noise came closer and closer, until it was right outside our door. A gang of young people stood there shouting, "Down with the Japanese imperialist running dogs! Eliminate the foreign secret agents!"

'My sister behaved like a grown-up. She opened the door and asked the students, who seemed to be the same age as her, "What are you doing? My parents aren't at home."

'A girl at the front of the crowd said, "Listen, you brats, your parents are Japanese imperialist secret agents. They have been placed under the control of the proletariat. You must make a clean break with them, and expose their spying activities!"

'My parents, secret agents! In the films I had seen, secret agents were always wicked. Noticing how frightened I was, my sister quickly shut the door and put her hands on my shoulders. "Don't be scared. Wait till Mama and Papa come home and we'll tell them about it," she said.

'My elder brother had been saying for some time that he wanted to join the Red Guards. Now he said quietly, "If they are secret agents, I'll go to Beijing to take part in the revolution against them."

'My sister glared at him and said, "Don't talk nonsense!"

'It was dark by the time the students stopped shouting outside our door. Later, somebody told me the group had intended to search our house, but couldn't bring themselves to do it when they saw my sister standing in the doorway protecting the three of us. Apparently, the Red Guard leader had given them a terrible tongue-lashing because of it.

'We did not see my father again for a long time.' Hua'er's face froze.

During the Cultural Revolution, anyone from a rich family, anyone who had received higher education, was an expert or scholar, had overseas connections or had once worked in the pre-1949 government was categorised as a counter-revolutionary.

There were so many political criminals of this kind that the prisons could not contain them. Instead, these intellectuals were banished to remote country areas to labour in the fields. Their evenings were occupied with 'confessing their crimes' to Red Guards, or else with lessons from the peasants, who had never seen a car or heard of electricity. My parents had endured many such periods of labour and re-education.

The peasants taught the intellectuals the songs they sang as they planted crops, and how to slaughter pigs. Having grown up in bookish, learned environments, the intellectuals shuddered at the sight of blood, and often astonished the peasants with their lack of practical skills and knowledge.

A woman university professor I once interviewed told me how the peasant who had been supervising her looked at the wheat seedlings she had uprooted by mistake and asked pityingly, 'You can't even tell the difference between a weed and a wheat sprout. What did the schoolchildren you taught learn from you? How did you command their respect?' The professor told me that the peasants in the mountain area she had been sent to had been extremely good to her, and she had learned a great deal from their poverty-stricken lives. She felt that human nature was basically simple and unsophisticated, and that it was only when people were taught about society that they learned to meddle with it. There was truth in what she said, but she had been lucky in her experience of the Cultural Revolution.

Hua'er continued her story. 'One day, my mother came home unusually late. Only my sister was still up. Dozing fitfully, I woke to hear my mother say to her, "Papa has been locked up. I don't know where they've put him. From now on, I'll have to go for special lessons every day, and may be back very late. I'll take Shi with me, but you'll have to look after Shan and Hua. Shu, you're grown up now, believe what I tell you: Papa and I aren't bad people. You must believe in us no matter what happens. We came here to China because we wanted more people to understand Japanese culture and help them to learn Japanese, not to do wrong . . . Help me look after your brother and sister. Pick wild plants on the way home from school and add them to the food when you cook. Coax your brother and sister to eat more; you're all growing, you need to eat enough. Be sure to put the lid on the stove before going to bed so you won't be poisoned by the coal gas. Shut the windows and doors properly when you leave the house, and be careful not to open the door to anyone. If the Red Guards come to search the house, take your brother and sister outside so that they aren't scared. From now on, go to bed at the same time as your little brother and sister. Don't wait up for me. If you need anything, write me a note, and I'll leave a note for you the next morning before I go. Don't stop studying Japanese language and culture. The knowledge will come in very useful some day. Study in secret, but don't be afraid. Things will get better."

'My sister's face was still, but two lines of tears trickled silently down her cheeks. I hid under the quilt and cried quietly. I didn't want my mother to see me.'

Remembering how my brother had cried for our mother, I could not hold back my tears as I imagined the scene Hua'er described. Hua'er was sad, but dry-eyed.

'For a very long time after that, we hardly ever saw my mother. My brother and I knew that our mother now slept in our room, but the only signs of her existence were the instructions and information she passed through Shu.

'Later, I discovered that I could see my mother if I woke up to go to the toilet at night. I started drinking as much water as possible before going to bed. My mother never seemed to sleep: every time I got up, she reached out to stroke me. Her hands were getting rougher and rougher. I wanted to rub my face against them, but I was afraid my sister would say that I was disturbing my mother's rest.

'I became increasingly listless and tired in the daytime because I was getting up to see my mother several times a night. Once I even fell asleep while studying "the highest directives" of the Party in school. Luckily, my teacher was a very kind woman. After class, she took me to a hidden place near the sports ground and said, "Falling asleep while studying the highest directives of Chairman Mao is seen as very reactionary by the Red Guards. You've got to be more careful."

'I didn't really understand what she meant, but I was frightened because my teacher's husband was the leader of the local Red Guard faction. I hurriedly explained why I hadn't been sleeping well. My teacher was silent for a long time, and I got even more anxious. Eventually, she patted my head affectionately, saying, "Don't worry, maybe your mother will be able to come home earlier soon."

'Not long after, my mother did start coming home earlier. She would arrive just as we were getting ready for bed. We could tell that she had changed a lot: she seldom spoke, and moved about very quietly; she seemed afraid of disturbing our faith in her and in our father. My elder brother, who had a strong personality, couldn't bear to argue with her now about going to Beijing to be one of Mao's Red Guards. Slowly, life became more normal. One day I heard my mother say with a sigh, "If only your father could come back too . . ."

'None of us could feel happy at the thought of seeing our father. We loved him, but if he were a secret agent we would still have to ignore him.

'Some time later, in the autumn of 1969, my sister was told that she had to attend an evening study group, to enable her to take a firm stand after our father's release, and draw a clear line between him and us.

'My sister came back very late from the first evening of the study group. My mother waited anxiously by the window, unable to sit still. I could not sleep either, because I was eager to know what the study group was like. The Red Guards only admitted to the group people whose thinking was revolutionary. I knew that after some people had joined it, they were no longer interrogated, their homes were no longer searched, and the people in their family who had been imprisoned were released. Would our father be back soon?

'My mother sent me to bed, and I rubbed my eyes repeatedly and put pen nibs on my pillow to keep myself from falling asleep. Finally, I heard footsteps and a man's low voice outside the window, but I could not hear what he was saying. When my sister came into the room, my mother rushed to her and asked, "How was it?" Her voice was full of fear.

'Shu lay down silently, fully clothed. When my mother tried to help her undress, my sister brushed her off, turned over and wrapped herself tightly in the quilt.

'I was very disappointed. We had waited up so long for nothing.

'That night, I heard my mother crying for a very long time. I fell asleep wondering if she was hurt by my sister's silence, or if she was afraid that we didn't love her. That night, I dreamed that I had got into the study group too, but as soon as I walked through the door to the class, I woke up.

'Shu spent an unusually long time in the study group, and she never told me anything about it. For several months, she came home very late every evening, long after I had fallen asleep. One evening, she came back not long after she had left for the study group. The man who brought her back told us, "Shu keeps on being sick, and today she fainted. The political instructor made me see her home."

'My mother had turned chalk white, and stood rooted to the spot as my sister fell to her knees before her and said, "Mama, there was nothing I could do. I wanted Papa to be released sooner."

'My mother shuddered, and seemed about to collapse. My elder brother rushed to support her and made her sit down on the bed. Then he led my little brother and me into the other room. I did not want to go, but I did not dare to stay.

'The next day, as I was leaving school, a man from the Red Guard faction was waiting for me. He told me that the political instructor had ordered me to join the study group. I hardly dared believe him. I was only eleven years old. How could I possibly go? Perhaps, I thought, the teacher had told them I was very obedient.

I was so happy I wanted to go home to tell my mother, but the man said that my mother had already been informed.

'The class was in a smallish room furnished like a home, with beds, a dining table and several chairs similar to the ones at school, but bigger. There was also a big bookcase full of revolutionary works. Quotations of Chairman Mao and revolutionary slogans written in red were pasted on all four walls of the room. I had only just started my fourth year of primary school, so I could not understand all of them.

'The Red Guard who had taken me there gave me a Little Red Book of quotations of Chairman Mao – I had always envied my sister hers – and asked, "Do you know that your parents are secret agents?"

'I nodded, wide-eyed. I was afraid they would not allow me to take part in the study group after all.

' "Do you know that everyone in the study group is a Red Guard?"

'I nodded again. I wanted to be a Red Guard so much, so that people would not curse me any longer, and so that I could sit on the back of a lorry and go out into the street to shout slogans; all that power and prestige!

' "So you mustn't let the secret agents know about the Red Guards' affairs, understand?" he said.

'Thinking of the stories about the underground Party and secret agents I knew from films, I stammered, "I – I won't tell my family."

' "Stand up now, and swear to Chairman Mao that you will keep the Red Guards' secrets."

' "I swear!"

' "Good. Now, first you will read Chairman Mao's quotations alone. After we've eaten we'll teach you how to study them."

'I was amazed to hear that I would be provided with food. No wonder, I thought, that my sister had never said anything about the study group. She had been sworn to secrecy, but she must also have been afraid that my little brother and I would be very envious at the mention of food. As these thoughts were going through my mind, I stared at the pages of my Little Red Book, not understanding a word.

'After I had finished eating, two more Red Guards came in. Both of them were very young, only a little older than my sister. They asked me, "Have you made your promise to Chairman Mao?" I nodded, wondering why they asked.

' "All right," they said, "we'll be studying until very late today, so you should rest for a while first."

'They took me in their arms and carried me to the bed, smiled at me and helped me unfold the quilt and undress, right down to the last piece of underclothing. They turned off the lights with a loud click of the switch.

'No one had ever told me about what goes on between men and women, not even my mother. All I knew about the difference between men and women was that men's trousers fastened in front, and women's trousers at the side. So when three men started to fumble with my body in the dark, I had no idea what this meant, or what was going to happen next.

'I felt very tired. For some reason, I could not keep my eyes open. In the confusion, I heard the men say, "This is your first lesson. We have to know if there are counter-revolutionary influences in your body."

'A hand pinched my undeveloped nipple and a voice said, "It's small, but there must be a bud in there."

'Another hand spread my legs apart, and a different voice cut in, saying, "Counter-revolutionary things are always hidden in the most secret places of a person's body, let's have a look."

'A wave of terror like nothing I had felt before swept over me. I started shaking with fear, but a thought flashed through my mind: only good people were in the study group, they wouldn't do bad things.

'Then a man said, "Jun'er, this one's for you. We brothers keep our word."

'I did not understand what they were talking about. By now, I had lost all control of my body. Later, when I was older, I realised they must have put sleeping pills in my food. Something thick and big stabbed my childish body as if it were going to pierce right through me. Countless pairs of hands rubbed my chest and bottom, and a foul tongue was stuffed into my mouth. There was urgent panting all around me and my body burned with pain as if I were being whipped.

'I don't know how long this hellish "lesson" lasted. I went completely numb.'

Hua'er's face was deathly white. I had to bite my lip to stop my teeth from chattering. When I reached out a hand to her, she ignored it.

'Finally, all the noise and movement stopped. I cried and cried.

'In the dark, several voices said to me, "Hua'er, later on you'll like it," "Hua'er, you're a good child, there is nothing evil about you. Your father will be let out very soon."

'I was passive as a rag doll as they bent and lifted my body to dress me.

'One of them said very quietly, "Hua'er, I'm sorry." I have always wanted to know who it was who said that.

'Several of the Red Guards took turns to carry me on their backs in the piercing autumn wind. They put me down a long way from home, saying, "Don't forget, you have sworn on Chairman Mao."

'I tried to take a step, but I couldn't move. My lower body felt as if it had been ripped to shreds. One of them picked me up in his arms and carried me to the door of my home, then he and his companions slipped away quickly in the darkness. My mother opened the door when she heard their voices, and took me in her arms.

' "What is it, Hua'er? Why are you back so late?" she asked.

'My mind was empty: I did not think about my promise to Chairman Mao. All I could do was cry. My mother carried me to bed as I wept. Seeing me in the light of the lamps, she understood everything.

' "Dear God!" she gasped.

'My sister Shu shook me and asked, "Did you go to the study group?" but I just continued crying and crying. Yes, I had gone to the "study group", a woman's study group, a . . .'

Finally, Hua'er was crying. Her shoulders shook with weak, exhausted sobs. I put my arms around her, and felt her whole body shivering.

'Hua'er, don't say any more, you won't be able to bear it,' I said. My face was wet with tears, and the weeping of the girls from the study group at my brother's school echoed in my ears.

It was noon, and a guard brought us some food. The two meals were completely different. I swapped my tray with Hua'er's, but she barely glanced at it. Still sobbing, she continued, 'I was so young. Despite the pain, I still managed to fall asleep to the sound of my mother and sister crying.

'I woke with a start. My elder brother Shan was standing outside our door, shouting, "Help, somebody! My mother's hanged herself!"

'My sister Shu was wailing, "Mama, why have you abandoned us?"

'My little brother Shi was clinging to something and crying. I got out of bed to look at what he was holding on to. It was my mother, hanging from the door lintel.'

Hua'er was gasping for breath. I rocked her in my arms, saying her name over and over again.

A few minutes later, I saw a slip of paper held up to the observation window. There was a message on it: 'Please maintain a suitable distance from the prisoner.'

I swore silently and knocked for the warden to open the door. Leaving Hua'er in the interview room, I went to the prison governor's office – Chief Constable Mei's letter in hand – and insisted that Hua'er be allowed to stay in my room for two nights. After much hesitation, he agreed, on condition that I gave him a written undertaking absolving him from responsibility if something unexpected occurred while Hua'er was with me.

Back in the interview room, I found that Hua'er had cried all over the food before her. I took her back to my room, but she barely said a word for the next twenty-four hours. I thought she was probably fighting her way out of the depths of her pain, and dared not imagine that she had yet more tragic experiences to grapple with.

When Hua'er had the strength to speak again, she told me that her father was released four days after her mother committed suicide, but he did not recognise his children. Years later, someone told them that Hua'er's father had lost his mind after being told that his beloved wife had taken her life. He had sat immobile in the same position for two nights running, asking, 'Where is Youmei?' over and over again.

Neither Hua'er nor her sister had ever dared to find out if their father had known about the 'study group', or if this knowledge had contributed to his breakdown. After his release, their father lived with them as if with strangers. In over twenty years, the only thing his children managed to teach him was that 'Papa' was their word for him. No matter who uttered this word, in whatever place, he would respond to it.

Hua'er's sister Shu never married. She had been taken home early from the study group that day because she was pregnant, and the men in the group had decreed that she could not continue 'studying'. She was fifteen at the time, and her mother did not dare to take her to the hospital because the Red Guards would condemn her as a 'capitalist' and 'a broken shoe', and take her away to be paraded through the streets. Instead, her mother planned to look for a medicinal herb to induce an abortion. Before she could do this, Hua'er's rape the next day pushed her over the edge.

Shu did not know what to do or who to turn to. Naively, she bound her swelling belly and breasts with strips of cloth, but to no avail. She did not know where to find the herb her mother had spoken of, but one day she remembered that her mother had once said that all medicine was three parts poison. She swallowed all the medicine in the house in one go, and collapsed at school, bleeding heavily. Although the hospital saved her life, the foetus died and her womb had to be removed. From then on, Shu was labelled a 'bad woman' and 'a broken shoe'. As the years passed and motherhood beckoned for her contemporaries, Shu changed into a cold, taciturn woman, quite unlike the kind, happy girl she had been.

The day before I left West Hunan Women's Prison, I interviewed Hua'er one last time.

A couple of years after Hua'er's experience in the study group, she found a book in the school storeroom called *Who Are You?*, about female biology and Chinese notions of chastity. Only after reading it did she realise the full implications of what had happened to her.

Hua'er entered adulthood with a shaky sense of identity and self-worth. She had not experienced the dreams of a young girl who is just beginning to understand love; she had no hope of a wedding night. The voices and fumbling in the blackness of that study-group room haunted her. Despite this, she eventually married a kind and good man whom she loved. When they married, virginity on the wedding night was the gold standard by which women were judged, and the lack of it often led to a bitter parting of ways. Unlike other Chinese men, Hua'er's husband had never had any suspicions about her virginity. He had believed her when she told him that her hymen had broken while she was playing sports.

Before 1990 or thereabouts, it was common for several generations of a family to live in the same room, with sleeping areas divided by thin curtains or by bunk beds. Sex had to take place in the dark, in silence and with caution; the atmosphere of restraint and suppression inhibited married couples' relationships and often led to marital strife.

Hua'er and her husband lived in one room with his family, so they had to make love with the lights off in order for their shadows not to show against the curtain separating their sleeping area. She was terrified of her husband touching her in the dark, his hands seemed to belong to the monsters of her childhood; involuntarily, she screamed in fear. When her husband tried to comfort her and asked her what was wrong, she could not tell him the truth. He loved her very much, but it was difficult for him to cope with her anxiety when they made love, so he suppressed his sexual desire instead.

Later, Hua'er discovered that her husband had become impotent. She blamed herself for his condition, and suffered dreadfully because she loved him. She did her best to help him recover, but was unable to suppress the fears that gripped her in the dark. In the end, she felt she ought to set him free, to give him the chance to have a normal sexual relationship with another woman, so she requested a divorce. When her husband refused and asked her for her reasons, she made up flimsy excuses. She said that he was not romantic, although he remembered every birthday and anniversary, and put fresh flowers on her desk every week. Everyone around them saw how he cheered her up, but she told him that he was small-minded and could not make her happy. She also said that he did not earn enough, even though her friends all envied the jewellery he gave her.

Unable to find a good reason for wanting a divorce, Hua'er finally resorted to telling her husband that he could not satisfy her physical needs, knowing that he was the only man who could ever do so. In the face of this, there was nothing Hua'er's husband could say. Heartbroken, he left for remote Zhuhai, which was still undeveloped at the time.

Hua'er's voice rang in my ears as I watched the changing scenery from the jeep taking me home after the few days in West Hunan Women's Prison.

'My beloved husband left,' she said. 'I felt as if my heart had been plucked from my chest . . . I would think: at eleven I could satisfy men, at twenty I could drive them mad, at thirty I could make them lose their souls, and at forty . . . ? Sometimes I wanted to use my body to give a chance to those men who could still say sorry, to help them understand what a sexual relationship with a woman could be; sometimes I wanted to seek out the Red Guards who had tortured me and watch their homes being broken up and their families scattered. I wanted to avenge myself on all men and make them suffer.

'My reputation as a woman has not meant much to me. I have lived with several men, and let them amuse themselves with me. Because of that, I have been sent to two labour re-education camps and been sentenced to prison twice. The political instructor in the camp called me an incorrigible female delinquent, but that didn't bother me. When people curse me for having no shame, I don't get angry. All the Chinese care about is "face", but they don't understand how their faces are linked to the rest of their bodies.

'My sister Shu understands me best. She knows that I will go to any lengths to put right my memories of sexual terror, that I want a mature sexual relationship to heal my scarred sexual organs. Sometimes I'm just as Shu says; then again, sometimes I'm not.

'My father doesn't know who I am, neither do I.'

The day after I got back to the radio station, I made two telephone calls. The first was to a gynaecologist. I told her about Hua'er's sexual behaviour and asked if there was any kind of treatment for the mental and physical traumas she had been through. The doctor seemed never to have thought about such a question. At that time in China, there was no concept of psychological illness, only physical.

Next, I called Chief Constable Mei. I told him that Hua'er was Japanese and asked whether she might be transferred to one of the prisons for foreigners where conditions were better.

He paused, then replied, 'Xinran, as far as Hua'er being Japanese is concerned, silence is golden. At the moment her crimes are sexual delinquency and illegal cohabitation; she shouldn't have too much longer to go. If it becomes known that she is foreign, she may be accused of having a political motivation for her actions and it could be much worse for her.'

Everyone who has lived through the Cultural Revolution remembers how women who committed the 'crime' of having foreign clothes or foreign habits were publicly humiliated. Their hair was shorn into all sorts of strange styles for the Red Guards' amusement; their faces were smeared with a mess of lipstick; high-heeled shoes were strung together and looped around their bodies; broken pieces of all manner of 'foreign goods' were dangled from their clothes at odd angles. The women were made to recount over and over again how they had come to possess foreign products. I was seven years old when I first saw what these women went through, paraded through the streets to be jeered at; I remember thinking that if there was a next life, I did not want to be reborn a woman.

Many of these women had returned with their husbands to the Motherland to devote their lives to the Revolution and the construction of the new China. Back in China, they had to manage the housework with the most basic of appliances, but this was nothing compared to having to suppress the comfortable habits and attitudes they had grown used to abroad. Every word and action was judged in a political context; they had to share their husbands' persecution as 'secret agents' and go through 'revolution' after 'revolution' for possessing women's goods from abroad.

I interviewed many women who had had such experiences. In 1989, a peasant woman in the mountains told me that she had once attended a music academy. Her face was scored with lines and her hands were coarse and callused; I could see no evidence of musical ability in her. It was only when she spoke with the special resonance peculiar to those who have had voice lessons that I began to think she might be telling the truth.

She showed me photographs that proved my doubts wholly unfounded. She and her family had spent some time in America; when they came back to China, she was not quite ten years old. She had been able to develop her musical gifts in a music college in Beijing, right up to the Cultural Revolution. Her parents' connection with America cost them their lives and ruined their daughter's.

At nineteen, she was sent to a very poor mountainous area and married off to a peasant by the village cadres. She had lived there ever since, in an area so poor that the villagers could not afford to buy any oil to cook with.

Before I left her, she asked, 'Are the American soldiers still in Vietnam?'

My father knew a woman who came back to China after many years in India, when she was over fifty. She was a teacher, and was extremely good to her students – she often used money from her life savings to help students in financial difficulties. At the start of the Cultural Revolution, nobody thought she would be affected, but she was 'struggled against' and 'remoulded' for two years because of her clothing.

This teacher had maintained that women ought to wear bright colours, and that the Mao suit was too mannish, so she often wore a sari under her regulation jacket. The Red Guards considered this disloyal to the Motherland, and condemned her for 'worshipping and having blind faith in foreign things'. Among the Red Guards who struggled against her were students whom she had given money to before. They apologised for their behaviour, but said, 'If we did not struggle against you, we would get into trouble, and our families with us.'

The teacher never wore her beloved saris again, but on her deathbed she had muttered, 'Saris are so beautiful,' over and over again.

Another woman teacher told me of her experience during the Cultural Revolution. A distant relative in Indonesia had sent her a lipstick and a pair of high-heeled shoes with an English trademark through a member of a government delegation. Realising that presents from abroad might bring with them suspicion of being a secret agent, she had hurriedly thrown them away without unwrapping them. She had not noticed a girl of eleven or twelve playing by the rubbish bin, who reported her 'crime' to the authorities. For many months, the teacher was driven through the town on the back of a lorry to be struggled against by the crowds.

Between 1966 and 1976, the dark years of the Cultural Revolution, there was little in either cut or colour to distinguish Chinese women's clothing from men's. Objects specifically for women's use were rare. Make-up, beautiful clothes and jewellery only existed in banned works of literature. But no matter how revolutionary Chinese people were at that time, not all could resist nature. A person could be 'revolutionary' in every other respect, but anyone who succumbed to 'capitalist' sexual desires was dragged on stage to be struggled against or put in the dock; some people took their own lives in despair. Others set themselves up as paragons of morality but took advantage of the men and women who were being reformed, making their sexual submission 'a test of loyalty'. The majority of people who lived through that time endured a barren sexual environment, most of all women. In the prime of their lives, husbands were imprisoned or sent to cadre schools for up to twenty years while their wives endured a living widowhood.

Now that the harm done to Chinese society by the Cultural Revolution is being weighed up, the damage to natural sexual instincts is a factor that must be counted in. The Chinese say, 'There is a book in every family that is best not read out loud.' There are many Chinese families who have not confronted what happened to them during the Cultural Revolution. The chapters of that book have been stuck together with tears and cannot be opened. Future generations or outsiders will only see a blurred title. When people witness the joy of families or friends reunited after years of separation, few dare to ask themselves how those people coped with their desires and pain during those years.

It was often children, particularly girls, who bore the consequences of frustrated sexual desire. Growing up during the Cultural Revolution as a girl was to be surrounded by ignorance, madness and perversion. Schools and families were unable and forbidden to give them even the most basic sex education. Many mothers and teachers were themselves ignorant in these matters. When their bodies matured, the girls fell prey to indecent assaults or rape, girls like Hongxue, whose only experience of sensual pleasure came from a fly; Hua'er, who was 'raped' by the revolution; the woman on the answering machine who was married off by the Party; or Shilin, who will never know that she has grown up. The perpetrators were their teachers, their friends, even their fathers and brothers, who lost control of their animal instincts and behaved in the ugliest and most selfish ways that a man can. The girls' hopes were destroyed, and their capacity to experience the pleasure of lovemaking damaged for ever. If we could listen to their nightmares, we could spend ten or twenty years hearing the same kinds of story.

It is too late now to bring back youth and happiness to Hua'er and other women who endured the Cultural Revolution. They drag the great dark shadows of their memories behind them.

I remember how, one day in the office, Mengxing read out a listener's request for a particular song and said, 'I just don't get it. Why do these old women like moth-eaten old songs so much? Why don't they look around them to see what the world is like today? They move too slowly for the times.'

Big Li rapped his desk smartly with a pen and admonished, 'Too slowly? Remember, these women never had the time to enjoy their youth!'

14

A Fashionable Woman

In the autumn of 1995, I submitted a request to resign as Director of Programme Development and Planning, arguing that I was juggling too many jobs simultaneously and that the workload created by my radio programme – reporting, editing, replying to my postbag, etc. – was constantly increasing. In fact, what I really wanted was space for myself. I had become weary of sifting through mountains of documents full of prohibitions and attending endless meetings. I needed to be able to spend more time getting to know Chinese women.

My superiors were far from happy with my decision, but they knew me well enough by now: if they forced me to keep my position, I might end up leaving completely. As long as I stayed, they would still be able to make use of my high public profile and extensive social network.

Once my decision was known, my future became a matter for endless conjecture and debate. Nobody understood why I was abandoning the guarantee of continued success in an official career. Some people said that I was going to join the tide of new entrepreneurs, some presumed that I was going to take a highly paid university lectureship, others thought that I would go to America. Most simply said, 'Whatever Xinran does, it will be fashionable.' Although being considered a trendsetter and a fashionable woman might seem like a good thing, I knew how much people had suffered at the hands of 'fashion'.

Fashion in China has always been political. In the 1950s, people made a fashion out of pursuing the lifestyle of Soviet Communism.

They shouted political slogans like 'Catch up with America and overtake England in twenty years!' and followed all Chairman Mao's latest directives to the letter. During the Cultural Revolution the fashion was to go into the countryside to be 're-educated'. Humanity and wisdom were banished to places which did not know there was anywhere in this world where women could say 'no' and men could read newspapers.

In the eighties, after the Reform and Opening Up policy, people started to make a fashion of going into business. In a short while, it said 'Business Director' on every business card; there was a saying: 'Out of one billion people, there were ninety million business people and ten million waiting to set up in business.'

The Chinese have never followed a trend by choice – they have always been driven into it by politics. In my interviews with Chinese women in particular, I discovered that many so-called 'fashionable' or 'trendsetting' women had been forced into being so, and then persecuted for the fashion they embodied. Chinese men say that strong women are the fashion these days – but women believe that 'behind every successful woman, there is a man who causes her pain'.

I once interviewed a famous businesswoman who lived her life in the public eye. She had always been considered a trendsetter and I had read a lot about her in the newspapers. I was interested to know how she felt about being high-profile, and how she had become so well known.

Zhou Ting had booked a luxury private room at a four-star hotel for our interview – she told me that it was to ensure that we had privacy. When she arrived, she gave every impression of enjoying being a woman of fashion. She wore expensive, elegant clothes in cashmere and silk, and a lot of jewellery that glittered and jingled as she moved. Her hands were laden with rings. I had been told that she gave extravagant dinners in all the big hotels, and that she changed cars as often as she changed clothes. She was the general manager in charge of health food sales for several large companies in the area. However, after I had interviewed her, I realised that there was a very different woman underneath the fashionable exterior.

At the start of our interview, Zhou Ting told me several times that she had not talked about her true feelings for a long time. I said that I always asked women about their true stories, because truth is a woman's lifeblood. She gave me a searching look and replied that the truth was never 'fashionable'.

During the Cultural Revolution, Zhou Ting's mother, a teacher, was forced by the Red Guards to attend political study classes. Her father was allowed to remain at home: he had a tumour on his adrenal gland, and was so ill that he could barely lift a chopstick. One of the Red Guards said later that they had not thought him worth bothering with. Her mother was eventually imprisoned for several years.

From her first year at primary school, Zhou Ting was bullied because of her family background. Sometimes her classmates beat her black and blue, sometimes they cut her arms viciously, leaving bloody wounds. But the misery of these attacks paled in comparison to the terror of being questioned about her mother by the workers, propaganda teams and political groups stationed at the school, who pinched her or hit her over the head when she remained silent. She was so scared of being interrogated that she would start quaking with fear if a shadow fell on the classroom window.

At the end of the Cultural Revolution, it was declared that Zhou Ting's mother was innocent, and had been falsely accused of being counter-revolutionary. Mother and daughter had suffered needlessly for ten years. Zhou Ting's father had not escaped either: later in the Cultural Revolution, the Red Guards had surrounded his hospital bed and submitted him to numerous interrogations until he died.

'Even now, I often wake with a start from nightmares of being beaten in my childhood,' Zhou Ting said.

'Was your experience unusual in your school?' I asked.

Sunlight was streaming into the room, and Zhou Ting drew a curtain to shield us from the glare.

'I stood out at school; at least I remember that my classmates always talked excitedly about going to the university to watch my mother being struggled against, or eavesdropping on me being interrogated by the political team.'

'And in your life since, you have stood out for different reasons.'

'Yes,' said Zhou Ting. 'First my mother, then the men around me made sure that people were always interested in me.'

'Was that in your professional or your personal life?'

'In my personal life, for the most part,' she replied.

'Some people say that traditional women cannot have modern feelings, and modern women cannot be chaste or loyal. Which of these paths would you say you have taken?'

Zhou Ting twisted her rings. I noticed she wasn't wearing a wedding ring.

'I am very traditional by nature, but, as you know, I was forced into leaving my marriage,' she said. I had once been invited to a talk in which she had set out proposals for a policy on marital break-up, but I knew nothing about her personal experience other than what I had read in the papers.

'My first marriage – actually there was just this one marriage – was just like many others in China. Friends introduced me to the man who became my husband. I was in Ma'anshan then, and he was in Nanjing, so we only saw each other once a week. It was an idyllic time: my mother had been released; I had a job and a relationship. When people urged me to take time to live and learn from experience before making decisions, I resisted, thinking their admonitions too much like those of the political workers who had interrogated me during the Cultural Revolution. My boyfriend and I were preparing to get married when he had an accident at work, and lost the fingers of his right hand. Friends and family told me to think twice about marrying him; he was crippled, and we would have many problems. In defence, I cited famous love stories, ancient and modern, from China and from abroad, and told everyone, "Love is unconditional, it is a kind of sacrifice. If you love someone, how can you abandon him when he is in trouble?" I gave up my job and moved to Nanjing to marry him.'

I had much sympathy for Zhou Ting's decision. 'Your behaviour was considered naive by people around you, but you must have been very proud of yourself, and very happy too,' I said.

Zhou Ting nodded. 'Yes, you're absolutely right, I really was very happy then. I did not fear marrying a crippled man at all. I felt like a heroine in a romantic novel.' She drew the curtain back slightly, and a weak ray of sunlight slanted in on the nape of her neck, glinting on her necklace to cast a bright spot on the wall.

'When our life together began, I found that everything had changed. The leaders of my husband's work unit at the Meishan iron mine in Nanjing had promised that they would give me a good job in the hospital to help us after we got married, but when I arrived, they only gave me a job as a primary-school matron. And they used the fact that I had no local registration documents as an excuse to stop me qualifying for a promotion or a pay rise that year. I had never expected those dignified, respectable leaders to go back on their word like that.

'But my new job was not the biggest problem. I soon realised that my husband was an incorrigible womaniser. He slept with any woman who was willing, from women decades older than him to young girls. Even tramps with matted hair and dirty faces were not beneath him. I was distraught. When I was pregnant, he stayed out all night, and made all sorts of excuses, but he always gave himself away.

'Eventually, I gave him a warning, and he agreed to stop. Not long after, he told me that he had to work late occasionally. When a colleague of his came to see him, I said that he was doing overtime. His colleague said, "He's not on overtime."

'I realised at once that my husband was at it again. I was furious. I asked my neighbour to look after my son, and rushed off to the house of the woman I knew my husband had been having an affair with before he agreed to stop. Her house was only a few streets away. As I approached it, I could see my husband's bicycle by the gate. I was shaking with anger as I knocked on the door. I waited a long time and knocked again, until a woman with her clothing in disarray eventually opened the side door, shouting, "Who is it, why are you making this racket so late at night?" The next moment, she recognised me and stammered, "You? What are you doing here? He . . . he isn't here with me."

'I didn't come here to look for him, I came to see you!' I said.

' "Me? What do you want me for? I haven't done anything to offend you."

' "Can I come in to talk?"

' "No, it's not very convenient."

' "All right, we can talk in the doorway. I just want to say to you, please don't carry on with my husband any longer. He's a family man."

'The woman exclaimed, "It's your husband who runs over to my place every day, I've never been to your house!"

' "Are you trying to tell me you won't refuse him? He . . ." I broke off suddenly, in a cold sweat. I was not used to confrontations.

' "What a joke," the woman mocked. "You can't keep a man and you blame me for not shutting the door?"

' "You? You . . ." I was speechless with anger.

' "Me? What about me? If you haven't got what it takes, don't come round yowling like a cat on heat. You'd do what I do yourself if you had it in you!" She sounded like a common prostitute, but this was an educated woman, a doctor.

'Suddenly, my husband appeared, doing up his flies. "What are you quarrelling about, you jealous bitches? Let me show you what a man is!" Before I could react, he picked up a bamboo cane and started thrashing me.

'His mistress screamed, "You should have taught her a lesson before now!"

'I felt a stabbing pain in my left shoulder where he had hit me. He was hindered by his crippled right hand, so I managed to avoid the next few blows.

'Many people in the residential compound had been drawn out of their houses by the noise. They stood watching passively as I was chased around and beaten by my husband, while his mistress screamed abuse. When the police finally came, I was covered in cuts and bruises, but I heard an old woman saying, "Those yellow dogs [the police] are really meddlesome, sticking their noses into people's family affairs."

'In hospital, twenty-two bamboo splinters were extracted from my body by the doctor. The nurse was so outraged at what had happened to me that she wrote a letter about it to the city newspaper. Two days later a photograph of me covered in bandages appeared in the paper accompanying an article about how women should be treated with respect. Many people, mostly women of course, came to visit me in hospital, bringing gifts of food. It was only several weeks later that I saw this article. I was wrongly described as a wife who had been abused over a long period of time. I did not know whether my situation had been exaggerated because someone had felt sorry for me, or because someone had wanted to strike back on behalf of all abused women by putting my husband in the dock.'

'Did you try to correct the misrepresentation?'

'No, I was all at sea, I didn't know what to do. It was the first time I had been in the newspaper. Besides, in my heart I was grateful for that article. If it had simply been considered that my husband was "putting his house in order", how would things ever get better for women?'

A man battering his wife or beating his children is considered to be 'putting his house in order' by many Chinese. Elderly peasant women, in particular, accept such practices. Having lived under the Chinese dictum 'a bitter wife endures until she becomes a mother-in-law' themselves, they believe that all women should suffer the same fate. Hence the people who saw Zhou Ting being beaten did not step in to help.

Zhou Ting sighed. 'Sometimes I think I haven't had it too bad. It would have been worse to be born a woman in earlier times. Never mind going to school – in those days, I would only have had my husband's leftover rice to eat.'

'You're good at comforting yourself,' I said, thinking to myself that many Chinese women consoled themselves with such thoughts.

'My husband said too much learning had spoiled me.'

'He didn't come up with that himself. It was Confucius who said that lack of talent in a woman was a virtue.' I paused, then asked, 'Didn't you later appear in the news in a case of attempted murder?'

'Yes, I suppose so. The papers made me the villain of the piece and taught me the power of the media. To this day, nobody believes me when I tell them what really happened. They all think that anything printed in the newspaper is gospel.'

'So you think that report was inaccurate,' I prompted blandly.

Zhou Ting became agitated. 'I believe in divine retribution – may I be struck by lightning if I tell a lie!'

'Please don't feel you have to swear like that,' I said soothingly. 'I wouldn't be here if I didn't want to hear your side of the story.'

Mollified, Zhou Ting continued. 'I applied for a divorce, but my husband grovelled for one last chance, saying that as a cripple, he couldn't survive without me. I was torn: after he had beaten me up so badly, I didn't believe that he could change, but I was afraid that he really wouldn't be able to live without me. Affairs were all very well, but would his lovers go through thick and thin with him?

'But one day I came home from work early to find my husband and a woman, both half naked. All my blood surged to my head, and I screamed at the woman, "Call yourself a woman, whoring in my house? Get out!"

'I shouted and cursed madly. The woman stumbled to my bedroom and gathered up her clothes from my bed. I grabbed a cleaver from the kitchen and said to my husband, "You tell me, what kind of man are you?"

'My husband kicked me in the groin in response. Incandescent, I threw the cleaver at him, but he ducked, and stood staring at me, shocked that I could have dared to attack him. I was trembling with fury; I could barely speak. "You – both of you – what – are you doing . . . ? If you don't come clean . . . one of us will die right here!" I said.

'I had grasped a leather belt hanging from the door. As I spoke, I lashed out with it like a mad thing, but they moved away. When I turned to hit my husband, the woman slipped out. I chased her all the way to the police station, whipping her with the belt as she screamed that she would never sleep with my husband again. As soon as she was through the gate of the police station, she rushed for the duty room shouting, "Help, I'm being attacked!"

'I did not know that the woman was related to one of the policemen in this station, nor that one of her lovers also worked there. When a policeman ran up and twisted my arm behind my back, I shouted, "You've got it all wrong!"

' "Shut up!" he said brusquely.

' "You've really got it all wrong. That woman committed adultery with my husband in my home, do you hear?" I struggled in his armlock.

' "What?" he exclaimed. The other policemen who had gathered were all shocked. As you know, sexual activity outside marriage was a serious offence then. It could lead to a prison sentence of more than three years.

'The policeman released me. "What evidence do you have?" he asked.

'"If I provide evidence, what will you do with her?" I asked, certain that I could find proof.

'He did not answer my question directly. "If you can't get any proof we're going to detain you for a false charge and assault," he said. There were no proper legal procedures then. Looking back now, I wonder if those policemen understood the law at all.

'"Give me three hours," I said, "If I can't get the evidence, you can go ahead and lock me up."

'One of the older policemen, perhaps the head of the station replied, "All right, we'll send someone with you to collect the evidence."

'My husband was sitting on the sofa smoking a cigarette when I arrived home with a policeman. He was surprised, but I ignored him and went straight to the bedroom, then to the toilet, but couldn't find anything suspicious. Finally, I opened the kitchen bin, and saw a pair of women's knickers, the crotch damp with semen.

'The policeman looked at me and nodded. My husband, who had been watching anxiously as I searched, blanched and stammered, "You . . . what are you doing?"

'"I'm going to turn you both in," I said decisively.

'"But you'll ruin me!" he said.

"You are the one who has already done so much to ruin me!" I said, then I took the evidence and left with the policeman.

'At the police station I was taken aside by one of the police officers who said he wanted to discuss something with me.

'I was taken aback. "Discuss? What do you want to discuss with me?" I asked.

'"Well, the woman you're accusing of adultery is the sister-in-law of the station head. If this came out, it would look bad for him. The woman's husband has also begged us to come to an arrangement with you. He says his wife is a nymphomaniac, and their daughter has just turned fourteen; if we imprison the woman, her family will be in a difficult position."

' "What about my family, what am I going to do?" I said, starting to get angry.

' "Aren't you getting a divorce at the moment? It's very difficult to get a divorce; you'll have to sit it out for three years at least. We can get someone to plead your case to the judge, and will even bear witness for you if you want, to speed up the process."

'I understood what he was getting at. "What sort of witness will you bear?" I asked.

'The policeman seemed helpful. He said, "We can testify that your husband had extra-marital affairs."

' "What evidence will you provide?' I thought of the bundle I held in my hands.

' "Well, there's so much gossip about your husband anyway. We can just testify that what is said about him is true."

' "Well you needn't bother cooking up a story," I said. "This is the evidence from tonight." Naively, I handed him the stained underwear without asking for a receipt or insisting on a record of our agreement being signed and filed. I just wanted to get the whole thing over with quickly.

'In the divorce court two weeks later, I stated that the police station would testify for me. The judge announced, "According to our inquiries, the said police station has no record of dealing with any matter concerning you." How can the People's Police swindle people like this?' Zhou Ting exclaimed.

I was not surprised at the lack of scruples in the police force, but asked, 'Did you report this to any government department?'

'Make a report? To whom? Before I could even go back to the police station to beg them to testify for me, the local paper had published a report headlined, "A Wife's Revenge". I was portrayed as a violent woman who was being divorced by her husband. The report was reprinted in other papers and every time it appeared it was touched up: by the end I was a madwoman cackling in a pool of blood!'

I felt ashamed of fellow journalists who had distorted Zhou Ting's story in this way. 'How did you react?'

'It was just one more thing to cope with then. My family had fallen apart, and I was living with my mother at the time.'

'And what about your former flat?' As soon as I asked this, I realised I knew the answer: in state-run work units, practically everything allocated to a family is in the man's name.

'The work unit said that the flat was in my husband's name, so it belonged to him.'

'Where did the work unit expect you to live?' Divorced women were treated like dead leaves, I thought.

'They said I would have to find somewhere temporary to live and wait for the next round of housing allocation.'

I knew that in official parlance, the 'next round' could take years to materialise. 'And how long did it take for you to be assigned a flat?' I asked.

Zhou Ting snorted derisively. 'It still hasn't happened nine years later.'

'They did absolutely nothing for you?'

'As good as nothing. I went to the president of the trade union, a woman of fifty or so, to ask for help. She said in a kind voice, "It's easy for a woman. Just find another man with a flat and you'll have everything you need."'

I struggled to grasp the world-view of the Party cadre who could have said such a thing. 'The president of the trade union said that?'

'That's what she said, word for word.'

I thought I had begun to understand Zhou Ting a little more. 'So you never considered taking action against your treatment by the media?' I asked, not expecting her to have done so.

'No, well, I did do something about it eventually. I telephoned the newspaper office, but they ignored me, so I complained directly to the chief editor. Half joking and half threatening, he said to me, "Zhou Ting, it's all over now; if you don't bring it up yourself, nobody will give it another thought. Do you want to be in the news again? Do you want to take on the paper this time?" Loath to put myself through any more unpleasantness, I agreed to let the matter drop.'

'You had a soft heart underneath,' I said.

'Yes, some of my friends say I have a "mouth of knives and a heart of tofu". What's the use of that? How many people see through your words to your heart?'

She paused, then continued. 'I'm not really sure why I got into the news the third time; I suppose it was because of love. There was a young teacher in my work unit called Wei Hai. He wasn't a local man, so he lived in the school dormitory. My divorce was going through the courts at the time. I loathed the sight of my husband, and was afraid he would beat me, so I often stayed on in the office after work, reading magazines. Wei Hai often sat in the teachers' office reading the newspapers. One day, he suddenly grasped my hand and said, "Zhou Ting, don't suffer like this. Let me make you happy!" Tears were shining in his eyes; I'll never forget the sight.'

'I wasn't divorced yet, but I had other misgivings besides this about starting a relationship with Wei Hai. He was nearly nine years younger than I; women age so quickly . . . we would attract so much gossip; I was scared. You know the saying, "The words of men are to be feared" – well, they can kill,' Zhou Ting said fiercely.

'When my divorce finally came through, I was already labelled a "bad woman". Luckily, this was the beginning of the period of economic reform. Everybody was busy chasing after money so they had less time to poke their noses into others' private lives. I started living with Wei Hai. He was very, very good to me, in every possible way. I was so happy with him, he became even more important to me than my son.'

This was no mean feat, I thought, given the traditional Chinese mindset of putting sons above all else.

'After a year of living together, a trade union representative and an administrator from my work unit came to our home to ask us to get a marriage certificate as soon as possible. Although China was starting to open up, cohabitation was considered "an offence against public decency" by some, especially women. But the happiness and strength our life together had given me far surpassed my fear of others' opinion. For us, marriage was just a matter of time. After the visit from the officials, we decided to request our respective work units to issue us with a certificate the following week, so we could register our marriage. Having lived together for over a year already, we did not celebrate or get particularly excited.

'On the following Monday evening, I asked Wei Hai if he had taken out a certificate yet. He said he had not. I had not managed to get mine either because I had been busy, so we agreed that we would definitely get our certificates before Wednesday. On Wednesday morning, I phoned Wei Hai to tell him I had already got mine, and asked if he had managed to get his. No problem, he said. At about three o'clock he phoned and told me that my mother wanted me to go to Ma'anshan to see her. He didn't tell me what for. I immediately thought that something had happened to her, so I asked for permission to leave early, and rushed to the bus station at four thirty. When I arrived at my mother's an hour later, breathless with worry, she asked in surprise, "What's happened? Wei Hai phoned to say he was coming to Ma'anshan, and asked me to stay in. What's going on with you two?"

' "I'm not sure," I said, confused. Without further thought, I left my mother and rushed to the bus station to meet Wei Hai off the Nanjing bus. More than a year together had not faded the first flush of love. I could hardly bear being apart from him then; leaving him to go to work was painful, and I looked forward to coming home every day. I was infatuated, in a trance.

'By about half past eight that evening, Wei Hai had still not arrived at the bus station. I was frantic. I asked the driver of every bus that arrived if there had been any accidents or breakdowns on the road, and if all the scheduled buses were running. Their replies were reassuring: nothing out of the ordinary had happened. Past nine, I decided I couldn't wait any longer so I boarded a bus back to Nanjing to see if Wei Hai was at home, ill. I didn't dare think what else might have happened to him. Thinking that Wei Hai might be on a bus to Ma'anshan while I travelled in the opposite direction on the same road, I switched on a torch I had with me, and shone it out of the bus window, straining to see the passing vehicles. I couldn't actually see anything, but it comforted me to try. After a while, our bus was pulled over by the traffic police. The policeman who boarded the bus said that someone on the bus seemed to have been signalling with torchlight, so they wanted all the passengers to get out for an inspection. I hurried to the front and explained that I had been using the torch because I was afraid my husband had taken the wrong bus. The furious traffic policeman sent us on our way, and the other passengers all swore at me for causing a delay. I wasn't bothered – I just apologised and continued looking out of the window.

'We lived not far from the bus station; as I approached our flat, I saw light from the windows, and my heart lifted. But both doors were locked, which was odd: the inner door wasn't usually locked when someone was home. A wave of terror washed over me when I saw the flat was empty. Instinct prompted me to open the wardrobe in the bedroom. I went cold all over: Wei Hai's clothes were missing. He had gone.'

'Wei Hai had gone? Left the house and gone?'

Zhou Ting's lower lip was quivering. 'Yes, he'd gone. He'd taken all his things. Just after we had decided to get married, he left.'

I felt for her deeply. 'Did he leave a note, a letter, an explanation, anything?'

'Not a word,' she said, lifting her chin to prevent a tear from rolling down her cheek.

'Oh, Zhou Ting,' I said, lost for words.

The tear rolled down her face. 'I collapsed. I don't know how long I lay on the ground, shaking all over. When I heard footsteps outside, a last thread of hope made me get to my feet. Wei Hai's cousin was at the door. He said that Wei Hai had told him to bring me the keys. With the door still closed, I told him that it was late, and it wasn't a good time, we'd talk the next day. He had no choice but to leave.

'I locked all the windows and doors, turned the gas tap on, sat down and started to make a tape recording. I wanted to apologise to my mother for not repaying the debt I owed her for bringing me up; I wanted to say sorry to my son for not fulfilling my natural duty to him; I didn't have the heart or the strength to go on living. I didn't plan to leave any words for Wei Hai, thinking that my soul would express my love and pain to him in the netherworld. My head and my body felt as if they were going to explode, and I could barely stay upright when I heard voices outside the window:

' "Ting, open the door, your mother is waiting for you outside!"

' "Don't do anything stupid, you're grown up now. What does a man matter? The world is full of good men!"

' "Don't light a match whatever you do!"

' "Quick . . . this window is big enough . . . smash it . . . hurry . . ."

'I don't know what happened after that. The next thing I was aware of was my mother holding my hand and crying. When she saw me open my eyes, she sobbed so hard she couldn't speak. Later, she told me that I had been unconscious for more than two days.

'Only I knew that I had not really come round: my heart remained unconscious. I was in hospital for eighteen days. When I left, I weighed less than six stone.'

'How long was it before you could leave this pain behind you?' I realised immediately how foolish my question sounded: it was impossible for Zhou Ting to forget her pain.

She wiped her eyes. 'For the best part of two years I slept badly. I developed a strange illness: the sight of a man, any man, sickened me. If a man bumped into me on the bus, I scrubbed at myself with soap as soon as I got home. This went on for nearly three years. I couldn't bear to stay on in my old work unit after Wei Hai had left, so I resigned. It was very difficult to leave a job then, but I had no demands and nothing to fear. I took up a job offer from a sales company. With my knowledge and a certain knack for business, I soon became a successful and popular sales agent in the food industry. I was headhunted by several big companies, and was able to accumulate experience in different places.

'Money was not a problem for me by then. I even started to become extravagant. But I still hadn't got over Wei Hai.' She stared at the ceiling for a long time, as if searching for something.

Eventually, she turned back to look at me. 'Because of my success in business, the press started to notice me again. They called me the "Sales Empress". My business activities were reported on, and journalists found all sorts of reasons to interview me. But now I knew how to protect myself and fend them off when necessary. So my personal life was never once mentioned in the articles.

'I got to know the director of a big Shanghai trading company, who pursued me for two reasons. First, his company needed me to help open up the market for them. Second, he had never married because he was impotent. Hearing about my hatred of men touching me, he thought that we might make a good match. He was quite persistent and offered me one-seventh of his portfolio of shares as an engagement present. I was happy with this arrangement: I no longer had to work for other people, and I had a boyfriend but did not have to put up with being pawed. A Shanghai business newspaper fought to publish an exclusive, which was headlined "Sales Empress to marry Shanghai Tycoon. Shake-up in Market expected." The news was quickly reprinted in many other papers.

'Is the marriage taking place soon?' I asked, genuinely hoping that Zhou Ting would find a place where she belonged.

'No, it was called off,' she said blandly, touching her ring finger.

'Why? Did the media get in the way again?' I feared that, once again, journalists might have made Zhou Ting's life difficult.

'No, not this time. It was because Wei Hai reappeared.'

'Wei Hai came looking for you?' I felt sick.

'No, he turned up at one of my training sessions for local sales personnel. My heart had been barren for so long; as soon as I set eyes on him, all my feelings flooded back,' she said, shaking her head.

I could not keep the incredulity out of my voice as I asked, 'Do you still love him?'

Zhou Ting ignored my tone. 'Yes. When I saw him, I instantly knew that I still loved him as deeply as before.'

'What about him? Does he still love you? As much . . . ?'

'I don't know, and I don't want to ask. I'm afraid of opening old wounds. Wei Hai seems very weak now. He has lost the spirit that he had when he held my hand and asked me to live with him all those years ago, but there's still a certain something that I yearn for in his eyes,' she said contentedly.

Unable to hide my disapproval, I exclaimed, 'You took him back?' I had met too many women who always excused the men in their lives for the pain they had caused them.

'That's right. I returned the shares to the Shanghai businessman, broke off my engagement and rented another flat with Wei Hai. We are still together.'

I noted the brevity of Zhou Ting's description. Concerned, I pressed her, 'Are you happy?'

'I don't know. Neither of us has brought up the subject of how he left me. There are things between us that I think we will never be able to touch.'

'Do you think that if you were still poor, he would have come back to you?' I probed.

Her reply was quite definite. 'No, he wouldn't.'

I was bewildered. 'Well, if he were to start a business of his own one day or become financially independent, do you think he would leave you?'

'Yes, if he had his own career, or if he met another successful woman, he would definitely go.'

I was even more perplexed. 'What about you then?'

'Why do I stay with him, you mean?' she asked defiantly, her eyes filled with tears. I nodded.

'Because of that first declaration he made me, and the happiness I have had with him; those are my happiest memories.'

To me, Zhou Ting sounded like any other besotted woman who stayed with a man unworthy of her. I hinted at my disapproval again, asking, 'Are you nurturing your feelings for Wei Hai now with memories?'

'Yes, you could say that. Women really are that pathetic.'

'Does Wei Hai know you think all this?'

'He is over forty. Time ought to have taught him.' Zhou Ting's weary reply made my question seem naive. 'Emotionally, men can never be like women; they will never be able to understand us. Men are like mountains; they only know the ground beneath their feet, and the trees on their slopes. But women are like water.'

I remembered hearing the same analogy from Jingyi, the woman who had waited forty-five years for her lover. 'Why are women like water?' I asked.

'Everybody says women are like water. I think it's because water is the source of life, and it adapts itself to its environment. Like women, water also gives of itself wherever it goes to nurture life,' Zhou Ting said in a considered tone. 'If Wei Hai gets the chance, he won't stay on in a home where he doesn't have much power, just for my sake.'

'Yes, if a man has no occupation, or lives off a woman, the reversal of roles is a recipe for disaster.'

Zhou Ting was silent for a few moments. 'Did you see the

headline "Tough Businesswoman rejects Strategic Marriage to renew Old Flame" or something like that? God knows what people must have thought of me after that piece of news had been worked over a few times. The media has made me into a monstrous figure of a woman: attempted murder, adultery, I'm made out to have done the lot. This has isolated me from other women, and my friends and family keep their distance too. But notoriety has brought me some unexpected benefits.' Zhou Ting laughed bitterly.

'Are you saying your business benefited from it?'

'That's right. All the gossip about me makes people open to my sales pitch because they are curious about me.' She spread her hands out, displaying the rings that adorned them.

'So your personal life has contributed to your professional achievements,' I mused, unhappy at the thought that this was how women became successful.

'You could say that. But people do not realise the price I have had to pay.'

I nodded. 'Some say that women always have to sacrifice emotion to success.'

'In China, that is almost always the case,' Zhou Ting said, choosing her words carefully.

'If a woman asked you for the secret of your success, how would you reply?' I asked.

'First, put away the tender emotions of a woman and let the media gasp in amazement about how different you are. Second, cut your heart out and create a good news story. Then use your scars as a business opportunity: exhibit them to the public; tell them your pain. As people exclaim over the wounds you must have suffered, lay out your products on their counters and take away the money.'

'Oh, Zhou Ting! It can't really be that way?'

'Yes, it is. From my understanding of it, it is,' she said earnestly.

'Then how do you cope with life?' I asked, marvelling once again at the courage of women.

'Do you have a callus on your hand? Or scars on your body? Touch them – do you feel anything?' Zhou Ting spoke gently, but her words made me despair.

She got up to go. 'I'm afraid it is six o'clock and I have to go to several big stores to check their stock levels. Thank you for this meeting.'

'Thank you. I hope the calluses on your heart will be softened by love,' I said.

Zhou Ting had completely regained her composure. She replied in a hard voice, 'Thank you, but it's much better to be numb than to be in pain.'

As I left the hotel, the sun was setting. I thought of how fresh it had been at dawn and how weary it must be after its day's work. The sun is giving; women love – their experience is the same. Many people believe that successful Chinese women are only interested in money. Few realise how much pain they have suffered to get to where they are today.

15

The Women of Shouting Hill

In 1995, there was a survey in China which found that, in the more prosperous areas of the country, the four professions that had the shortest life expectancy were chemical-factory workers, long-distance lorry drivers, policemen and journalists. Factory workers and lorry drivers suffered from the lack of proper safety regulations. The lot of Chinese policemen was one of the hardest in the world: under an imperfect judicial system and in a society where political power was all, criminals with influential connections often swaggered off scot-free, and some subsequently took revenge on the police officers involved. The police struggled between what they knew to be right and their orders; the frustration, uncertainty and self-reproach led them to early death. But why did journalists, who in some ways lived such a privileged life, share the same fate?

Journalists in China had witnessed many shocking and upsetting events. However, in a society where the principles of the Party governed the news, it was very difficult for them to report the true face of what they had seen. Often they were forced to say and write things that they disagreed with.

When I interviewed women who were living in emotionless political marriages, when I saw women struggling amid poverty and hardship who could not even get a bowl of soup or an egg to eat after giving birth, or when I heard women on my telephone answering machines who did not dare speak to anyone about how their husbands beat them, I was frequently unable to help them because of broadcasting regulations. I could only weep for them in private.

When China started to open up, it was like a starving child devouring everything within reach indiscriminately. Afterwards, while the world saw a flushed, happy China in new clothes, no longer crying out with hunger, the journalistic community saw a body racked by the pain of indigestion. But it was a body whose brain they could not use, for China's brain had not yet grown the cells to absorb truth and freedom. The conflict between what they knew and what they were permitted to say created an environment in which their mental and physical health suffered.

It was just such a conflict that made me give up my journalistic career.

In the autumn of 1996, on his return from the Party Conference, Old Chen told me that several poverty-alleviation groups were being sent to north-west China, south-west China and other poor, economically backward areas. There was a shortage of qualified government personnel to undertake such research trips so the government often made use of skilled journalists to gather information. Old Chen said he planned to join a group going to the old military base area in Yan'an to see what the life of ordinary people there was now like. According to Old Chen, this was a corner forgotten by the Revolution.

I saw an excellent opportunity for me to extend my knowledge of Chinese women's lives and immediately asked to join one of the groups. I was allocated to the 'north-western' group, but we were actually travelling to the area west of Xi'an in central China. When most Chinese people speak of the 'north-west', they are actually referring to central China since the western deserts of the country do not figure in their mental map.

While packing for the trip, I decided not to include many of the useful items I usually carried on reporting trips. There were two reasons for this. First, there would be a long mountain trek during which we would have to carry our own luggage. I did not want to burden my male fellow journalists with any of my load when they too would be exhausted. The second reason was more important:

the loess plateau we were visiting was said to be a very poor place and I thought I would feel awkward with all my handy conveniences in front of the people there. They had never seen anything of the outside world, and perhaps had never had the luxury of being warm and well fed.

We travelled first to Xi'an, where the group split into three. There were four other people in my group – two male journalists, a doctor and a guide from the local government. We set off for our final destination with great zeal; although I do not think ours was the hardest route, the area we saw was probably the most poverty-stricken. There are countless degrees of wealth and poverty, which are manifested in many different ways. During our journey, the scene before us grew simpler and simpler: the tall buildings, hubbub of human voices and bright colours of the city were gradually replaced by low brick houses or mud huts, clouds of dust and peasants wearing uniform greyish clothes. Further into the journey, people and traces of human activity grew scarce. The unbroken yellow earth plateau was scoured by swirling dust storms, through which we could only squint with great difficulty. The motto of our mission had been: 'Helping the poorest people in the poorest places.' The extreme implied by the comparative suffix '-est' is hard to define. Every time one encounters an extreme situation, one is never sure whether it is the *most* extreme. However, to this day, I have never witnessed poverty to compare with what I saw on that trip.

When, after two and a half days' jolting in an army jeep, the guide finally announced that we had arrived, we all thought he had made a mistake. We had not seen so much as the shadow of a person, let alone a village in the surrounding landscape. The jeep had been winding its way through bare hills, and had stopped beside a relatively large one. On closer inspection, we realised that cave dwellings had been cut into the side of the hill. The guide introduced this as the place we had wanted to come to – Shouting Hill, a tiny village not on any map – and said that it was his first time here too. I wondered at this and mused over the village's strange name.

A few inquisitive villagers had been drawn over by the roar of the jeep. Surrounding the vehicle, they started making all sorts of comments, calling the jeep a 'horse that drank oil'; they wondered where its black 'tail' had disappeared to now that it had stopped moving, and the children among them chattered about how to find it. I wanted to explain to them that the tail was formed by the exhaust, but the village cadres had appeared to welcome us and ushered us into a cave house that served as the village headquarters.

That first meeting was taken up with exchanges of conventional greetings. We had to concentrate very hard to understand each other because of regional differences in speech and accent, so I was unable to observe the surroundings closely. We were given a welcome banquet: a few pieces of white-flour flatbread, one bowl of very thin wheat-flour gruel and a small saucer of egg fried with chilli. It was only later I discovered that the regional government had asked the guide to bring the eggs along especially for us.

After we had eaten, we were led to our accommodation by the light of three candles. The two male journalists had a cave house to themselves, the doctor was staying with an old man, and I was to share a cave house with a young girl. I could not make out much of the cave in the candlelight, but the quilt smelled pleasantly sun-bleached. I politely refused the help of the villagers who had escorted me there, and opened my bag. Just as I was about to ask the girl how I could wash, I realised that she had already climbed on to the *kang*. I remembered what the guide had said on the journey here: this was a place where water was so precious that even an emperor couldn't wash his face or brush his teeth every day.

I undressed and got on to the part of the *kang* that had obviously been left for me. I had wanted to spend a few minutes chatting to the girl, but she was already snoring lightly. She seemed not to feel any novelty at having a guest, but had fallen asleep immediately. I was exhausted, and had also taken travel sickness pills, so I fell quickly into a dazed sleep myself. My ability to sleep in unfamiliar places was a matter of desperate envy for my colleagues, who said I was natural journalist material because of it. As soon as they had acclimatised to a new place, they had to move on somewhere else, where they would suffer insomnia again. For them, a long-distance reporting trip was torture.

Light filtering into the cave house woke me. I got dressed and walked outside to find the young girl already making breakfast.

Heaven and earth seemed to have merged. The sun had not yet risen, but its light already spilled from a great distance across this immense canvas, touching the stones on the hills, and gilding the yellow-grey earth gold. I had never seen such a beautiful dawn. I mused over the possibility of tourism helping this area out of poverty. The magnificent sunrise on this loess plateau was a match for those which people climbed Mount Tai or rushed to the sea to see. When I mentioned later that those people ought to come to Shouting Hill instead, a teenage boy dismissed my idea as pure ignorance: Shouting Hill did not even have enough water for the villagers' most basic daily needs, how could it provide for an influx of visitors?

The choking fumes from the young girl's cooking fire brought me back from my reverie. The dried cow dung she used for fuel gave off a pungent odour. The fire had been lit between a few large stones, over which the girl had placed a pot and a flat stone. She made a thin flour gruel in the pot, and toasted a coarse flatbread on the stone. The girl's name was Niu'er (girl). She told me that dung was their only fuel for heating during the winter. Occasionally, when there was a death or a marriage, or when family or friends visited, they would cook with dung fires as a solemn expression of friendship. Their normal cooking fuel was the roots of cogon grass (a grass found in extremely arid terrain with a large root system and only a few short-lived leaves), with which they heated a mouthful of hot water for gruel. The coarse flatbread, *mo*, was only baked once a year, on the scorching stones of the hill in summer. It was then stored underground, and was so dry and hard that it would keep for almost a year. I was being honoured by being served the *mo*. Only men who did farming work had the right to eat it. Women and children survived on the thin wheat gruel – years of struggle had accustomed them to hunger. Niu'er said that the greatest honour and treat in a woman's life was to have a bowl of egg mixed with water when she had a son. Further into my visit, I remembered this when I heard quarrelling women retort: 'And how many bowls of egg and water have *you* eaten?'

After the special breakfast of gruel and *mo* on the first day, our group went to work. I explained to the village cadres that I wanted to report on the women of Shouting Hill. The cadres, who could not even write their own names but considered themselves cultured, shook their heads, taken aback. 'What's to be said about women?'

I persisted, so they eventually relented. To them, I was just another woman who understood nothing, but simply followed in the footsteps of men, trying to impress with novelty. Their attitude did not disturb me. Many years' experience as a journalist had taught me that access to my sources was more important than others' opinion of me.

When I had first heard the name 'Shouting Hill', I had felt a nameless excitement and a sense that my visit was predestined. The name conjures up a noisy, bustling place bursting with life, quite the opposite of the reality. The hill of yellow earth stands in a landscape of bare earth, sand and stones. There is no sign of flowing water or green plant life. The rare small beetle scuttling away seems to be fleeing the barren land.

Shouting Hill lies in the belt of land where the desert encroaches on the loess plateau. All through the year, the wind blows tirelessly, as it has for thousands of years. It is often difficult to see more than a few paces in a sandstorm, and villagers labouring on the hill have to shout to communicate. For this reason, the people of Shouting Hill are famous for loud, resonant voices; nobody could confirm if this was how Shouting Hill got its name, but I thought it a likely reason. It is a place entirely shut off from the modern world: between ten and twenty families with only four surnames live in small, low cave dwellings. Women there are valued solely for their utility: as reproductive tools, they are the most precious items of trade in the villagers' lives. The men do not hesitate to barter two or three girl children for a wife from another village. Marrying a woman from the family into another village and getting a wife for a man in the family in exchange is the most common practice, hence most of the women of Shouting Hill come from outside the village. After they become mothers, they in turn are forced to give up their own daughters. Women in Shouting Hill have no rights of property or inheritance.

The unusual social practice of one wife being shared by several husbands also occurs in Shouting Hill. In the majority of these cases, brothers from extremely poor families with no females to barter buy a common wife to continue the family line. By day they benefit from the food the woman makes and the household chores she does, by night they enjoy the woman's body in turn. If the woman has a child, she herself may not even know who the father is. To the child, the brothers are Big Papa, Second Papa, Third Papa, Fourth Papa, and so on. The villagers do not regard this practice as illegal, because it is an established custom passed down from the ancestors, making it more powerful to them than the law. Neither do they mock the children with many fathers, because they have the protection and property of several men. None of them feels compassion for the shared wives; to them, women's existence is justified by their utility.

No matter which village the women come from originally, they very soon enter into the customs that have been passed from generation to generation in Shouting Hill. They lead an extremely hard life. In their one-roomed cave houses, of which half the space is occupied by a *kang*, their domestic tools consist of a few stone slabs, grass mats and crude clay bowls; an earthenware pitcher is regarded as a luxury item for the 'wealthy families'. Children's toys or any household items specifically for the use of women are unthinkable in their society. Because wives are bought with the currency of female blood kin, they have to endure the resentment of family members who miss their own daughters or sisters, and have to labour day and night to see to the food, drink and other daily needs of the whole family.

It is the women who greet the dawn in Shouting Hill: they have to feed the livestock, sweep the yard and polish and repair the blunt, rusty tools of their husbands. After seeing their men off to work on the land, they have to collect water from an unreliable stream on the far side of a mountain two hours' walk away, carrying a pair of heavy buckets on their shoulders. When cogon grass is in season, the women also have to climb the hill to dig up the roots for use as cooking fuel. In the afternoon, they take food to their menfolk; when they come back they spin thread, weave cloth, and make clothes, shoes and hats for the family. All through the day, they carry small children almost everywhere with them in their arms or on their backs.

In Shouting Hill, 'use' is the term employed for men wanting to sleep with a woman. When the men return at dusk and want to 'use' their wives, they often yell impatiently at them: 'What are you dawdling for? Are you getting on the *kang* or what?' After being 'used', the women tidy up and attend to the children while the men lie snoring. Only with nightfall can the women rest, because there is no light to work in. When I tried to experience a very small part of these women's lives through joining in their daily household tasks for a short while, I found my faith in the value of life severely shaken.

The only day a woman of Shouting Hill can hold her head high is the day she gives birth to a son. Drenched in sweat after the torment of labour, she hears the words that fill her with pride and satisfaction: 'Got him!' This is the highest recognition of achievement she will ever get from her husband, and the material reward is a bowl of egg with sugar and hot water. There is no prejudice against a woman who gives birth to a girl, but she does not enjoy this treat. Shouting Hill has a unique social structure, but it does not differ from the rest of China in valuing sons more than daughters.

During my first few days at Shouting Hill, I wondered why most of the children who were playing beside or helping the women as they busied themselves about the cave dwellings were boys, and thought this could be another village in which female infanticide was practised. Later, I found out that this was due to a shortage of clothes. When a family got new clothes, once every three to five years, they dressed the boys first, often leaving several sisters to share one set of outer clothing, which had to fit all of them. The sisters would sit on the *kang* covered by a large sheet and put on the set of clothes in rotation to go outside and help their mother.

There was a family of eight daughters with only one pair of trousers between them, so covered in patches that the original fabric had been obscured. Their mother was pregnant with their ninth child, but I could see that this family's *kang* was no bigger than the ones in families with three or four children. The eight girls sat close together on the *kang* sewing shoes in a strict division of labour, like an assembly line in a small workshop. They were laughing and chatting as they worked. Whenever I spoke to them, they talked about what they had seen and heard on the day they 'wore clothes'. Every girl counted the days to her turn to 'wear clothes'. They chatted happily about which family was having a wedding or funeral or had a new son or daughter, which man beat his wife, or who had called who bad names. They talked most about the males in their village; even the traces on the ground from where a little boy had relieved himself was a matter for discussion and laughter. However, over the two weeks I spent with them, I almost never heard them talk about women. When I deliberately led the conversation round to topics like hairstyles, clothes, figures, make-up or other matters of concern to women in the outside world, the girls would often have no idea what I was talking about. The way women lived in Shouting Hill was the only conceivable way of life to them. I did not dare tell them about the world beyond, or the way women lived there, for I knew that living with the knowledge of what they could never have would be far more tragic than living as they did.

I noticed a bizarre phenomenon among the female villagers of Shouting Hill: when they reached their teens or thereabouts their gait suddenly became very strange. They began walking with their legs spread wide apart, swaying in an arc with each step. There was no trace of this tendency in the little girls, though. For the first few days I puzzled over this riddle, but did not like to enquire too deeply into it. I hoped to find the answer in my own way.

It was my habit to make sketches of the scenery I thought typified each place I was reporting on. No colour was necessary to depict Shouting Hill, a few lines were enough to bring out its essential qualities. While I was sketching, I noticed some small piles of stones that I could not recall having seen before. Most of them were in out-of-the-way spots. On closer inspection, I found blackish-red leaves under these stones. Only cogon grass grew in Shouting Hill; where had these leaves come from?

I examined the leaves carefully: they were mostly about ten centimetres long and five centimetres wide. They had clearly been cut to size, and seemed to have been beaten and rubbed by hand. Some of the leaves were slightly thicker than the others, and were moist to the touch, with a fishy odour. Other leaves were extremely dry from the pressure of the rocks and the burning heat of the sun; these were not brittle but very tough, and they too had the same strong salty smell. I had never seen leaves like this before. I wondered what they were used for and decided to ask the villagers.

The men said, 'Those are women's things!' and refused to say any more.

The children shook their heads in bewilderment, saying: 'I don't know what they are, Mama and Papa say we're not to touch them.'

The women simply lowered their heads silently.

When Niu'er noticed that I was puzzled about the question of these leaves, she said: 'You'd best ask my granny, she'll tell you.' Niu'er's grandmother was not so very old, but early marriage and childbearing had made her part of the village's senior generation.

Her grandmother slowly explained that the leaves were used by women during their periods. When a girl in Shouting Hill had her first period, or a woman had just married into the village, she would be presented with ten of these leaves by her mother or another woman of the older generation. These leaves were gathered from trees very far away. The older women would teach the girls what to do with the leaves. First, each leaf had to be cut to the right size, so that it could be worn inside trousers. Then small holes had to be pricked into the leaves with an awl, to make them more absorbent. The leaves were relatively elastic and their fibres very thick, so they would thicken and swell as they absorbed the blood. In a region where water was so precious, there was no alternative but to press and dry the leaves after each use. A woman would use her ten leaves for her period month after month, even after childbirth. Her leaves would be her only burial goods.

I exchanged some sanitary towels I had with me for a leaf from Niu'er's grandmother. My eyes filled with tears as I touched it: how could this coarse leaf, hard even to the hand's touch, be put in a woman's tenderest place? It was only then that I realised why the women of Shouting Hill walked with their legs splayed: their thighs had been repeatedly rubbed raw and scarred by the leaves.

There was another reason for the strange gait of the women in

Shouting Hill, which shocked me even more.

In written Chinese, the word 'womb' is made up of the characters for 'palace' and 'children'. Almost every woman knows that the womb is one of her key organs. But the women in Shouting Hill do not even know what a womb is.

The doctor who had come with us told me that one of the villagers had asked him to examine his wife, as she had been pregnant many times but never managed to carry a child to full term. With the villager's special permission, the doctor examined the woman, and was dumbfounded to find that she had a prolapsed womb. The friction and infection of many years had hardened the part of the womb that was hanging outside to cutin, tough as a callus. The doctor simply could not imagine what had caused this. Surprised by his reaction, the woman told him disapprovingly that all the women in Shouting Hill were like this. The doctor asked me to help him confirm this; several days later I confirmed the truth of that woman's words after much surreptitious observation of the village women as they relieved themselves. Prolapsed wombs were another reason why the women walked with their legs spreadeagled.

In Shouting Hill, the course of nature is not resisted, and family planning an alien concept. Women are treated as breeding machines, and produce one child a year or as many as three every two years. There is no guarantee that the children will survive. To the best of my knowledge, the only curb to the ever-growing families is infant mortality, or miscarriage from exhaustion.

I saw many pregnant women in Shouting Hill, but there was no sense of eager anticipation of a child among them or their men. Even while heavily pregnant, they had to labour as before and be 'used' by their men, who reasoned that 'only children who resist being squashed are strong enough'. I was appalled by all this, especially at the thought of shared wives being 'used' by several men throughout their pregnancy. The children that the women bore were indeed very strong: the notion of 'the survival of the fittest' certainly held true in Shouting Hill. This brutal pragmatism had led to severely prolapsed wombs among the fearless, selfless village women.

The evening after I had established that prolapsed wombs were an everyday phenomenon in Shouting Hill, I was unable to sleep for a very long time. I lay on the earthen *kang* weeping for these women, who were of my generation and of my time. That the women of Shouting Hill had no concept of modern society, let alone any awareness of the rights of women, was a small comfort; their happiness lay in their ignorance, their customs and the satisfaction of believing that all women in the world lived as they did. To tell them about the outside world would be like peeling away the calluses from a work-worn hand and letting thorns prick the tender flesh.

On the day I left Shouting Hill, I found that the sanitary towels I had given to Niu'er's grandmother as a souvenir were stuck in her sons' belts; they were using them as towels to wipe away sweat or protect their hands.

Before my visit to Shouting Hill, I had thought that Chinese women of all ethnic groups were united, each developing in a unique way, but essentially walking in step with the times. During my two weeks at Shouting Hill, however, I saw mothers, daughters and wives who seemed to have been left behind at the beginning of history, living primitive lives in the modern world. I was worried for them. Would they ever be able to catch up? One cannot walk to the end of history in one single step, and history would not wait for them. However, when I got back to the office and saw that trips like ours were bringing hidden communities to the attention of the rest of the country, I felt as if I was at the beginning of something. This beginning contained my hope. Perhaps there was a way of helping the women of Shouting Hill to move a little more quickly . . .

Big Li listened to my account of the women of Shouting Hill, then asked, 'Are they happy?'

Mengxing exclaimed, 'Don't be ridiculous! How can they be?'

I said to Mengxing that, out of the hundreds of Chinese women I had spoken to over nearly ten years of broadcasting and journalism, the women of Shouting Hill were the only ones to tell me they were happy.

Epilogue

In August 1997, I left China for England. My experience of Shouting Hill had shaken me. I felt I needed to breathe new air – to know what it was like to live in a free society. On the plane to London I sat next to a man who told me he was coming back from his seventh visit to China. He had visited all the important historical sites. He spoke knowledgeably about tea, silk and the Cultural Revolution. Curious, I asked him what he knew about the position of Chinese women in society. He replied that China seemed to him a very equal society: everywhere he went he saw men and women doing the same work.

I had boarded the plane with the idea that I might find a way of describing the lives of Chinese women to people in the West. Suddenly, confronted with the very limited knowledge of this man, the task seemed much more daunting. I would need to reach far back into my memory to recapture all the stories I had collected over the years. I would have to relive the emotions I felt on first hearing them and try to find the best words to describe all the misery, bitterness and love that the women had expressed. And even then, I wasn't sure how Western readers would interpret these stories. Having never visited the West, I had little idea how much people there knew about China.

Four days after I arrived in London, Princess Diana died. I remember standing on the platform of Ealing Broadway tube station surrounded by people carrying bunches of flowers that they intended to lay at the gates of Buckingham Palace. I couldn't resist the journalistic impulse to ask a woman next to me in the crowd what Princess Diana had meant to her. We started talking about the position of women in British society. After a while, she asked me what life was like for women in China. For Westerners, she said, the modern Chinese woman still seemed to wear an ancient veil. She believed it was important to try and see behind that veil. Her words inspired me. Perhaps there would, after all, be an interested audience in the West for my stories. Later, when I went to work at London University's School of Oriental and African Studies, other people were encouraging. I told one of the teachers about a few of my interviews and she was adamant that I should write them down. Most of the books written so far, she said, had been about particular Chinese families. These stories would give a broader perspective.

However, the defining moment for me came when a twenty-two-year-old Chinese girl asked me for help. She was studying at SOAS and sat next to me one day in the student canteen. She was very depressed. Her mother, without any concern for the cost of long-distance calls, was phoning her daily to warn her that Western men were 'sexual hooligans' and she wasn't to let them near her. Unable to turn to anyone for advice, the girl was desperate to know the answers to the most basic questions about the relationship between men and women. If you kissed a man, were you still considered a virgin? Why did Western men touch women so much and so easily?

There were students sitting near us in the canteen who were studying Chinese and understood what she was saying. They laughed in disbelief that anyone could be so innocent. But I was very moved by her unhappiness. Here, ten years after Xiao Yu had written to me to ask whether love was an offence against public decency and committed suicide when I failed to answer, was another young girl whose mother was responsible for keeping her in a position of complete sexual ignorance. The Western students whom she studied alongside, who hugged each other without a thought, had no notion of what she was suffering. Indeed, in China, there are many sexually experienced young women – usually living in cities – who would laugh at her. But I had talked to so many women in a similar position. After her cry for help, it seemed to me even more imperative that I use their tears, and my